Contents

III Route planning

iii Key to map symbols

iv Route planner

viii Distance table

1 Road maps

1 Key map

2 Great Britain at 12 miles to 1 inch

32 Ireland at 12 miles to 1 inch

41 Town and city plans

41 Town plan locator

42 London approaches map

44 London city plan

46 Town and city plans

73 Index to road maps

GW00514883

First published in 1996 by

George Philip Ltd
an imprint of Reed Consumer Books Ltd
Michelin House, 81 Fulham Road, London SW3 6RB
and Auckland and Melbourne

Fourth edition 1998

All rights reserved. Apart from any fair dealing for the purpose of private
study, research, criticism or review, as permitted under the Copyright
Designs and Patents Act, 1988, no part of this publication may be
reproduced, stored in a retrieval system, or transmitted in any form or by
any means, electronic, electrical, chemical, mechanical, optical,
photocopying, recording, or otherwise, without prior written permission.
All enquiries should be addressed to the Publisher.

To the best of the Publisher's knowledge, the information in this atlas was
correct at the time of going to press. No responsibility can be accepted
for any errors or their consequences.

The representation in this atlas of any road, drive or track is no evidence
of the existence of a right of way.

The mapping on pages 42-43 is based upon the Ordnance Survey
1:250 000 Digital Database with the permission of the Controller of
Her Majesty's Stationery Office © Crown copyright 399817.

The mapping on page 47 is based upon the Ordnance Survey map with
the permission of the Controller of Her Majesty's Stationery Office
© Crown Copyright. Permit No. 1092

The mapping on page 54 is based upon the Ordnance Survey Map by
permission of the Government of the Republic of Ireland. Permit No. 6572

The other town plans are based upon the Ordnance Survey maps with the
permission of the Controller of Her Majesty's Stationery Office
© Crown Copyright.

Cartography by Philip's
Copyright © 1997 George Philip Ltd

Printed and bound in Spain by Cayfosa

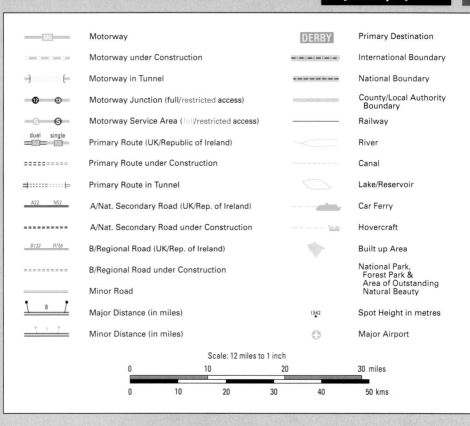

M6	Motorway	DERBY	Primary Destination
	Motorway under Construction		International Boundary
	Motorway in Tunnel		National Boundary
12 13	Motorway Junction (full/restricted access)		County/Local Authority Boundary
S S	Motorway Service Area (full/restricted access)		Railway
dual single A5 N6	Primary Route (UK/Republic of Ireland)		River
	Primary Route under Construction		Canal
	Primary Route in Tunnel		Lake/Reservoir
A22 N52	A/Nat. Secondary Road (UK/Rep. of Ireland)		Car Ferry
	A/Nat. Secondary Road under Construction		Hovercraft
B133 R756	B/Regional Road (UK/Rep. of Ireland)		Built up Area
	B/Regional Road under Construction		National Park, Forest Park & Area of Outstanding Natural Beauty
	Minor Road		
8	Major Distance (in miles)	1342	Spot Height in metres
6	Minor Distance (in miles)		Major Airport

Scale: 12 miles to 1 inch

```
0        10        20        30  miles
0    10    20    30    40    50 kms
```

NUMERICAL LIST OF REFERENCED UNITARY AUTHORITIES

① Dundee City	25 K18	⑭ Stockton-on-Tees	21 N21	㉗ Bridgend	9 U16
② Clackmannanshire	24 K16	⑮ Darlington	16 N20	㉘ Rhondda Cynon Taff	9 U17
③ West Dunbartonshire	24 L15	⑯ Middlesbrough	16 N21	㉙ Torfaen	4 U17
④ Inverclyde	19 L14	⑰ Redcar and Cleveland	17 N22	㉚ Caerphilly	4 U17
⑤ Renfrewshire	19 L14	⑱ Kingston upon Hull	17 Q23	㉛ Cardiff	4 U17
⑥ East Dunbartonshire	19 L15	⑲ North East Lincolnshire	17 Q23	㉜ Newport	4 U18
⑦ City of Glasgow	19 L15	⑳ Stoke-on-Trent	10 R19	㉝ City of Bristol	4 V18
⑧ East Renfrewshire	19 L15	㉑ Derby City	11 S21	㉞ Thamesdown	5 U20
⑨ Falkirk	24 L16	㉒ Leicester City	11 S21	㉟ Southampton	5 W21
⑩ North Lanarkshire	19 L16	㉓ Luton	12 U23	㊱ Poole	5 W20
⑪ West Lothian	24 L16	㉔ Neath Port Talbot	9 U16	㊲ Bournemouth	5 W20
⑫ City of Edinburgh	25 L17	㉕ Merthyr Tydfil	9 U17	㊳ Portsmouth	5 W21
⑬ Hartlepool	21 N21	㉖ Blaenau Gwent	9 U17	㊴ Brighton and Hove	6 W23

ALPHABETICAL LIST OF REFERENCED UNITARY AUTHORITIES

㉖ Blaenau Gwent	9 U17	⑥ East Dunbartonshire	19 L15	⑩ North Lanarkshire	19 L16
㊲ Bournemouth	5 W20	⑧ East Renfrewshire	19 L15	㊱ Poole	5 W20
㉗ Bridgend	9 U16	⑨ Falkirk	24 L16	㊳ Portsmouth	5 W21
㊴ Brighton and Hove	6 W23	⑬ Hartlepool	21 N21	⑰ Redcar and Cleveland	17 N22
㉚ Caerphilly	4 U17	④ Inverclyde	19 L14	⑤ Renfrewshire	19 L14
㉛ Cardiff	4 U17	⑱ Kingston upon Hull	17 Q23	㉘ Rhondda Cynon Taff	9 U17
㉝ City of Bristol	4 V18	㉒ Leicester City	11 S21	㉟ Southampton	5 W21
⑫ City of Edinburgh	25 L17	㉓ Luton	12 U23	⑭ Stockton-on-Tees	21 N21
⑦ City of Glasgow	19 L15	㉕ Merthyr Tydfil	9 U17	⑳ Stoke-on-Trent	10 R19
② Clackmannanshire	24 K16	⑯ Middlesbrough	16 N21	㉞ Thamesdown	5 U20
⑮ Darlington	16 N20	㉜ Newport	4 U18	㉙ Torfaen	4 U17
㉑ Derby City	11 S21	⑲ North East Lincolnshire	17 Q23	③ West Dunbartonshire	24 L15
① Dundee City	25 K18			⑪ West Lothian	24 L16

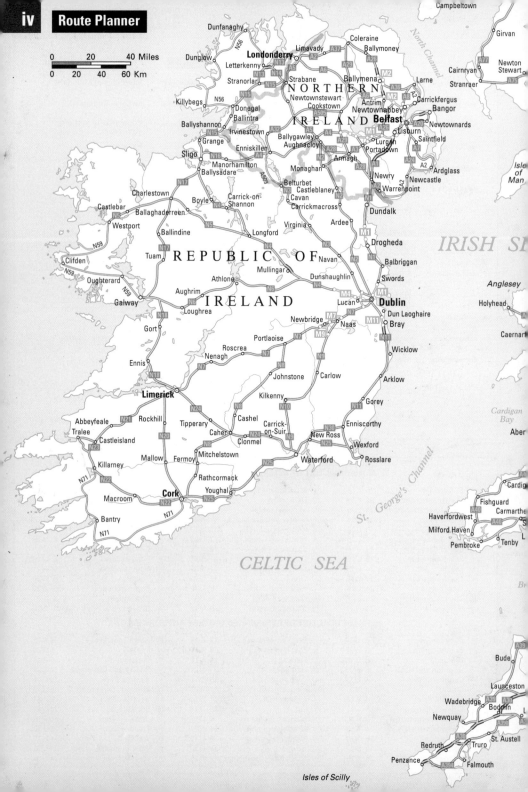

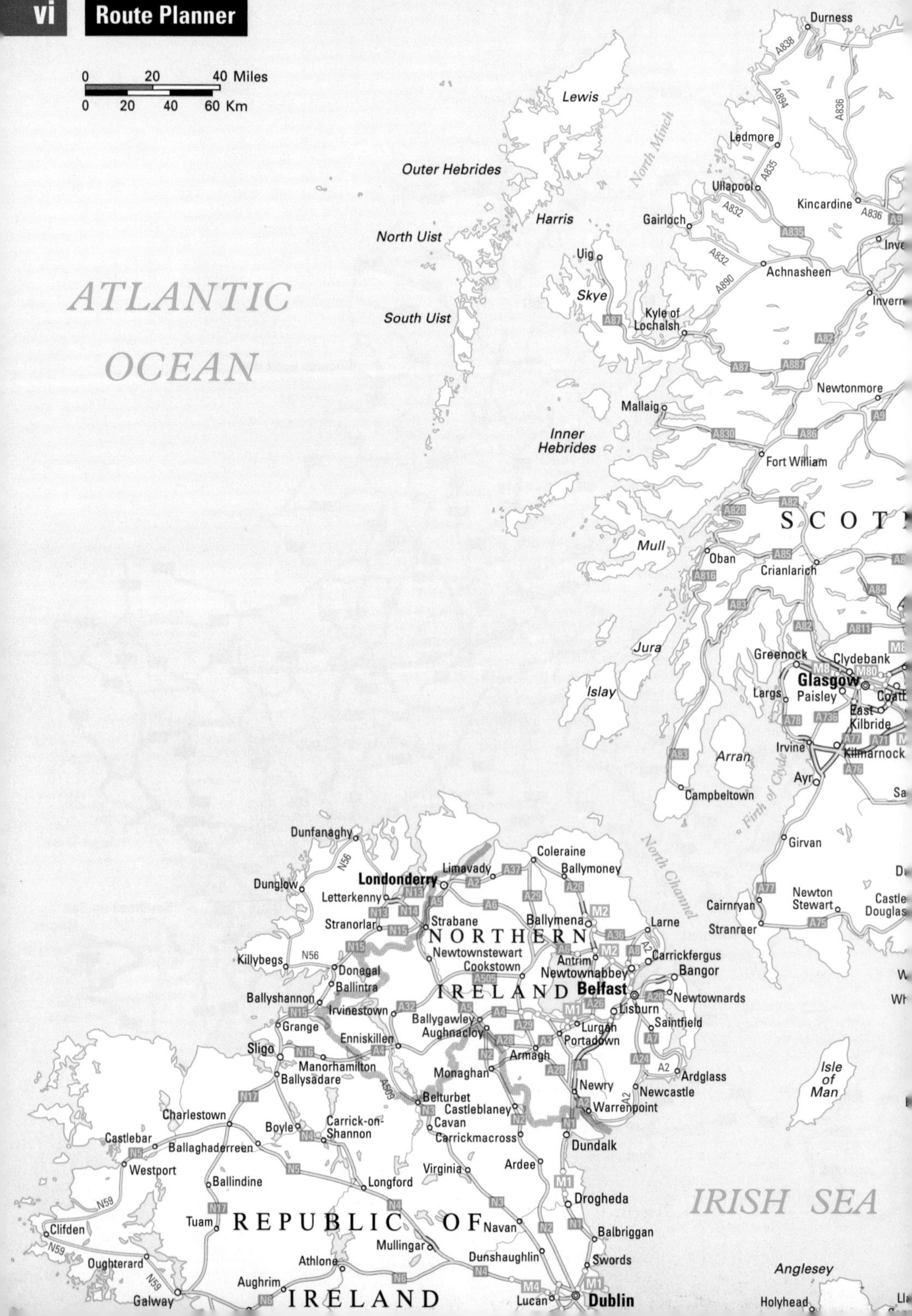

0 20 40 Miles
0 20 40 60 Km

ATLANTIC

OCEAN

Durness

Lewis

Ledmore

Outer Hebrides

Ullapool

Kincardine

Harris

Gairloch

North Uist

Inve

Uig

Achnasheen

Skye

Inver

South Uist

Kyle of
Lochalsh

Newtonmore

Mallaig

Inner
Hebrides

Fort William

SCOT

Mull

Oban

Crianlarich

Jura

Greenock Clydebank

Glasgow Coatb

Islay

Largs Paisley

East
Kilbride

Arran

Irvine

Kilmarnock

Campbeltown

Ayr

Sa

Girvan

Dunfanaghy

Coleraine

Newton
Stewart

Castle
Douglas

Dunglow

Limavady

Ballymoney

Cairnryan

Londonderry

Letterkenny

Stranraer

Stranorlar

Strabane

Ballymena

Larne

NORTHERN

Newtownstewart

Antrim

Carrickfergus

Killybegs

Cookstown

Newtownabbey

Bangor

Donegal

IRELAND

Belfast

Newtownards

Ballyshannon Ballintra

Ballygawley

Lisburn

Saintfield

Irvinestown

Aughnacloy

Lurgan

Grange

Enniskillen

Portadown

Isle
of
Man

Sligo

Armagh

Manorhamilton

Monaghan

Ardglass

Ballysadare

Belturbet

Newry

Charlestown

Carrick-on-
Shannon

Castleblaney

Newcastle

Boyle

Cavan

Warrenpoint

Castlebar

Carrickmacross

Ballaghaderreen

Dundalk

Westport

Virginia

Ardee

Ballindine

Longford

IRISH SEA

Clifden

Tuam

REPUBLIC OF

Navan

Drogheda

Balbriggan

Oughterard

Mullingar

Dunshaughlin

Swords

Anglesey

Athlone

Aughrim

Galway

IRELAND

Lucan

Dublin

Holyhead

HOW TO USE THIS TABLE

Distances are shown in miles

Example: the distance from Cambridge to Dover is 125 miles

Cambridge	169			
Cardiff	190	45		
Carlisle	289	264	277	
Dover	389	238	125	202
Dundee	523	152	441	406	430

Distance table (distances in miles):

London	
Aberdeen	517
Aberystwyth	445 211
Birmingham	114 420 117
Bournemouth	147 207 564 107
Brighton	92 163 253 573 52
Bristol	147 82 81 125 493 122
Cambridge	169 116 154 100 214 471 54
Cardiff	190 45 182 117 103 105 505 157
Carlisle	289 264 277 370 343 196 224 221 301
Dover	389 238 125 202 82 174 194 292 588 71
Dundee	523 152 441 406 430 517 495 349 376 67 448
Edinburgh	56 462 96 385 345 373 456 439 292 320 125 390
Fishguard	399 460 331 297 112 270 154 291 222 170 56 504 260
Fort William	486 144 127 596 206 485 479 486 575 539 392 430 149 510
Glasgow	101 376 44 83 488 96 385 372 373 468 439 292 320 145 397
Gloucester	346 454 153 349 410 191 247 56 123 35 159 99 56 102 468 109
Harwich	196 432 543 337 413 469 125 336 246 67 217 128 187 167 281 535 76
Holyhead	349 191 330 438 167 333 394 360 231 216 270 206 334 288 148 111 439 269
Inverness	474 569 504 166 66 542 158 132 622 262 549 505 539 617 597 458 486 105 550
John o' Groats	129 603 693 628 295 195 671 285 259 747 391 680 630 668 741 724 574 601 232 663
Kingston upon Hull	518 394 231 196 198 254 369 280 234 295 256 158 244 139 233 245 264 134 223 364 184
Land's End	421 868 741 405 390 235 573 686 353 574 642 381 477 245 374 200 308 205 281 313 692 297
Leeds	405 55 487 360 176 223 174 215 329 237 202 258 260 119 232 145 194 260 255 113 169 327 189
Lincoln	68 371 44 554 427 216 155 159 291 399 272 258 314 202 191 208 85 183 197 209 90 199 383 131
Liverpool	129 75 361 130 511 382 102 265 140 216 329 160 216 286 299 120 165 194 161 272 234 93 104 341 202
Manchester	35 84 40 361 95 500 373 124 228 126 215 329 197 215 285 276 119 183 165 161 257 227 80 129 340 185
Newcastle upon Tyne	132 168 159 92 498 132 395 268 272 308 266 148 253 329 110 166 358 57 325 241 299 352 347 207 257 235 286
Norwich	264 185 220 105 176 421 149 654 529 311 73 204 385 504 343 366 422 174 289 262 62 252 175 214 166 276 496 114
Oban	492 233 307 308 387 307 665 346 244 117 427 524 441 92 49 481 123 117 585 188 477 468 465 565 530 384 412 178 499
Oxford	462 145 260 144 172 137 168 274 192 656 532 238 145 52 356 472 205 372 433 141 260 108 83 74 108 90 64 154 483 57
Plymouth	199 587 343 410 283 283 293 316 89 355 790 664 328 309 157 495 595 264 496 552 300 399 167 293 122 224 128 203 237 615 218
Sheffield	283 135 339 146 125 38 72 46 33 361 65 520 393 186 187 126 248 348 215 235 291 245 152 194 120 161 226 216 76 159 360 159
Shrewsbury	82 225 106 364 205 201 69 58 133 109 303 169 567 438 113 240 77 272 382 145 274 330 251 176 111 159 103 226 185 45 77 399 160
Southampton	185 199 151 64 530 206 324 221 239 204 232 228 256 723 598 293 164 105 433 541 233 438 500 143 324 121 148 76 61 31 128 201 547 77
Stranraer	445 277 263 500 379 148 403 158 220 221 298 220 585 259 379 262 338 435 343 84 195 392 124 167 496 101 390 379 378 475 444 297 325 228 402
Swansea	417 161 118 217 206 141 506 301 347 187 195 233 248 285 264 696 572 184 267 89 409 496 67 412 473 274 309 41 227 85 222 167 119 73 507 194
York	272 222 258 133 52 333 181 309 181 84 64 99 75 24 411 37 479 352 204 228 189 217 330 261 194 250 282 121 244 165 222 275 269 130 195 319 207

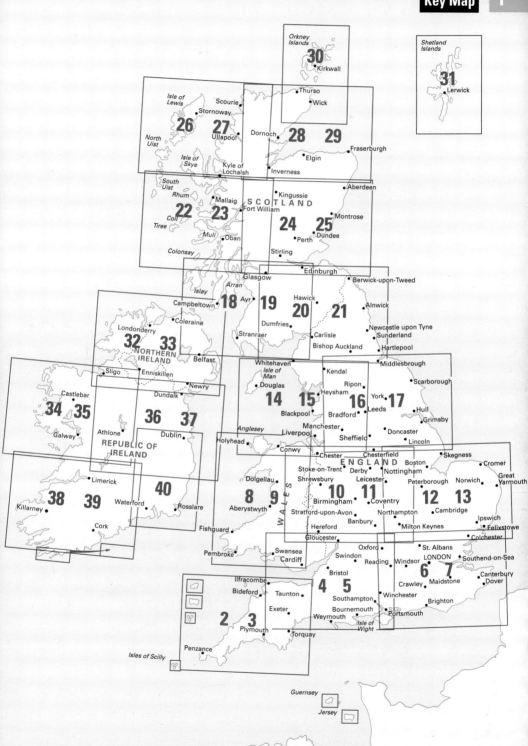

12   13   14

GUERNSEY map inset:

Y

V

POOLE
ALDERNEY

GUERNSEY
St. Sampson
St. Peter Port
Herm
Rocquaine Bay
GUERNSEY
St. Martin
Sark

Z

Torteval
JERSEY

18   19

JERSEY map inset:

Z

Grosnez Pt.
JERSEY
Rozel
Trinity
St. Martin
St. Ouens Bay
JERSEY
St. Peter
St. Helier
St. Brelade
Gorey
St. Aubin
la Rocque Pt.

W

GUERNSEY

19 ST. MALO

ISLES OF SCILLY map inset:

Tresco
St. Martin's
Bryher
Crow Sound
Hugh Town
ST. MARY'S
St. Mary's
Broad Sd.
St. Agnes
St. Mary's Sd.

Y

11   PENZANCE

Main Cornwall map:

Lundy

Hartland Pt.
Ha

Morwenstow

Kilkhampto

Bude Bay

Bude

Widemouth

Dizzard Pt. Poundstock

CORNWALL

Tintagel Hd.
Boscastle
B3263
A39
Hallwort
Tintagel
B3266
B3263
A39
Delabole
Camelford
Altar
Port Isaac Bay
419
BROWN WILLY
St. Breward
Pentire Pt.
Polzeath
Port Isaac
St. Teath
Trevose Hd.
Padstow
St. Minver
St. Tudy
B O D M
Padstow Bay
St. Merryn
St. Mabyn
M O O
Wadebridge
Washaway
Colliford
Lake Res.
St. Issey
A389
Camel
BODMIN
Trenance
B3276
A30
B3274
Dobwalls
Watergate Bay
St. Columb
Major
A30
A38
C O R N W
NEWQUAY
St. Columb Minor
Roche
Bugle
Lostwithiel
Perranporth
A392
St. Enoder
St. Dennis
Blazey
Du
St. Agnes Hd.
B3285
Newlyn East
Fraddon
A3058
St. Stephen
Tywardreath
Bodinnick
St. Agnes
Goonhavern
A390
Fowey
Perranzabuloe
50
Ladock
B3275
A39
ST.
Polruan
Portreath
Probus
Grampound
AUSTELL
P
Illogan
A30
Chacewater
A390
Tresillian
B3287
Mevagissey Bay
REDRUTH
St. Day
Kea
TRURO
Mevagissey
St. Ives Bay
Pool
B3301
Gwennap
A39
Tregony
Gorran Haven
St. Ives
Carbis Bay
Hayle
Camborne
B3297
Probus
Veryan
Dodman Pt.
Gurnard's Hd.
Zennor
Lelant
Leedstown
Penryn
Feock
Veryan B.
Pendeen
252
Ludgvan
St. Erth
A393
Gerrans B.
C. Cornwall
PENZANCE
HELIPORT
A30
Marazion
FALMOUTH
St. Mawes
St. Just
Newlyn
B3280
Breage
HELSTON
Kelynack
A30
PENZANCE
A394
Falmouth Bay
Sennen
B3315
Mousehole
Praa Sands
Helford
CORNWALL
Land's End
St. Buryan
Porthleven
Gweek
St. Levan
Mount's Bay
Mawgan
St. Keverne
The Manacles
Mullion
B3083
Coverack
Wolf Rock
Ruan Minor
Black Hd.
Lizard
Lizard Pt.

X

Y

12   13   14

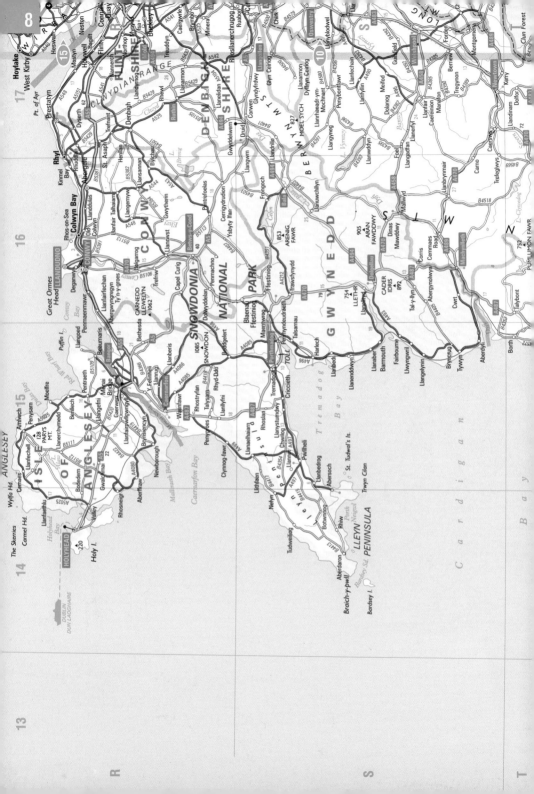

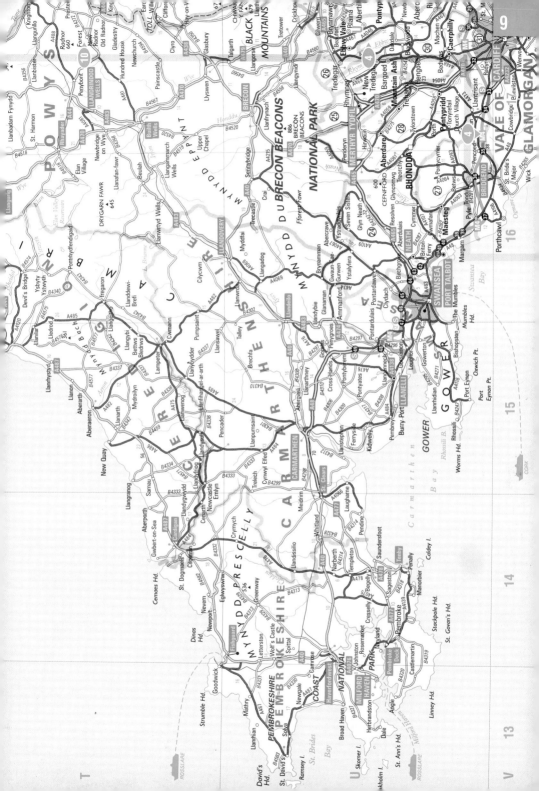

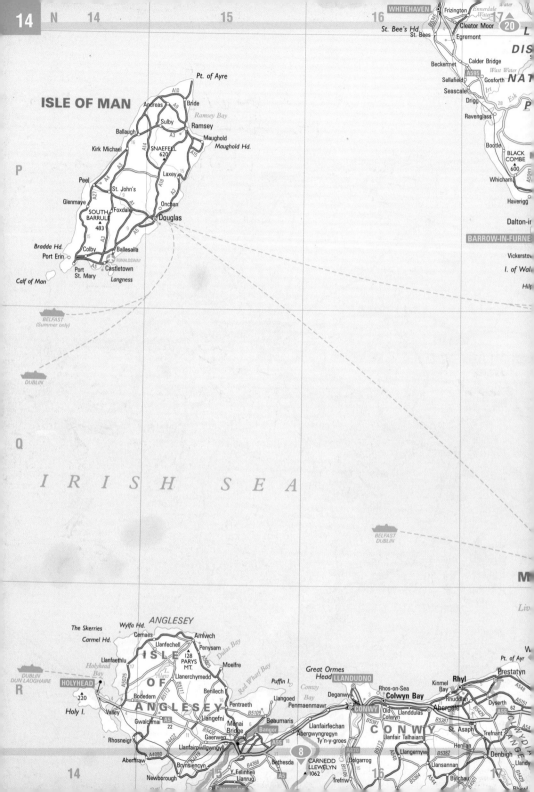

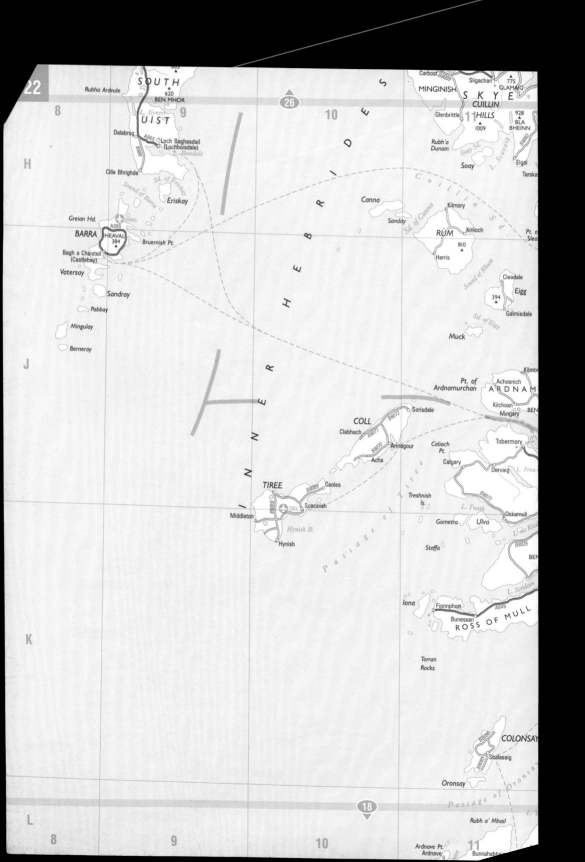

SOUTH

Rubha Ardvule

663
620
BEN MHOR

8   9   10

UIST

Dalabrog   A865   Loch Baghasdail
(Lochboisdale)
B890
L. Bonsdale

Cille Bhrighde

H

Sd. of Eriskay

Eriskay

Greian Hd.

Sound of Barra

BARRA   HEAVAL
384
Bruernish Pt.

Bagh a Chaisteil
(Castlebay)

Vatersay

Sandray

Pabbay

Mingulay

J

Berneray

TIREE   B8069   Caoles

B8068

Scarinish

Middleton   TIREE

Hynish B.

Hynish

K

I N N E R

H E B R I D E S

26

Canna

Sanday

Sd. of Canna

Kilmory

RUM   Kinloch

810
Harris

Carbost   B8009   Sligachan   775
GLAMAIG
MINGINISH   SKYE   18
CUILLIN
Glenbrittle   11 HILLS   928
1009   BLA
BHEINN   B8083

Rubh'a
Dunain   Soay Sd.

Soay   L. Scavaig   Elgol

Tarskav

Pt. o
Slea

Sound of Rhum

Cleadale

Eigg
394
Galmisdale

Sd. of Eigg

Muck

Pt. of
Ardnamurchan   Achosnich   Kilmor
ARDNAM

Kilchoan   BEN
Mingary

COLL   B8072   Sorisdale
Clabhach   B8071   Arinagour   Caliach
Pt.   Tobermory
B8070   Acha   Calgary
Dervaig   L. Frisa

Treshnish
Is.   L. Tuath   Oskamull

Gometra   Ulva

Staffa   BEN

B8077

B8035

L. Sridnan

Iona   Fionnphort   A849
Bunessan   ROSS OF MULL

Torran
Rocks

COLONSAY
B898
Scalasaig

B936

Oronsay

Passage of Oronsa

18

Rubh a' Mhail

L

8   9   10   11

Ardnave Pt.
Ardnave   Bunnahabhai

THE BUCK
Badenyon
Lumsden
Tullynessle
Inverurie
Newmachar
A947
B888
Balmedie

17
18
Alford
29
Monymusk
Kemnay
Kintore
Dyce
A90
20
LERWICK
STROMNESS
FAROE ISLANDS

MOR
Strathdon
Don
Ordhead
A944
Dunecht
Bankhead
Bucksburn
19
Bridge of Don
ABERDEEN

MAR
872
MORVEN
Tarland
Lumphanan
Echt
B9119
Westhill
ABERDEEN
CITY
Girdle Ness

Ordie
Torphins
B977
Petercutter
Cults
Cove Bay

Aboyne
Dee
Banchory
A93
A957
B9077
Portlethen
Cammachmore

Ballater
Marywell
B976
Strachan
A979
Newtonhill
Muchalls

DEENSHIRE
Ballochan
KINCARDINE
Stonehaven

938
MT. KEEN
Auchronie
Auchenblae

Spittal of
Glenmuick
Glen Esk
HOWE OF THE MEARNS
A92
Todhead Point

endoll
Lodge
Clova
Waterhead
Fettercairn
B967
Inverbervie

Glenprosen
Lodge
Rottal
Edzell
B966
Laurencekirk
Gourdon
Johnshaven

ANGUS
B955
Dykehead
Tannadice
Marykirk
St. Cyrus

Backwater
Res.
B951
Kirriemuir
B957
67
Brechin
A935
MONTROSE

Meigle
A928
A94
Glamis
Inverarity
A932
Friockheim
Inverkeilor
Lunan B.

Angus
A928
B9127
Monikie
Carmyllie
Marywell

SIDLAW HILLS
455
B978
B961
Muirdrum
ARBROATH

DUNDEE
1
A92
Monifieth
Carnoustie

ongforgan
Invergowrie
TAY BRIDGE
Broughty
Ferry
Barry
Buddon Ness

Inchture
Wormit
Tayport
Inchcape Rock

Errol
Newport-on-Tay
Leuchars

A913
Kilmany
Guard Bridge

A92
Cupar
B939
ST. ANDREWS
Kingsbarns

miglo
Ladybank
Ceres
Dunino
B940
Fife Ness

Park
Freuchie
B940
Crail

A916
Kirkton
of Largo
B9171
Kilrenny
Anstruther

Markinch
A911
Windygates
A917
Pittenweem
St. Monance
I. of May

thes
Leven
Methil
Earlsferry
Elie

Buckhaven
East Wemyss

Dysart
Firth of Forth

KIRKCALDY

Kinghorn
Bass Rock

Burntisland
Inchkeith
North
Berwick

Leith
Dirleton
Whitekirk

Prestonpans
Cockenzie
Gullane
Drem
Dunbar

URGH
Musselburgh
Tranent
EAST
Barns Ness

Dalkeith
A1
Haddington
East
Linton
Spott

LOTHIAN
Macmerry
Garvald
Cockburnspath
St. Abb's Head

21
Gifford
Ecclaw
St. Abb's
Eyemouth

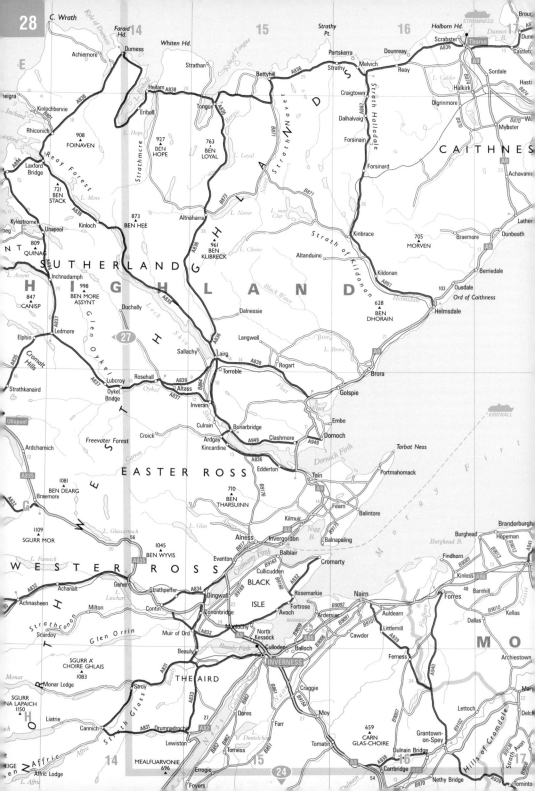

E

F

G

H

18   19   20

John o' Groats
Canisbay
Duncansby Head
Duncansby
Freswick
Nybster
Gortat   Keiss
A99
Sinclair's B.
B876
Reiss
Noss Hd.
Staxigoe
Wick
A882
Thrumster
Ulbster
A99
Halberry Head

17   18   19   20

mouth
Findochty   Portknockie
Cullen
Buckie   Portsoy
Spey B.
Garmouth   Portgordon
anbryde   A98
Fochabers   Craibstone
A96   B9022
Newmill   B9018
Mulben   B9121
Keith   Aberchirder
AY   B9014
Craigellachie   B9025
arlestown of Aberlour   A920
fftown   Huntly
A941   STRATHBOGIE
Laggan   A96
Ardwell   Kennethmont
Cabrach   B9002
722   Rhynie
THE   GARIOCH
BUCK   Lumsden   Tullynessle
Badenyon

Fordyce   Macduff
A97   Banff
Weachyburn   B9031
Aberchirder   B9121   50
Newbyth   B9025
Turriff   Cuminestown
B9170   A947
Fortrie   BUCHAN
B9024   New Deer
Badenscoth   B9001   B9005   Maud
Fyvie   B9170
Rothienorman   A947   Methlick   Hatton
A920   Tarves   49
Colpy   FORMARTINE   Ellon
Insch   53   Oldmeldrum   A920
25   Inverurie   B9000   Newburgh
Newmachar

Troup Hd.   Rosehearty   *Kinnairds Hd.*
B9031   **FRASERBURGH**
Gardenstown   Pennan   Inverallochy
New   St. Combs
Aberdour   A98   Rathen
B9031   Crimond   *Rattray Hd.*
B9093   Strichen   A952
New   A981   St. Fergus
Pitsligo   B9033
Mintlaw   **PETERHEAD**
Old   A950   Longside
Deer   A952   *Buchan Ness*
B9030   Boddam
A948   A90
Hatton   Cruden Bay
A975

ABERDEENSHIRE
A96
A90

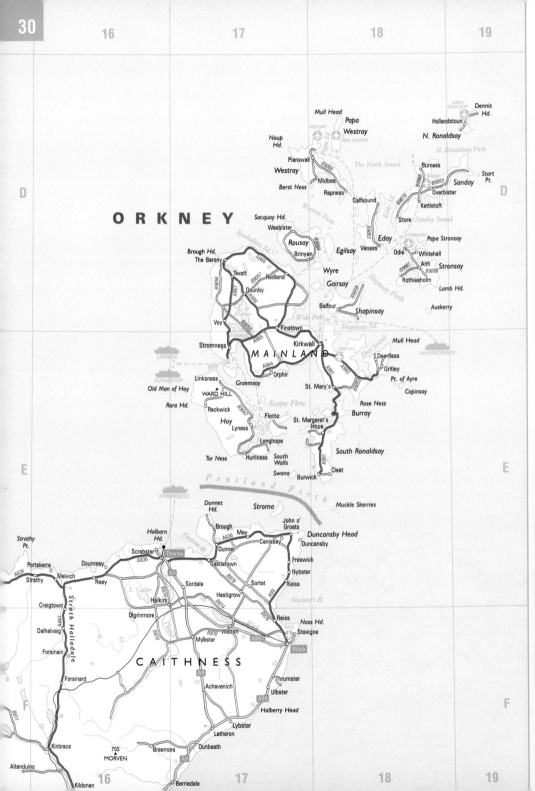

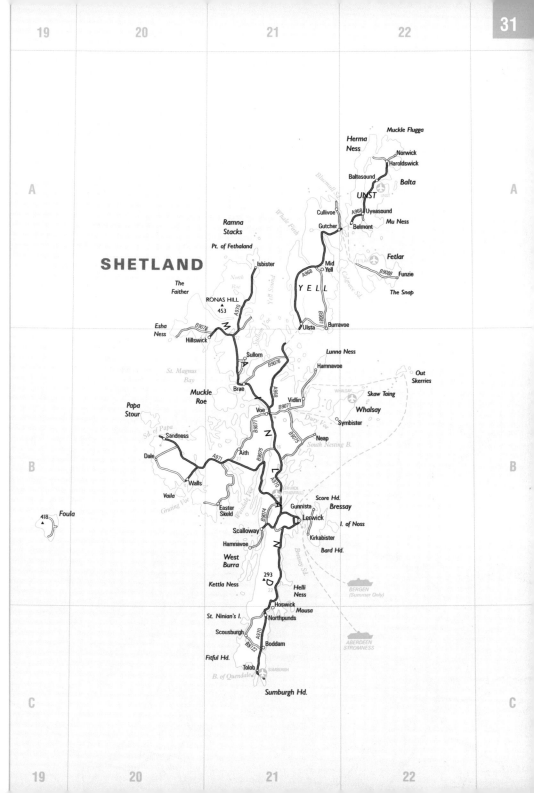

SHETLAND

Muckle Flugga

*Herma
Ness*

Norwick
Haroldswick

Baltasound   *Balta*

UNST   UYEA

A968 Uyeasound
Cullivoe   Mu Ness
Gutcher   Belmont

Fetlar

*Ramna
Stacks*

Pt. of Fethaland

Isbister   Mid
Yell   B9088 Funzie

Y E L L   *The Snap*

*The
Faither*

*North
Roe*   A968

RONAS HILL
453   A970   B9081

*Esha
Ness*   B9078   Ulsta Burravoe

Hillswick   Sullom   *Lunna Ness*

B9076   Hamnavoe   *Out
Skerries*

*St. Magnus
Bay*   Brae   *Muckle
Roe*   Vidlin   WHALSAY   Skaw Taing

Voe   B9071   *Whalsay*

*Papa
Stour*   B9075   Symbister

Sandness   A971   Aith   Neap

Dale   B9075   *South Nesting B.*

Sd. of Papa

B   Walls   A970

Vaila   THINGWALL
VOE

418 *Foula*   Easter
Skeld   B9074   Gunnista Score Hd. *Bressay*

Scalloway   Lerwick   I. of Noss

Hamnavoe   Kirkabister

*West
Burra*   Bard Hd.

293   *BERGEN
(Summer Only)*

Kettla Ness   22   *Helli
Ness*

St. Ninian's I.   Hoswick Mousa
Northpunds

Scousburgh   A970   *ABERDEEN
STROMNESS*

Fitful Hd.   B9122 Boddam

Tolob   SUMBURGH
B. of Quendale

Sumburgh Hd.

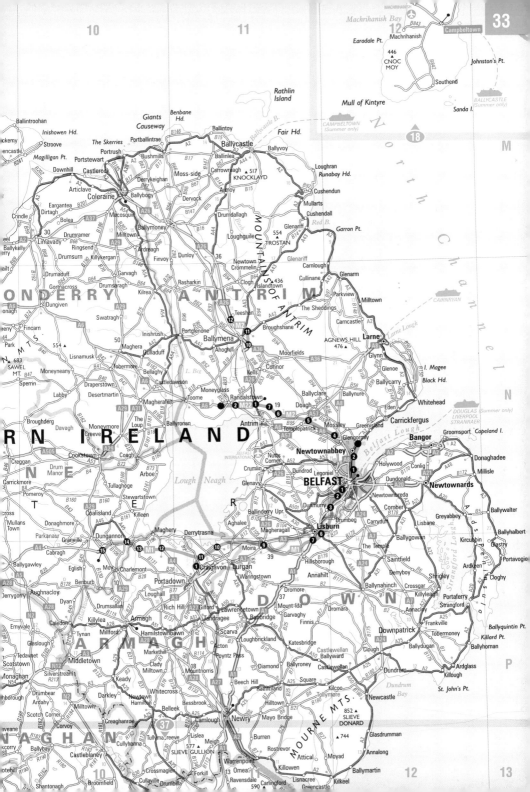

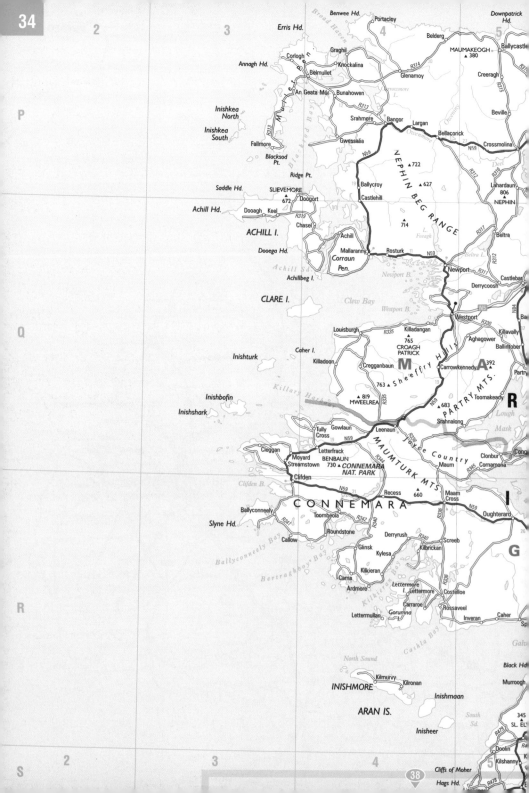

Benwee Hd.
Portacloy
Broad Haven
Downpatrick Hd.
Erris Hd.
Belderg
Ballycastle
MAUMAKEOGH ▲ 380
Annagh Hd.
Corlogh
Graghil
Glenamoy
Creeragh
Knockalina
R314
Belmullet
Beville
An Geata Mór
Bunahowen
R315
Inishkea North
R313
Srahmore
Bangor
Largan
Crossmolina
Inishkea South
Fallmore
Gwessalia
Bellacorick
N59
Blacksod Pt.
NEPHIN BEG RANGE
Laherdaun 806 ▲ NEPHIN
Ridge Pt.
▲ 722
Saddle Hd.
SLIEVEMORE
Ballycroy
▲ 627
R317
Achill Hd.
672 ▲ Doogort
Castlehill
Beltra
Dooagh Keel
R319
▲ 714
R312
Chasel
L. Feeagh
ACHILL I.
Achill
Rosturk
N59
Dooega Hd.
Mallaranny
Newport
R311
Castlebar
Corraun Pen.
Rosturk
Derrycoosh
Achillbeg I.
Newport B.
CLARE I.
Clew Bay
Westport
Westport B.
Louisburgh
R335
Killadangan
Aghagower
Killavally
Ballintober
765 ▲ CROAGH PATRICK
Caher I.
Killadoon
Cregganbaun
Carrowkennedy ▲ 392
Party
Inishturk
Sheeffry Hills
PARTRY MTS.
R
763 ▲
Inishbofin
819 ▲ MWEELREA
R335
N59
683 ▲
Toomakeady
Lough
Mask
Inishshark
Killary Harbour
Srahnalong
Gowlaun
Leenaun
Joyce Country
Tully Cross
N59
Clonbur
Cong
Cleggan
Letterfrack
R344
Maum
Cornamona
R345
Moyard Streamstown
BENBAUN 730 ▲ CONNEMARA NAT. PARK
MAUMTURK MTS.
Maam Cross
I
Clifden
Recess
N59
Clifden B.
N59
660 ▲
Oughterard
CONNEMARA
R336
N59
Ballyconneely
Toombeola
R342
Derryrush
R340
Screeb
G
Slyne Hd.
R341
Roundstone
Glinsk
Kilbrickan
Callow
Kylesa
Kilkieran
R336
Ballyconneely Bay
Carna
Lettermore
Costelloe
Ardmore
Lettermore I.
Rossaveel
Bertraghboy Bay
Carraroe
Inveran
Caher
Lettermullan
Gorumna
Kilkieran Bay
Cashla Bay
Gal
North Sound
Black Hd.
Kilmurvy
Kilronan
Murroogh
INISHMORE
Inishmaan
345 ▲ SL. EL.
ARAN IS.
South Sd.
Inisheer
Doolin
R479
Kilshanny
Cliffs of Moher
R478
38
Hags Hd.

P

Q

R

S

2   3   4   5

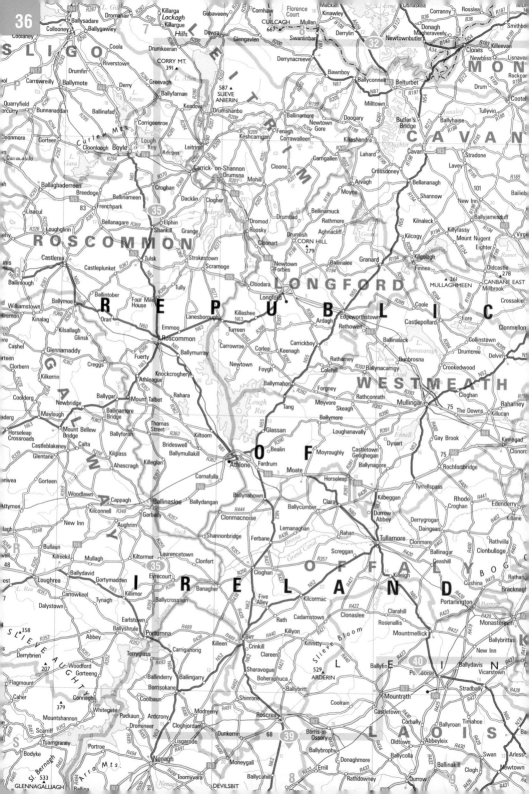

Key to Town Plan Symbols

Through Route(dual/single)	✝	Abbey/Cathedral	✿	Garden	_i_	Tourist Information Centre open all year
Secondary Road(dual/single)		Ancient Monument	⛴	Historic Ship	_i_	summer only
Minor Road		Aquarium		House		Zoo
Pedestrian Roads		Art Gallery		House & Garden	✦	Other Place of Interest
Restricted Access Roads		Bird Garden		Museum	H	Hospital
Shopping Streets		Building of Public Interest		Preserved Railway	P	Parking
Railway		Castle		Railway Station		Police Station
Railway/Bus Station		Church of Interest		Roman Antiquity	PO	Post Office
Shopping Precinct		Cinema		Theatre	▲	Youth Hostel
Park						

London

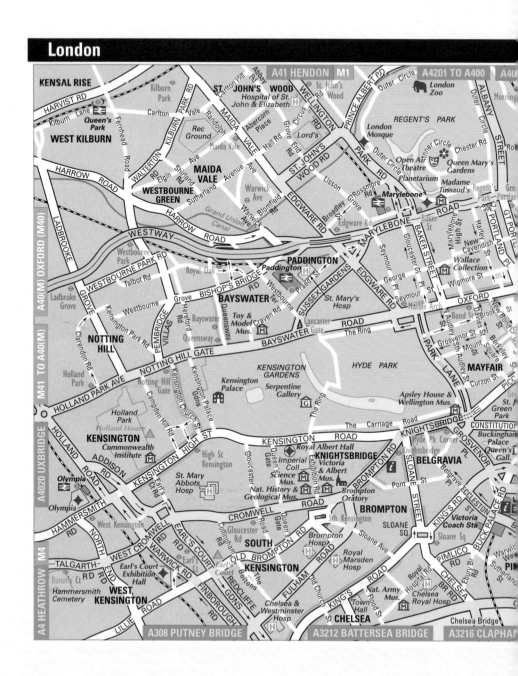

KENSAL RISE

ST. JOHN'S WOOD
A41 HENDON M1
A4201 TO A400
London Zoo

Abbey Rd
St. John's Rd

Kilburn Park

Carlton Hill
Hospital of St. John & Elizabeth

WELLINGTON RD
PRINCE ALBERT RD
Outer Circle
ALBANY STREET

HARVIST RD
Carlton
Vale
REGENT'S PARK

Kilburn Lane
Queen's Park
Fernhead
Randolph Ave
Abercorn Place
London Mosque
Morning

WEST KILBURN
Maida Vale
Grove End Rd
Hall Rd
Outer Circle
Open Air Theatre
Chester Rd

HARROW ROAD
Road
WALTERTON
Elgin
Shirland Ave
MAIDA VALE
Warwick Ave
Blomfield
ST. JOHN'S WOOD RD
Lord's
Park Rd
Planetarium
Queen Mary's Gardens
Madame Tussaud's
Regent

WESTBOURNE GREEN
Sutherland
Warwick
Grand Union Canal
Lisson
Edgware Rd
Marylebone
Baker St
High St
Harley
New Cavendish
GT PORTLA
PORTLAND PL

WESTWAY
HARROW ROAD
Westbourne Park Rd
Praed St
Bishop's Bridge Rd
Westbourne Ter
MARYLEBONE ROAD
Gloucester
Seymour
George
Wigmore St
Wallace Collection

LADBROKE
A40(M) OXFORD (M40)
Ladbroke Grove
Westbourne
Talbot Rd
PADDINGTON
Paddington
SUSSEX GARDENS
St. Mary's Hosp
OXFORD

M41 TO A40(M)
GROVE
Kensington Park Rd
Hereford Rd
Bayswater
BISHOP'S BRIDGE RD
Craven Rd
Lancaster Gate
Bond St
Marble Arch
Davies St
New Bond

NOTTING HILL
PEMBRIDGE VILLAS
Queensway
BAYSWATER
Toy & Model Mus.
The Ring
BAYSWATER ROAD
Grosvenor St
Berkeley

A4020 UXBRIDGE
Clarendon Rd
Holland Park
NOTTING HILL GATE
Notting Hill Gate
KENSINGTON GARDENS
HYDE PARK
MAYFAIR
Curzon St
PICC

HOLLAND PARK AVE
Kensington Gdns
Kensington Palace
Serpentine Gallery
The Ring
Apsley House & Wellington Mus.
St. James's Green Park

HOLLAND ROAD
Holland Park
Holland House
Campden Hill Rd
The Carriage Road
KNIGHTSBRIDGE
CONSTITUTION

KENSINGTON
Commonwealth Institute
KENSINGTON HIGH ST
KENSINGTON ROAD
Hyde Pk Corner
Buckingham Palace
Queen's Gall.
BELGRAVIA

Olympia
ADDISON RD
KENSINGTON CT RD
High St Kensington
Gloucester
Royal Albert Hall
Kensington Gore
Imperial Coll
KNIGHTSBRIDGE
Victoria & Albert Mus.
BROMPTON RD
SLOANE STREET
GROSVENOR PL
Belgrave

Olympia
St. Mary Abbots Hosp
Science Mus.
Nat. History & Geological Mus.
Brompton Oratory
BROMPTON
Victoria Coach Sta

A4 HEATHROW M4
HAMMERSMITH RD
NORTH END RD
West Kensington
CROMWELL ROAD
Gloucester Rd
Queen's Gate
Sth Kensington
SLOANE SQ
Sloane Sq
KING'S RD
BUCK PALACE RD
PIMLICO

TALGARTH RD
WEST CROMWELL RD
WARWICK RD
EARL'S COURT
OLD BROMPTON RD
SOUTH KENSINGTON
Brompton Hosp
Sloane Ave
Royal Marsden Hosp
PIMLICO
Ebury Br Rd
CHELSEA BR RD

Baron's Ct
Earl's Court Exhibition Hall
Earl's Ct
The Boltons
FULHAM ROAD
Royal Hospital Rd
Nat. Army Mus.
Chelsea Royal Hosp

Hammersmith Cemetery
WEST KENSINGTON
REDCLIFFE GDNS
FINBOROUGH RD
Chelsea & Westminster Hosp
KING'S RD
Townhead St
CHELSEA
Chelsea Bridge

LILLIE ROAD
A308 PUTNEY BRIDGE
A3212 BATTERSEA BRIDGE
A3216 CLAPHAM

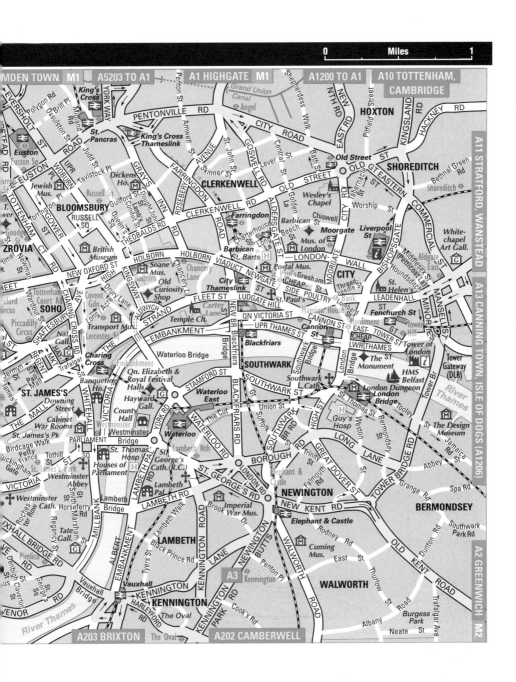

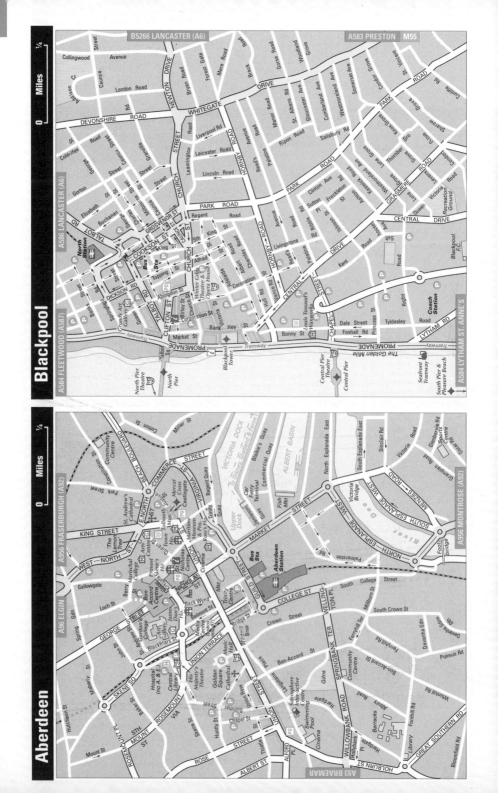

Blackpool

Aberdeen

Belfast

¼   0   Miles

A2 CARRYDUFF, BALLYNAHINCH
A24 CARRYDUFF, BALLYNAHINCH
A1 LISBURN
A12 TO M1. LISBURN, CRAIGAVON
A12 ANTRIM (M2), CARRICKFERGUS (M2, M5, A2)
M3 ANTRIM (M2)
A501 CRUMLIN

River Lagan

Ormeau Park

Central Station
Bridge End Station
Botanic Station
Gt. Victoria St Rail Station
City Hospital Station
Bus Sta
Bus Sta

City Hall
Grand Opera House
St. Peter's Cathedral
Royal Victoria Hospital
Maternity Hospital
City Hospital
Queen's University
Waterfront Hall
Castlecourt Centre
Belfast Waterfront Hall
Royal Courts of Justice
Ulster Hall
Group Theatre
Technical College
Recreation Centre

Car Ferry Terminal
Sea Cat Terminal

FALLS ROAD
SPRINGFIELD ROAD
SHANKILL ROAD
CRUMLIN ROAD
GROSVENOR ROAD
DIVIS STREET
WESTLINK
DONEGALL ROAD
ORMEAU ROAD
CROMAC ST
RAVENHILL ROAD
ALBERT BRIDGE
EAST BRIDGE ST
QUEEN'S BRIDGE
QUEEN ELIZABETH BR
LAGANBANK
OXFORD STREET
MAY STREET
CHICHESTER ST
ADELAIDE ST
BEDFORD ST
DUBLIN RD
GREAT VICTORIA STREET
UNIVERSITY RD
BRADBURY
DONEGALL PASS
SHORT STRAND
NEWTOWNARDS ROAD
MIDDLEPATH ST
ALBERT BRIDGE RD
WOODSTOCK ROAD
QUEEN'S QUAY
DONEGALL QUAY
CORPORATION ST
YORK ST
DUNBAR LINK
VICTORIA ST
ANN ST
COLLEGE SQ
DONEGALL PL
ROYAL AVE
PETER'S HILL
CARRICK HILL
MILLFIELD

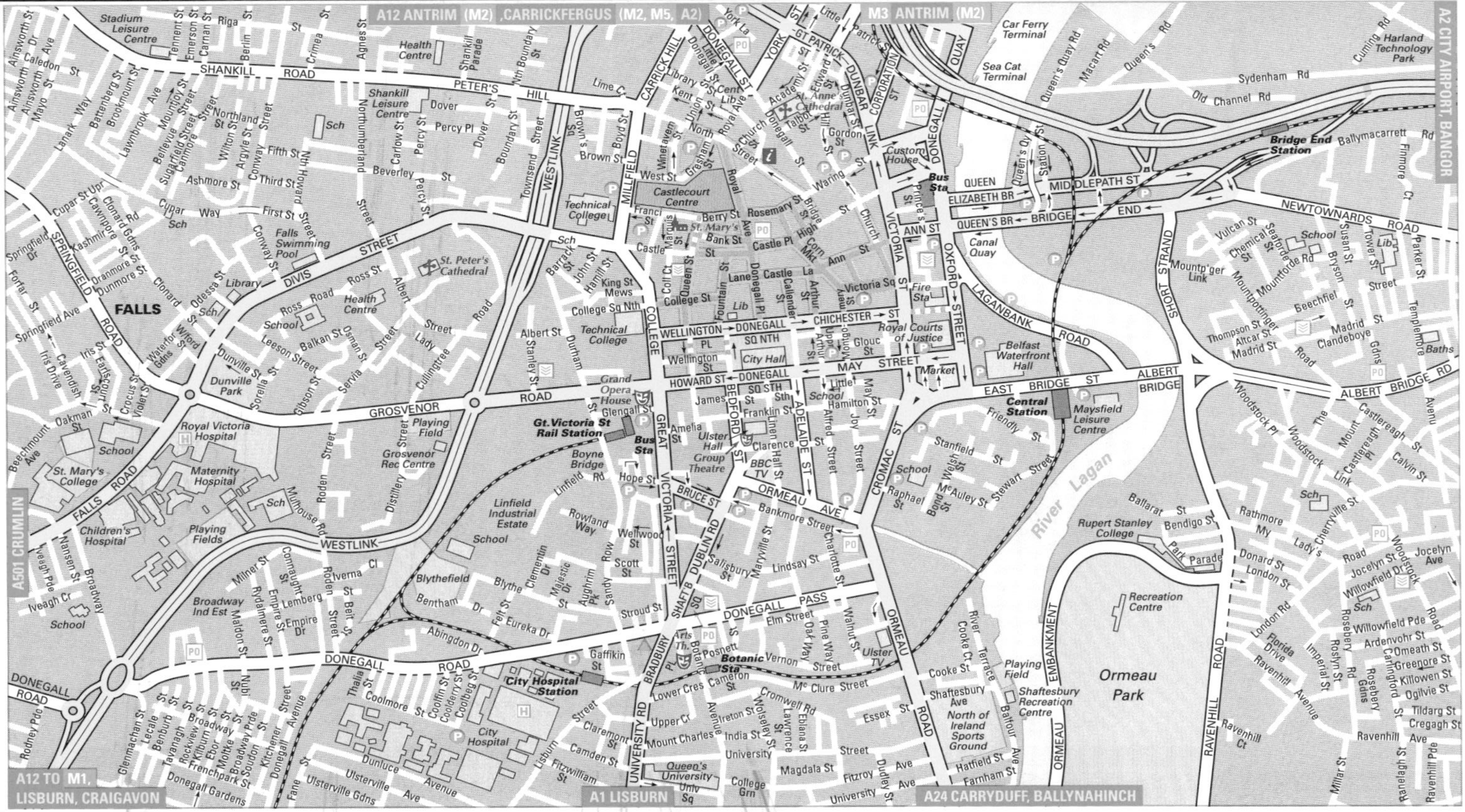

Birmingham

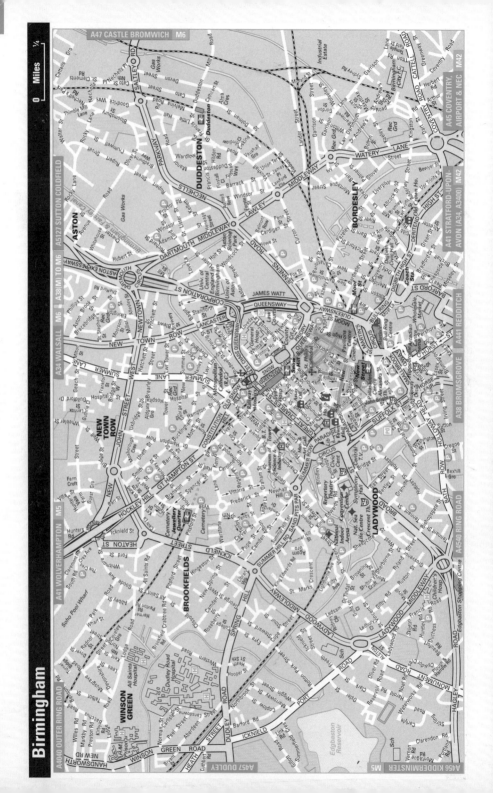

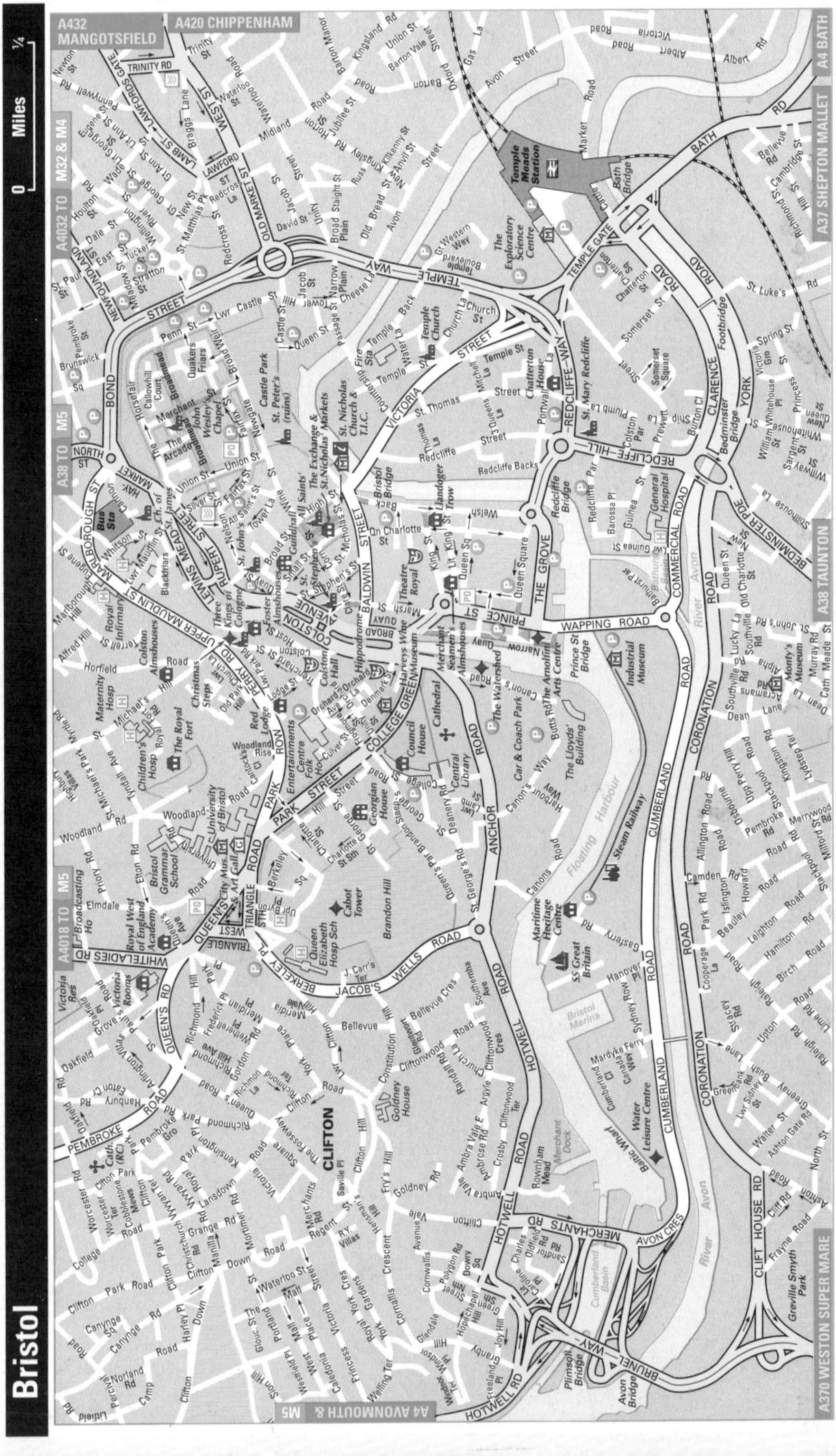

Bristol
0
Miles
¼
A432 MANGOTSFIELD
A420 CHIPPENHAM
A4032 TO M32 & M4
A38 TO M5
A4018 TO M5
A4 AVONMOUTH & M5
A370 WESTON SUPER MARE
A38 TAUNTON
A37 SHEPTON MALLET
A4 BATH
Temple Meads Station
The Exploratory Science Centre
Temple Church
St. Mary Redcliffe
Castle Park
St. Peter's (ruins)
The Exchange & St. Nicholas' Markets
St. Nicholas Church & T.I.C.
Bristol Bridge
Llandoger Trow
Theatre Royal
Bus Sta
Royal Infirmary
Colston Almshouses
Christmas Steps
Three Kings of Cologne
Foster Almshouses
Colston Hall
Hippodrome
Harveys Wine Museum
Cathedral
Council House
Central Library
Georgian House
Merchant Seamen's Almshouses
The Watershed
The Arnolfini Arts Centre
Industrial Museum
Prince St Bridge
The Lloyds' Building
Car & Coach Park
Floating Harbour
Steam Railway
Maritime Heritage Centre
SS Great Britain
Bristol Marina
Water Leisure Centre
Baltic Wharf
Merchant Dock
Cumberland Basin
Plimsoll Bridge
Avon Bridge
River Avon
Cabot Tower
Brandon Hill
Queen Elizabeth Hosp Sch
University of Bristol
City Mus. & Art Gall.
Bristol Grammar School
Royal West of England Academy
Victoria Rooms
Broadcasting Ho
The Royal Fort
Children's Hosp
Maternity Hosp
Red Lodge
Entertainments Centre
Goldney House
CLIFTON
Cath. (RC)
Greville Smyth Park
Monty's Museum
General Hospital
Queen Square
The Grove
Redcliffe Bridge
Bedminster Bridge
Footbridge
John Wesley Chapel
The Arcade
Broadmead
Quakers Friars
Temple Way
Victoria Street
Redcliffe Way
Baldwin Street
Colston Avenue
College Green
Park Row
Park Street
Anchor Road
Hotwell Road
Cumberland Road
Coronation Road
Commercial Road
Clarence Road
Bath Road
York Road
Bedminster Pde
Wapping Road
Prince St
Marlborough St
Bond Street
Newfoundland St
Old Market St
West St
Lawford St
Upper Maudlin St
Whiteladies Rd
Queen's Rd
Pembroke Road
Jacob's Wells Road
Merchants Rd
Brunel Way
Clift House Rd
Avon Cres

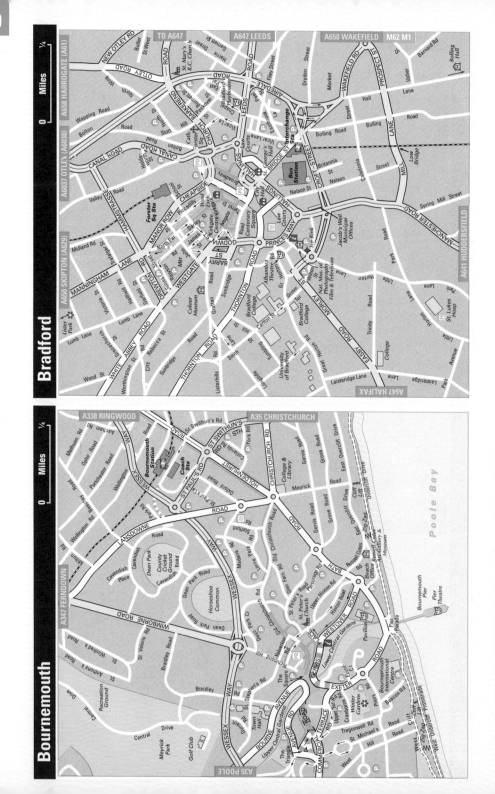

Bradford

¼

Miles

0

A658 HARROGATE (A61)

A6037 OTLEY (A6038)

A650 SKIPTON (A629)

TO A647

A647 LEEDS

A650 WAKEFIELD

M62 M1

A641 HUDDERSFIELD

A647 HALIFAX

NEW OTLEY RD

OTLEY ROAD

AIREDALE ROAD

WAKEFIELD RD

PROSPECT ST

MANCHESTER ROAD

St. Mary's R.C. Church

Harris Street

St West

King

North

Butler

Street

Street

St West

Chapel

Bradford Playhouse

Vicar La.

Vicar Lane

Leeds

Rd

Fley Street

Dryden Street

Market

Barnard Rd

Bolling Hall

Usher

Hall

Lane

Wapping Road

Bolton

Road

Foster Sq.

St. Peter's Cath.

Bolling Road

Bolling

Street

Low Bridge

CANAL ROAD

Bolton Road

Canal Road

Valley

Road

Holds

Broadway

Britannia

Caledonia

Spring Mill Street

CHEAPSIDE

Wool Exchange

Piccadilly

Tyrrel St

City Hall

St. George's Hall

Nelson St

Nelson St

Road

THAMES TRADE

Forster Sq Sta

MANOR ROW

Darley St

James St

Kirkgate

Centenary Square

Law Courts

Municipal Offices

Jacob's Well

Midland Rd

North Park

Rawson Mkt

GODWIN

Ice Rink

MANNINGHAM LANE

DREWTON RD

WESTGATE

BARRY ST

PRINCESS WAY

Sunbridge

Alhambra Theatre

Gt Horton

Nat. Mus. of Photography Film & Television

Sunwin St

Horton

Little Horton Lane

St. Lukes Hosp

Lister Park

Lumb Lane

Lumb Lane

Grattan

Colour Museum

Bradford College

Carlton St

Pier

Bradford College Rd

Little Horton Lane

Park

WHITE ABBEY ROAD

Rebecca St

City

Sunbridge

Hill St

Smith

Great Horton Rd

EASBY ROAD

Trinity

Road

Avenue

Worthington St

Wood St

Listerhills

THORNTON ROAD

Longside

University of Bradford

Laisteridge Lane

College

Laisteridge Lane

Park

MORLEY

MILL LANE

CROFT STREET

HALL INGS

Interchange Sta

Bus Station

BRIDGE ST

Bournemouth

¼

Miles

0

A338 RINGWOOD

A35 CHRISTCHURCH

A347 FERNDOWN

A35 POOLE

Poole Bay

WESSEX WAY

ST SWITHUN'S

St Swithun's Rd

ST PAUL'S RD

CHRISTCHURCH RD

HOLDENHURST ROAD

LANSDOWNE

WESSEX WAY

WIMBORNE ROAD

BOURNE AVENUE

COMMERCIAL

GERVIS ROAD

WESTOVER ROAD

BATH ROAD

EXETER ROAD

AVENUE RD

Ascham Rd

Methuen Rd

Oxford Road

Queen's Road

Porchester Road

Wellington

Wellington

Milton Rd

St. Anthony's Road

St. Winifred's Road

St. Valarie Rd

Bournemouth Station

Coach Sta

St. Paul's Rd

York Rd

5TH

College & Library

Meyrick

Gervis Road

Grove Road

East Overcliff Drive

Undercliff Drive

Cavendish Road

Dean Park

County Cricket Ground

Cavendish Place

Dean Park Road

Horseshoe Common

Stafford Rd

Lorne Park Rd

Madeira

Old Christchurch Road

Gervis Road

Russell Cots Art Gallery & Museum

Cliff

Bournemouth Pier

Pier Theatre

Braidley Rd

Dean Road

Glen Fern Rd

St. Peter's Road

Upper Hinton Rd

Hinton Road

Beach Office

Pier Approach

Pier

Richmond Hill

The Square

St. Stephen's Rd

Town Hall

The Triangle

Upper Central Gardens

BOURNE

Lower Central Gardens

Pavilion

Bournemouth International Centre

Meyrick Park

Golf Club

Recreation Ground

Central Drive

Braidley

Durant Rd

Cranborne Rd

Priory

Winter Gardens

West Cliff

Tregonwell Rd

St. Michael's Road

Beacon Rd

West Hill

West Cliff Road

West Undercliff Promenade

Zig-Zag Lift

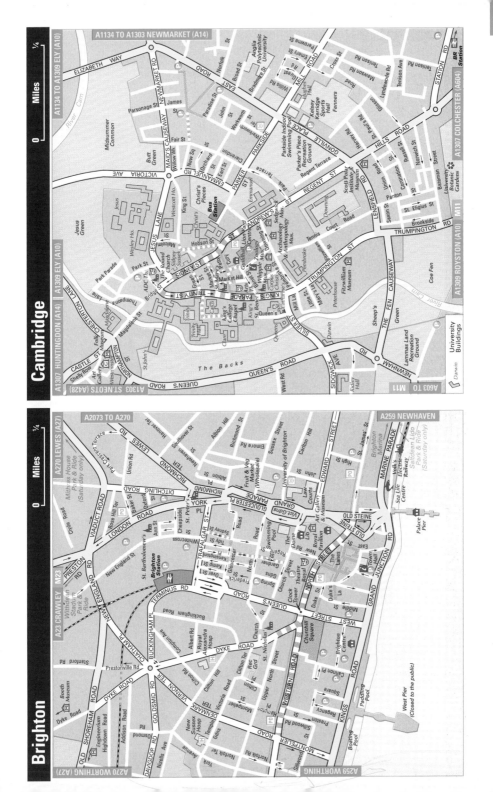

Brighton

Cambridge

Cardiff

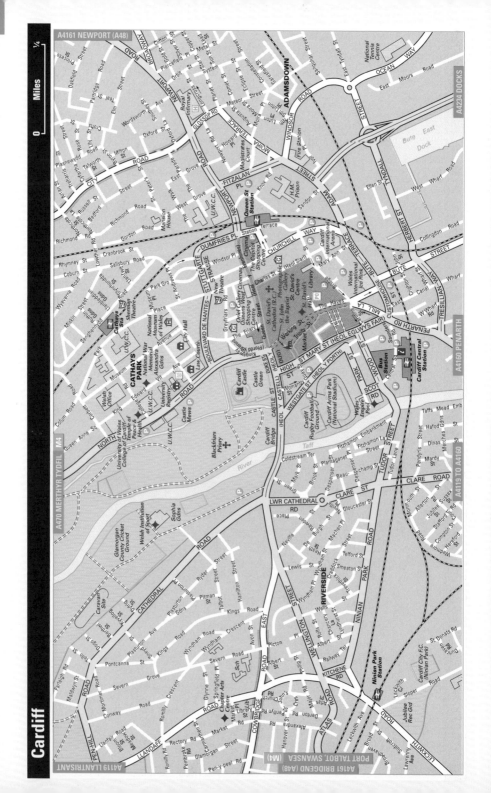

A4234 DOCKS

A4160 PENARTH

A4119 TO A4160

A470 MERTHYR TYDFIL M4

A4119 LLANTRISANT

A4161 BRIDGEND (A48) PORT TALBOT, SWANSEA (M4)

0 ¼ Miles

ADAMSDOWN

National Tennis Centre

OCEAN WAY

Bute East Dock

HERBERT ST

TYNDALL

CUSTOMHOUSE ST

PENARTH RD

TRESILLIAN

Queen St Station

CATHAYS PARK

National War Memorial
National Museum of Wales
City Hall
Law Courts

Cathays Sta

Welsh Office

University of Wales College of Cardiff

U.W.C.C.

Temple of Peace & Health

Sherman Theatre

NORTH ROAD

Blackfriars Priory

Cardiff Castle
Castle Green
Castle Mews

Cardiff Bridge

River Taff

Glamorgan County Cricket Ground

Welsh Institution of Sport

Sophia Gdns

Caravan Site

St David's Hall
St David's Centre
Capitol Shopping Centre
New Theatre
Oriel Gallery
Queen's West Shopping Centre
Photographic Gallery
Wales International Ice Rink

St John the Baptist
St David's Cathedral (R.C.)
Central Market

The Hayes

Cardiff Central Station

Bus Station

Cardiff Arms Park (National Stadium)
Cardiff Rugby Football Ground
Wales Empire Pool

WESTGATE ST
HIGH ST
ST MARY ST (HEOL EGLWYS FAIR)

CLARE ROAD

RIVERSIDE

CATHEDRAL ROAD

WELLINGTON STREET

NINIAN PARK ROAD

Ninian Park Station

Cardiff City F.C. (Ninian Park)

Jubilee Rec Grd

Chapter Arts Centre

COWBRIDGE ROAD

LLANDAFF ROAD

PEN-HILL ROAD

LECKWITH ROAD

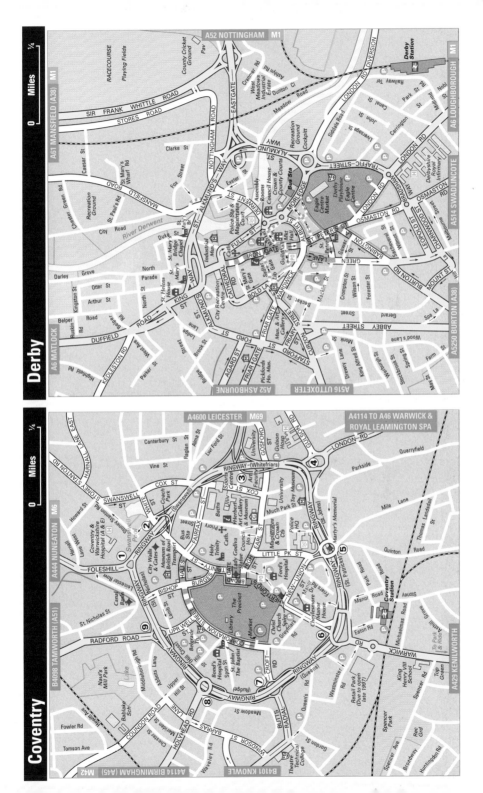

Derby

Coventry

Dublin

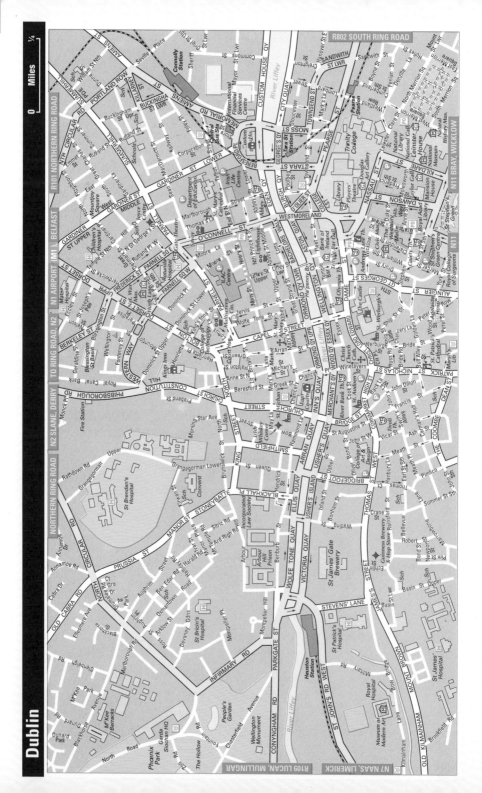

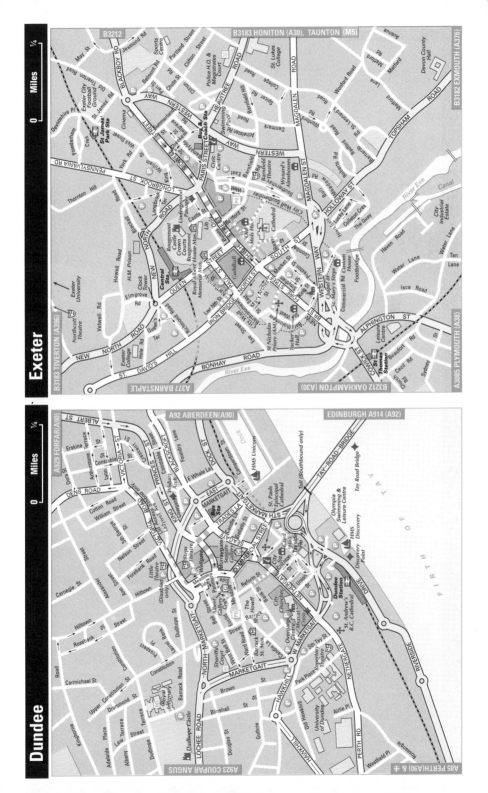

Exeter

Dundee

Edinburgh

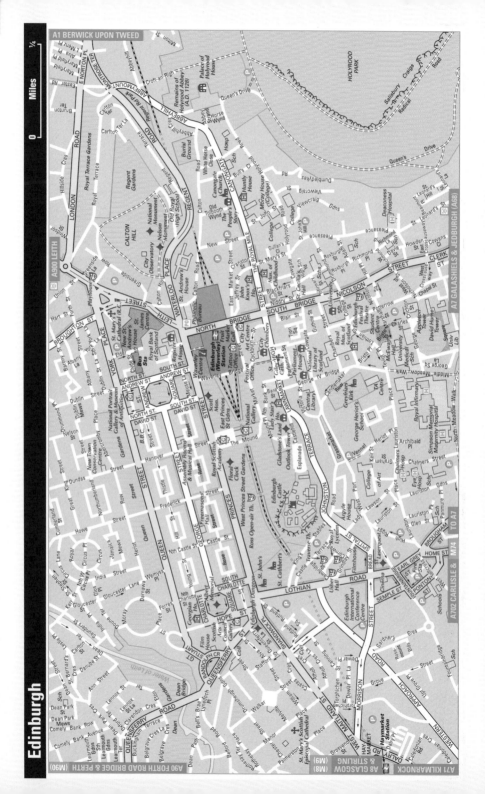

Glasgow

Miles ¼ 0

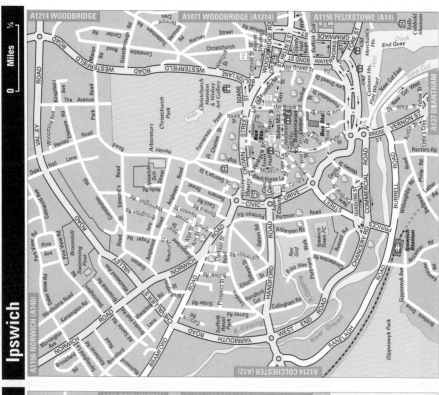

Ipswich

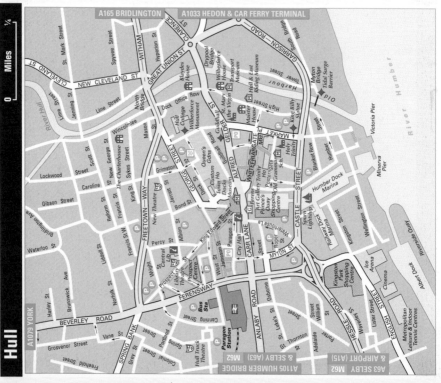

Hull

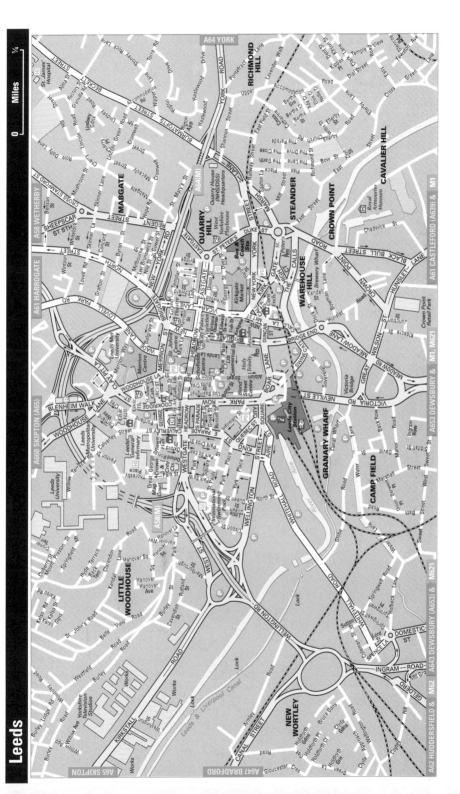

Leeds

59

Liverpool

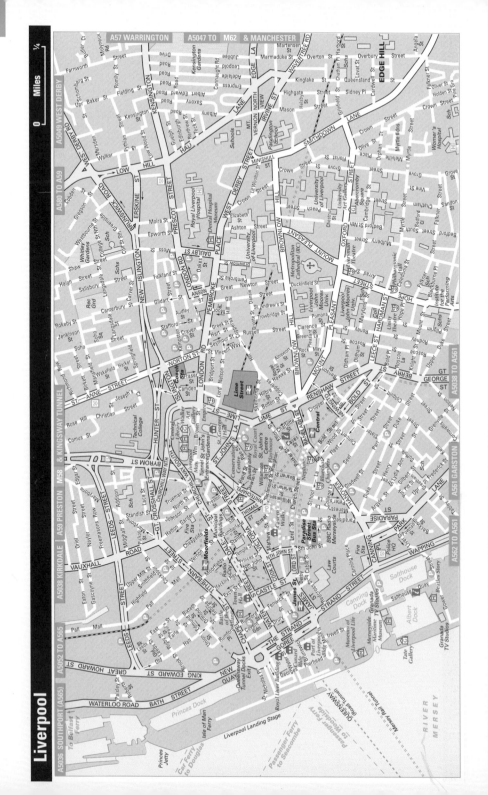

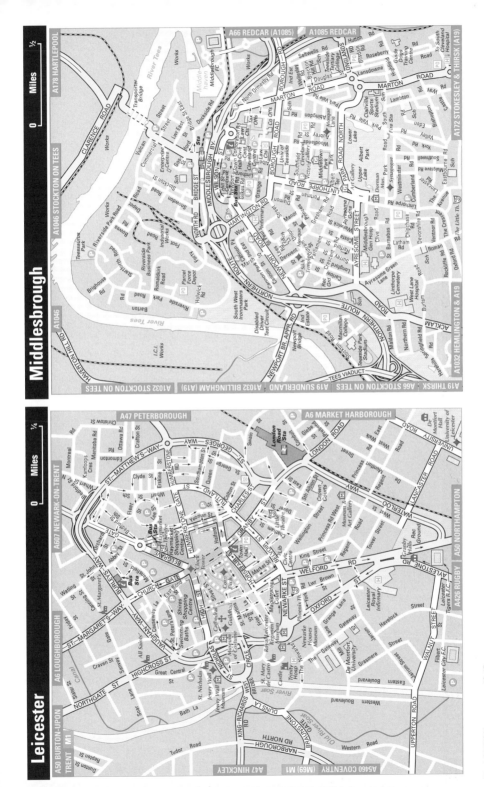

Middlesbrough

CLARENCE ROAD

River Tees

River Tees

A66 REDCAR (A1085) | A1085 REDCAR

A172 STOKESLEY & THIRSK (A19)

A1032 HEMLINGTON & A19

Leicester

A607 NEWARK-ON-TRENT

A6 LOUGHBOROUGH

A50 BURTON-UPON-TRENT | M1

UNIVERSITY ROAD

A50 NORTHAMPTON

A26 RUGBY

For LONDON see pages 42-45

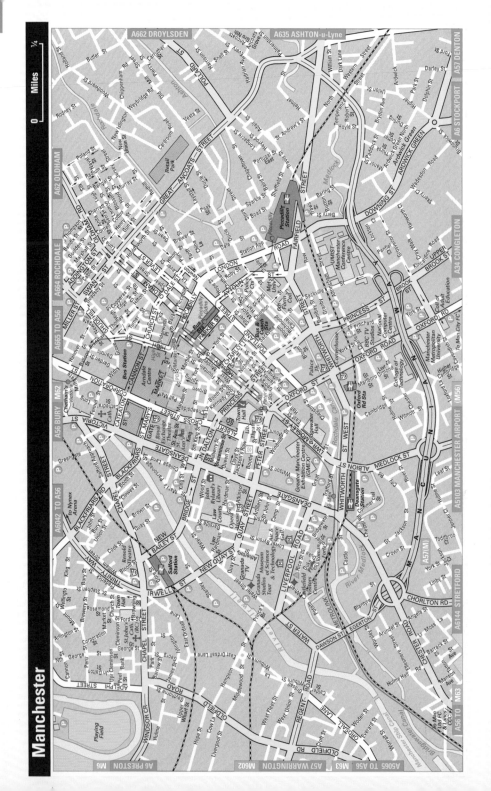

Manchester

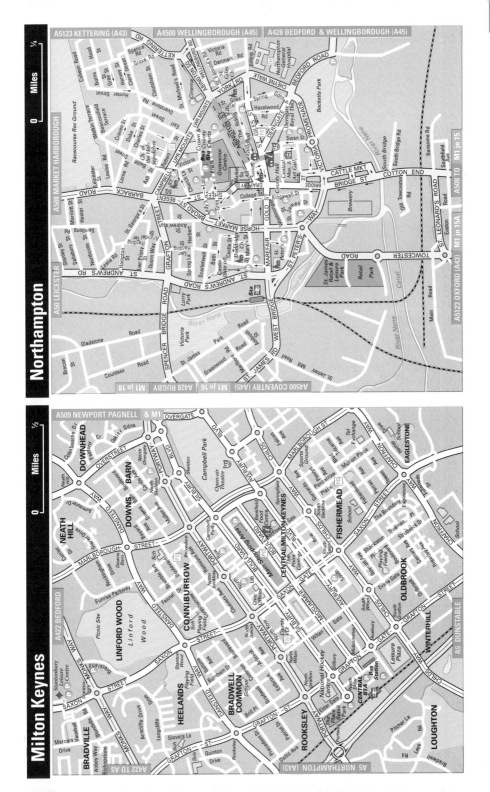

Milton Keynes

Northampton

Newcastle

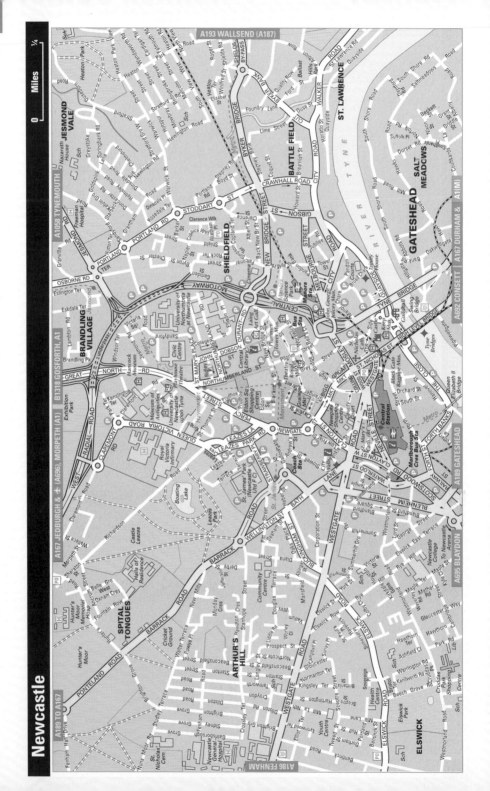

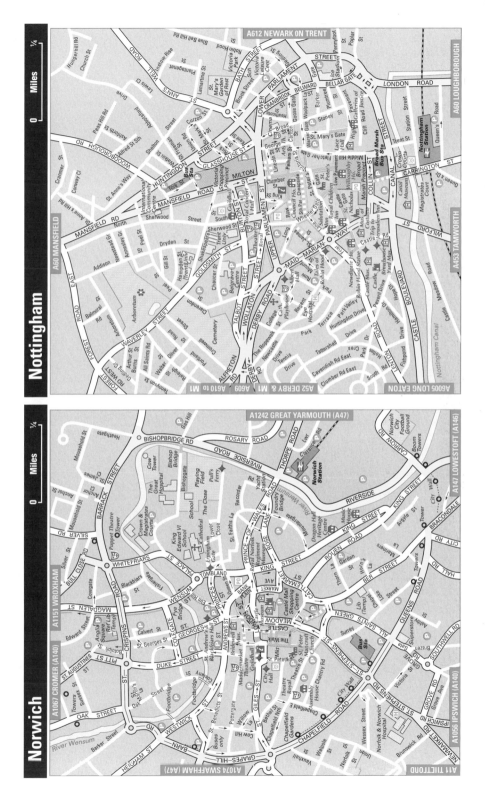

Norwich

Nottingham

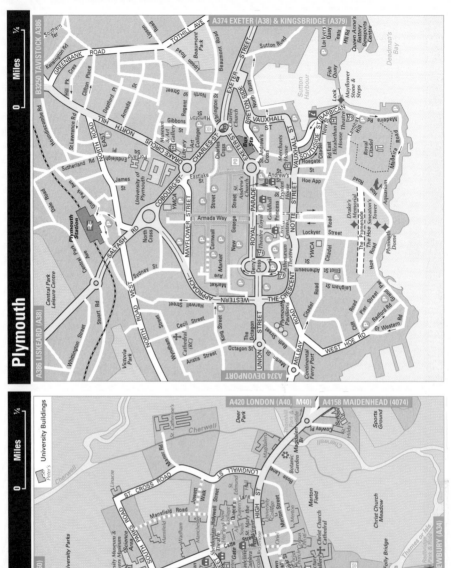

Plymouth

B3250 TAVISTOCK A386

A374 EXETER (A38) & KINGSBRIDGE (A379)

A386 LISKEARD (A38)

A374 DEVONPORT

0   Miles   ¼

Central Park Leisure Centre
Plymouth Station
Sutton Harbour
Royal Citadel
Barbican
Hoe
The Promenade

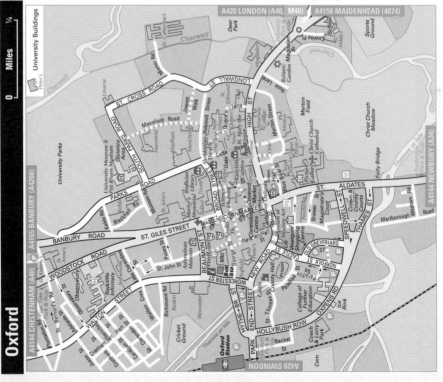

Oxford

A4144 CHELTENHAM (A40) | A4165 BANBURY (A4260)

A420 LONDON (A40, M40) | A4158 MAIDENHEAD (4074)

A4144 NEWBURY (A34)

A420 SWINDON

0   Miles   ¼

University Buildings

University Parks
University Museum & Pitt Rivers Museum
Christ Church Meadow
Oxford Station
Cricket Ground

Portsmouth

Reading

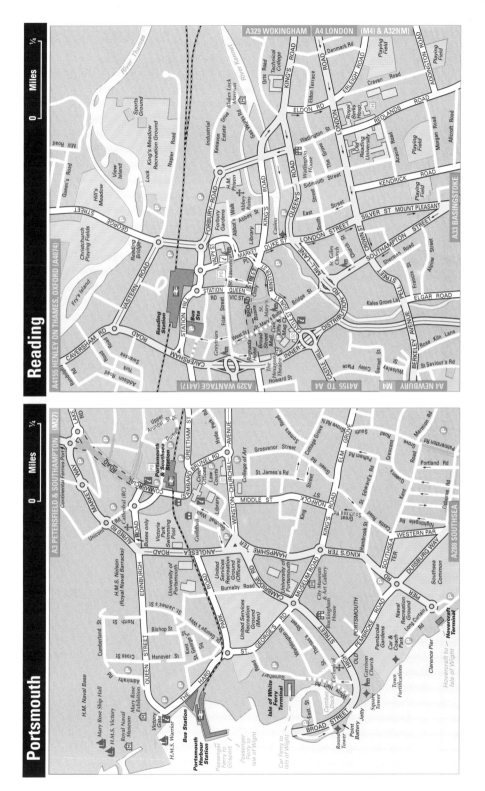

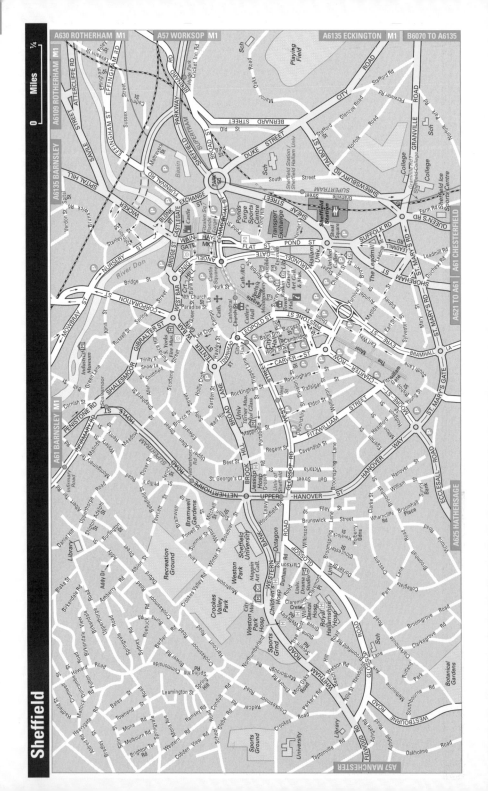

Sheffield

Southend

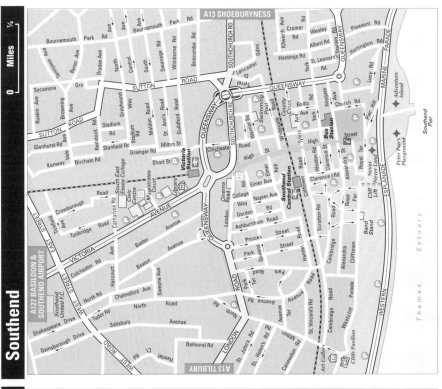

Southampton

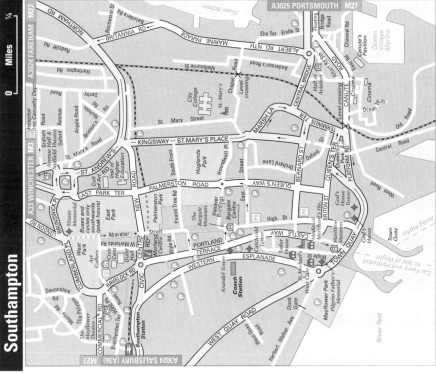

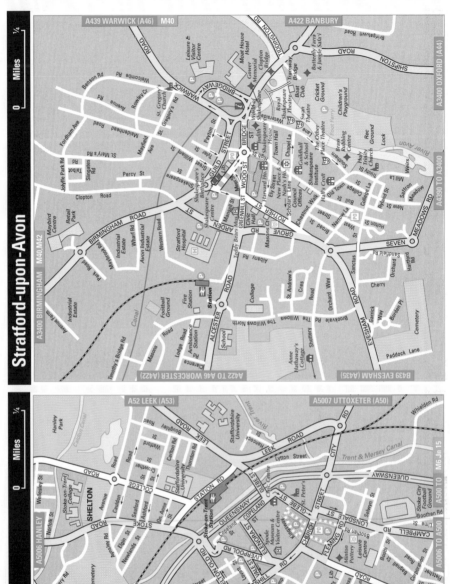

Stratford-upon-Avon

A439 WARWICK (A46) M40

A422 BANBURY

A3400 OXFORD (A44)

A3400 BIRMINGHAM M40.M42

A4390 TO A3400

A422 TO A46 WORCESTER (A422)

B439 EVESHAM (A435)

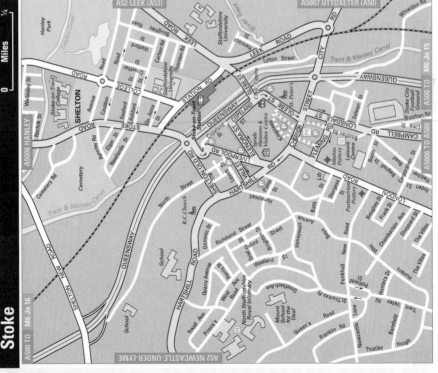

Stoke

A52 LEEK (A53)

A5007 UTTOXETER (A50)

A5006 HANLEY

M6 Jn 15

A500 TO A500

A5006 TO A500

A500 TO M6 Jn 16

A52 NEWCASTLE-UNDER-LYME

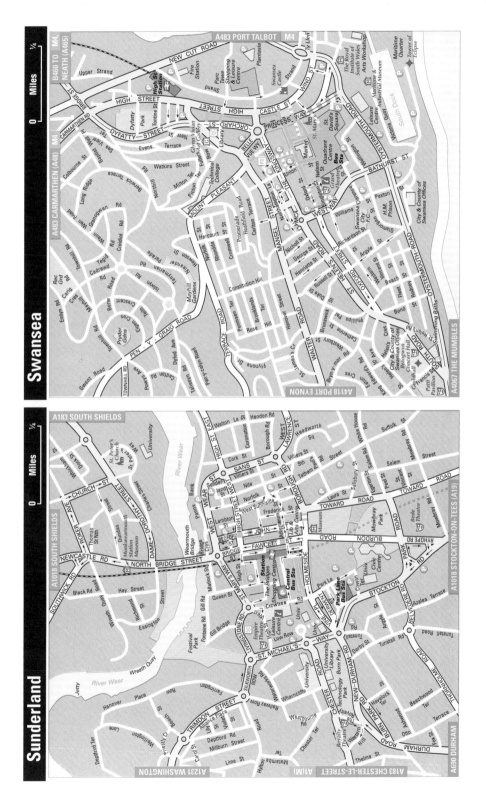

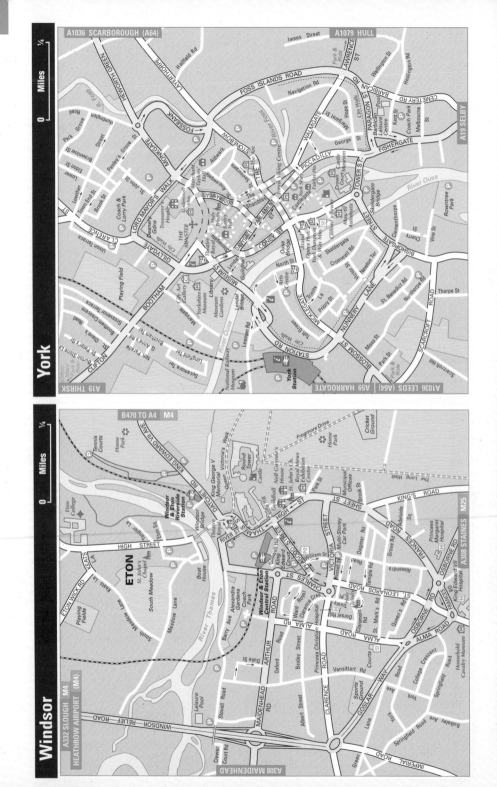

York

A1036 SCARBOROUGH (A64)
A1079 HULL
A19 SELBY
A19 THIRSK
A1036 LEEDS (A64)
A59 HARROGATE

Windsor

B470 TO A4 M4
M25
A308 STAINES
A332 SLOUGH M4
HEATHROW AIRPORT (M4)
A308 MAIDENHEAD

ETON

Abbr.	Full	Abbr.	Full	Abbr.	Full
Aberd C	Aberdeen City	Chan Is	Channel Islands	Gtr Man	Greater Manchester
Aberds	Aberdeenshire	Ches	Cheshire	Gwyn	Gwynedd
Angl	Isle of Anglesey	Clack	Clackmannanshire	Hants	Hampshire
Arg/Bute	Argyll & Bute	Cornw'l	Cornwall	Hartlep'l	Hartlepool
Bath/NE Som'set	Bath & North East Somerset	Cumb	Cumbria	Heref/Worcs	Hereford & Worcester
Beds	Bedfordshire	Denbs	Denbighshire	Herts	Hertfordshire
Berks	Berkshire	Derby	Derbyshire	H'land	Highland
Bl Gwent	Blaenau Gwent	Derby C	Derby City	I of Man	Isle of Man
Borders	Scottish Borders	D'lington	Darlington	I of Scilly	Isles of Scilly
Bournem'th	Bournemouth	Dumf/Gal	Dumfries & Galloway	I of Wight	Isle of Wight
Bridg	Bridgend	Dundee C	Dundee City	Invercl	Inverclyde
Brighton/Hove	Brighton and Hove	E Ayrs	East Ayrshire	Kingston/Hull	Kingston upon Hull
Bristol	City & County of Bristol	E Dunb	East Dunbartonshire	Lancs	Lancashire
Bucks	Buckinghamshire	E Loth	East Lothian	Leics	Leicestershire
C of Edinb	City of Edinburgh	E Renf	East Renfrewshire	Leics C	Leicester City
C of Glasg	City of Glasgow	E Riding Yorks	East Riding of Yorkshire	Lincs	Lincolnshire
C of York	City of York	E Sussex	East Sussex	Mersey	Merseyside
Caerph	Caerphilly	Falk	Falkirk	Merth Tyd	Merthyr Tydfil
Cambs	Cambridgeshire	Flints	Flintshire	Middlesbro'	Middlesbrough
Card	Cardiff	Glos	Gloucestershire	Midloth	Midlothian
Carms	Carmarthenshire	Gtr Lon	Greater London	M/Keynes	Milton Keynes
Ceredig'n	Ceredigion			Monmouths	Monmouthshire
				N Ayrs	North Ayrshire

Abbr.	Full	Abbr.	Full	Abbr.	Full
N Lanarks	North Lanarkshire	Shetl'd	Shetland		
N Lincs	North Lincolnshire	Shrops	Shropshire		
N Som'set	North Somerset	Som'set	Somerset		
N Yorks	North Yorkshire	Staffs	Staffordshire		
NE Lincs	North East Lincolnshire	S'thampton	Southampton		
Neath P Talb	Neath Port Talbot	Stirl	Stirling		
Newp	Newport	Stockton	Stockton on Tees		
Northants	Northamptonshire	Stoke	Stoke-on-Trent		
Northum	Northumberland	Swan	Swansea		
Notts	Nottinghamshire	Thamesd'n	Thamesdown		
Oxon	Oxfordshire	Torf	Torfaen		
Pembs	Pembrokeshire	Tyne/Wear	Tyne & Wear		
Perth/Kinr	Perth & Kinross	V of Glam	Vale of Glamorgan		
Portsm'th	Portsmouth	W Dunb	West Dunbartonshire		
Redcar/Clevel'd	Redcar & Cleveland	W Isles	Western Isles		
Renf	Renfrewshire	W Loth	West Lothian		
Rh Cyn Taff	Rhondda Cynon Taff	W Midlands	West Midlands		
Rutl'd	Rutland	W Sussex	West Sussex		
S Ayrs	South Ayrshire	W Yorks	West Yorkshire		
S Gloucs	South Gloucestershire	Warwick	Warwickshire		
S Lanarks	South Lanarkshire	Wilts	Wiltshire		
S Yorks	South Yorkshire	Wrex	Wrexham		

A

Abbey Galway 35 R7
Abbey Town Cumb 20 N17
Abbeydorney Kerry 38 T4
Abbeyfeale Limerick 38 T5
Abbeyleix Laois 40 S9
Abbots Bromley Staffs 11 S20
Abbotsbury Dorset 4 W18
Aberaeron Ceredig'n 9 T15
Aberarth Ceredig'n 9 T15
Abercarn Caerph 4 U17
Aberchirder Aberds 29 G18
Abercrave Powys 9 U16
Aberdare Rh Cyn Taff 9 U16
Aberdaron Gwyn 8 S14
Aberdeen Aberd C 25 H19
Aberdour Fife 24 K17
Aberdulais Neath P Talb 9 U16
Aberdyfi Gwyn 8 S15
Aberfeldy Perth/Kinr 24 J16
Aberffraw Angl 8 R15
Aberfoyle Stirl 24 K15
Abergavenny Monmouths 4 U17
Abergele Conwy 8 R16
Abergwili Carms 9 U15
Abergwyngregyn Gwyn 8 R15
Abergynolwyn Gwyn 8 S16
Aberlady E Loth 25 K18
Abernethy Perth/Kinr 24 K17
Aberporth Ceredig'n 9 T14
Abersoch Gwyn 8 S14
Abersychan Torf 4 U17
Abertillery Bl Gwent 4 U17
Aberystwyth Ceredig'n 9 T15
Abingdon Oxon 5 U21
Abington Limerick 39 S7
Abington S Lanarks 20 L16
Aboyne Aberds 25 H18
Accrington Lancs 15 Q19
Acha Arg/Bute 22 J10
Achanalt H'land 27 G13
Achaphubuil H'land 23 J13
Acharacle H'land 23 J12
Achavanich H'land 28 F17
Achavraie H'land 27 G13
Achill Mayo 34 Q4
Achiltibuie H'land 27 F13
Achnacroish Arg/Bute 23 J12
Achnasheen H'land 27 G13
Achnashellach H'land 27 G13
Achosnich H'land 22 J11
Achriabhach H'land 23 J13
Acklam N Yorks 17 P22
Aclare Sligo 35 P6
Acle Norfolk 13 S27
Acomb C of York 16 Q21
Acton Armagh 37 P11
Acton Burnell Shrops 10 S18
Adamstown Waterford 40 T9
Adare Limerick 39 S6
Adcarn Roscommon 35 Q7
Addingham W Yorks 15 P20
Adlington Lancs 15 Q18
Adrigole Cork 38 U4
Adwick le Street S Yorks 16 Q21

Affric Lodge H'land 27 H13
Aghagower Mayo 34 Q5
Aghalee Antrim 33 N11
Aghavannagh Wicklow 40 S11
Aghaville Cork 38 U5
Aghern Cork 39 T7
Aghnacliff Longford 36 Q8
Aglish Waterford 39 T8
Ahascragh Galway 35 R7
Ahoghill Antrim 33 N11
Ainsdale Mersey 15 Q17
Aird Arg/Bute 23 K12
Aird a Mhulaidh W Isles 26 G10
Aird Asaig Tairbeart W Isles 26 G10
Aird Uig W Isles 26 F9
Airdrie N Lanarks 19 L16
Airor H'land 23 H12
Airth Falk 24 K16
Aisgill Cumb 15 P19
Aith Orkney 30 D18
Aith Shetl'd 31 B21
Akeley Bucks 11 T22
Albrighton Shrops 10 S19
Alcester Warwick 11 T20
Aldborough N Yorks 16 P21
Aldbourne Wilts 5 V20
Aldbrough E Riding Yorks 17 Q23
Aldeburgh Suffolk 13 T27
Aldbury Wilts 5 V20
Alderley Edge Ches 15 R19
Aldermaston Berks 5 V21
Aldershot Hants 6 V22
Aldridge W Midlands 11 S20
Aldsworth Glos 5 U20
Aldwick W Sussex 6 W22
Alexandria W Dunb 24 L14
Alford Aberds 25 H18
Alford Lincs 17 R24
Alfreton Derby 11 R21
Alfriston E Sussex 6 W24
Alkham Kent 7 V26
Allen Kildare 37 R10
Allendale Town Northum 21 N19
Allenheads Northum 21 N19
Allenwood Kildare 37 R10
Allihies Cork 38 U3
Alloa Clack 24 K16
Allonby Cumb 20 N17
Almondsbury S Gloucs 4 U18
Alness H'land 28 G15
Alnmouth Northum 21 M20
Alnwick Northum 21 M20
Alphington Devon 4 W16
Alrewas Staffs 11 S20
Alsager Ches 10 R19
Alston Cumb 21 N19
Alt na h'Airbhe H'land 27 G13
Altanduino H'land 28 F15
Altarnun Cornw'l 2 W14
Altass H'land 28 G14
Althorne Essex 7 U25
Althorpe N Lincs 17 Q22
Altnaharra H'land 28 F15
Alton Hants 6 V22
Alton Staffs 11 S20
Altrincham Gtr Man 15 R19
Alva Clack 24 K16
Alvechurch Heref/Worcs 11 T20

Alveley Shrops 10 T19
Alveston S Gloucs 4 U18
Alvie H'land 24 H16
Alwinton Northum 21 M19
Alyth Perth/Kinr 25 J17
Amble Northum 21 M20
Ambleside Cumb 15 P18
Ambrosden Oxon 11 U21
Amersham Bucks 6 U22
Amesbury Wilts 5 V20
Amlwch Angl 8 R15
Ammanford Carms 9 U16
Ampleforth N Yorks 16 P21
Ampthill Beds 12 T23
Amulree Perth/Kinr 24 J16
An Geata Mór Mayo 34 P3
An t-Ob W Isles 26 G9
Anacotty Limerick 39 S6
Anascaul Kerry 38 T3
Ancaster Lincs 12 S22
Ancroft Northum 21 L19
Ancrum Borders 21 L18
Andover Hants 5 V21
Andoversford Glos 11 U20
Andreas I of Man 14 P15
Angle Pembs 9 U13
Angmering W Sussex 6 W23
Annacarty Tipperary 39 S7
Annacloy Down 33 N12
Annagassan Louth 37 Q11
Annahilt Down 33 P12
Annalong Down 37 P12
Annan Dumf/Gal 20 N17
Annbank S Ayrs 19 M14
Annestown Waterford 40 T9
Annfield Plain Durham 21 N20
Anstey Leics 11 S21
Anstruther Fife 25 K18
Antrim Antrim 33 N11
Appleby-in-Westmorland Cumb 21 N19
Applecross H'land 27 H12
Appledore Devon 3 V15
Appledore Kent 7 V25
Araglin Tipperary 39 T7
Arboe Tyrone 33 N10
Arbroath Angus 25 J18
Archiestown Moray 28 G16
Ardagh Limerick 38 T5
Ardagh Longford 36 Q8
Ardahy Monaghan 33 P10
Ardara Donegal 32 N7
Ardarroch H'land 27 H12
Ardcharnich H'land 27 G13
Ardchyle Stirl 24 K15
Ardcrony Tipperary 36 S8
Ardee Louth 37 Q10
Ardentinny Arg/Bute 23 K14
Ardersier H'land 28 G15
Ardessie H'land 27 G13
Ardfert Kerry 38 T4
Ardfinnane Tipperary 39 T8
Ardgay H'land 28 G15
Ardglass Down 33 P12
Ardgroom Cork 38 U4
Ardhasig W Isles 26 G10
Ardingly W Sussex 6 V23
Ardkearagh Kerry 38 U3
Ardkeen Down 33 P12
Ardleigh Essex 13 U26
Ardley Oxon 11 U21
Ardlui Arg/Bute 24 K14
Ardlussa Arg/Bute 23 K12

Ardmore Galway 34 R4
Ardmore Waterford 39 U8
Ardnacrusha Clare 39 S6
Ardnamona Donegal 32 N7
Ardnaree Mayo 35 P5
Ardnasodan Galway 35 R6
Ardnave Arg/Bute 18 L11
Ardpatrick Limerick 39 T6
Ardrahan Galway 35 R6
Ardreagh Londonderry 33 M10
Ardrishaig Arg/Bute 23 K13
Ardrossan N Ayrs 18 L14
Ardscull Kildare 40 R10
Ardstraw Tyrone 32 N9
Ardtalnaig Perth/Kinr 24 J15
Ardvasar H'land 23 H12
Ardwell Dumf/Gal 18 N14
Ardwell Moray 29 H17
Arinagour Arg/Bute 22 J10
Arisaig H'land 23 J12
Arklow Wicklow 40 S11
Arless Laois 40 S9
Armadale H'land 23 H12
Armadale W Loth 24 L16
Armagh Armagh 33 P10
Armathwaite Cumb 20 N18
Armitage Staffs 11 S20
Armoy Antrim 33 M11
Armthorpe S Yorks 16 Q21
Arncliffe N Yorks 15 P19
Arncott Oxon 6 U21
Arney Fermanagh 32 P8
Arnisdale H'land 23 H12
Arnold Notts 11 R21
Arnside Cumb 15 P18
Arreton I of Wight 5 W21
Arrochar Arg/Bute 24 K14
Arthurstown Wexford 40 T10
Articlave Londonderry 33 M10
Artigarvan Tyrone 32 N9
Arundel W Sussex 6 W22
Arvagh Cavan 36 Q8
Ascot Berks 6 V22
Asfordby Leics 11 S22
Ash Kent 7 V26
Ash Surrey 6 V22
Ashbourne Meath 37 Q11
Ashbourne Derby 11 R20
Ashburton Devon 3 W16
Ashbury Oxon 5 U20
Ashby de-la-Zouch Leics 11 S21
Ashchurch Glos 10 U19
Ashford Wicklow 40 R11
Ashford Derby 16 R20
Ashford Kent 7 V25
Ashington Essex 7 U25
Ashington Northum 21 M20
Ashley Staffs 10 S19
Ashton Ches 15 R18
Ashton-in-Makerfield Gtr Man 15 R18
Ashton Keynes Wilts 5 U20
Ashton under Hill Heref/Worcs 11 T20
Ashton under Lyne Gtr Man 15 R19
Ashurst Hants 5 W20
Ashville Louth 37 Q10
Ashwater Devon 3 W15
Ashwell Herts 12 T23
Ashwick Som'set 4 V18
Askam-in-Furness Cumb 15 P17

Askern S Yorks 16 Q21
Askrigg N Yorks 15 P19
Aslackby Lincs 12 S23
Aspatria Cumb 20 N17
Astee Kerry 38 S4
Astwood Bank Heref/Worcs 11 T20
Athboy Meath 37 Q10
Athea Limerick 38 T5
Athenry Galway 35 R6
Atherstone Warwick 11 S20
Atherton Gtr Man 15 Q19
Athlacca Limerick 39 T6
Athleague Roscommon 35 Q7
Athlone Westmeath 36 R8
Athy Kildare 40 S10
Attical Down 37 P11
Attleborough Norfolk 13 S26
Attymon Galway 35 R6
Atworth Wilts 5 V19
Auchenblae Aberds 25 J19
Auchencairn Dumf/Gal 19 N16
Auchengray S Lanarks 20 L16
Auchertool Fife 25 K17
Auchinleck E Ayrs 19 M15
Auchronie Angus 25 J18
Auchterarder Perth/Kinr 24 K16
Auchterderran Fife 24 K17
Auchtermuchty Fife 25 K17
Auchtertyre H'land 27 H12
Aucloggeen Galway 35 R6
Audlem Ches 10 S18
Audley Staffs 10 R19
Augher Tyrone 32 P9
Aughnacloy Tyrone 33 P10
Aughrim Clare 35 R6
Aughrim Galway 35 R7
Aughrim Wicklow 40 S11
Auldearn H'land 28 G16
Aultbea H'land 27 G12
Austwick N Yorks 15 P19
Avebury Wilts 5 V20
Avening Glos 5 U19
Aveton Gifford Devon 3 X16
Aviemore H'land 24 H16
Avoca Wicklow 40 S11
Avoch H'land 28 G15
Avonmouth Bristol 4 U18
Axbridge Som'set 4 V18
Axminster Devon 4 W17
Axmouth Devon 4 W17
Aylesbury Bucks 6 U22
Aylesford Kent 7 V24
Aylesham Kent 7 V26
Aylsham Norfolk 13 S26
Aynho Northants 11 U21
Ayr S Ayrs 19 M14
Aysgarth N Yorks 15 P19
Ayton N Yorks 17 P23
Ayton Borders 21 L19

B

Bac W Isles 26 F11
Backwell N Som'set 4 V18
Bacton Norfolk 13 S26
Bacup Lancs 15 Q19
Badenscoth Aberds 29 H19
Badenyon Aberds 25 H17

Badrallach *H'land* 27 G13
Bagh a Chaisteil *W Isles* 22 J8
Bagillt *Flints* 15 R17
Bagshot *Surrey* 6 V22
Baildon *W Yorks* 15 Q20
Baile Ailein *W Isles* 26 F10
Baileborough *Cavan* 37 Q10
Bainbridge *N Yorks* 15 P19
Bainton *E Riding Yorks* 17 Q22
Bakewell *Derby* 11 R20
Bala *Gwyn* 8 S16
Balbeggie *Perth/Kinr* 24 K17
Balblair *H'land* 28 G15
Balbriggan *Dublin* 37 Q11
Balcombe *W Sussex* 6 V23
Balderton *Notts* 11 R22
Baldoyle *Dublin* 37 R11
Balfour *Orkney* 30 D18
Balfron *Stirl* 24 K15
Balintore *H'land* 28 G16
Balla *Mayo* 35 Q5
Ballachulish *H'land* 23 J13
Ballagh *Galway* 35 R5
Ballagh *Limerick* 38 T5
Ballagh *Tipperary* 39 S8
Ballaghaderreen *Roscommon* 35 Q6
Ballantrae *S Ayrs* 18 M14
Ballasalla *I of Man* 14 P14
Ballater *Aberds* 25 H17
Ballaugh *I of Man* 14 P14
Ballickmoyler *Laois* 40 S9
Ballin Cloher *Kerry* 38 T4
Ballina *Mayo* 35 P5
Ballina *Tipperary* 39 S7
Ballinadee *Cork* 39 U6
Ballinafad *Sligo* 35 P7
Ballinagar *Offaly* 36 R9
Ballinakill *Laois* 40 S9
Ballinalack *Westmeath* 36 Q9
Ballinalea *Wicklow* 40 R11
Ballinalee *Longford* 36 Q8
Ballinamallard *Fermanagh* 32 P8
Ballinameen *Roscommon* 35 Q7
Ballinamore *Leitrim* 36 P8
Ballinamore Bridge *Galway* 35 R7
Ballinascarty *Cork* 39 U6
Ballinasloe *Galway* 35 R7
Ballincollig *Cork* 39 U6
Ballincurrig *Cork* 39 U7
Ballindaggan *Wexford* 40 S10
Ballinderreen *Galway* 35 R6
Ballinderry *Tipperary* 35 R7
Ballinderry Upr. *Antrim* 33 N11
Ballindine *Mayo* 35 Q6
Ballindooly *Galway* 35 R5
Ballineen *Cork* 39 U6
Ballingarry *Limerick* 38 T6
Ballingarry *Tipperary* 39 S7
Ballingarry *Tipperary* 39 S8
Ballingeary *Cork* 38 U5
Ballinhassig *Cork* 39 U6
Ballinlea *Antrim* 33 M11
Ballinlough *Roscommon* 35 Q6
Ballinluig *Perth/Kinr* 24 J16
Ballinrobe *Mayo* 35 Q5
Ballinskelligs *Kerry* 38 U3
Ballinspittle *Cork* 39 U6
Ballintober *Mayo* 34 Q5
Ballintober *Roscommon* 35 Q7
Ballintoy *Antrim* 33 M11
Ballintra *Donegal* 32 N7
Ballintroohan *Donegal* 33 M9
Ballinunty *Tipperary* 39 S8
Ballinure *Tipperary* 39 S8
Ballitore *Kildare* 40 R10
Ballivor *Meath* 37 Q10
Balloch *H'land* 28 H15
Ballochan *Aberds* 25 H18
Ballon *Carlow* 40 S10
Ballure *Donegal* 32 N7
Ballyagran *Limerick* 39 T6
Ballybay *Monaghan* 37 P9
Ballybofey *Donegal* 32 N8
Ballyboghil *Dublin* 37 Q11
Ballybogy *Antrim* 33 M10
Ballybritt *Offaly* 36 R8

Ballybrittas *Laois* 36 R9
Ballybrophy *Laois* 39 S8
Ballybunion *Kerry* 38 S4
Ballycahill *Tipperary* 39 S8
Ballycanew *Wexford* 40 S11
Ballycarney *Wexford* 40 S10
Ballycarry *Antrim* 33 N12
Ballycastle *Mayo* 34 P5
Ballycastle *Antrim* 33 M11
Ballyclare *Antrim* 33 N12
Ballyclerahan *Tipperary* 39 T8
Ballyclogh *Cork* 39 T6
Ballycolla *Laois* 40 S9
Ballyconneely *Galway* 34 R3
Ballyconnell *Cavan* 36 P8
Ballyconnell *Sligo* 32 P6
Ballycotton *Cork* 39 U7
Ballycrossaun *Galway* 36 R7
Ballycroy *Mayo* 34 P4
Ballycumber *Offaly* 36 R8
Ballydangan *Roscommon* 36 R7
Ballydavid *Galway* 35 R7
Ballydavid *Kerry* 38 T3
Ballydavis *Laois* 40 S9
Ballydehob *Cork* 38 U5
Ballydonegan *Cork* 38 U3
Ballyduff *Kerry* 38 T4
Ballyduff *Waterford* 39 T7
Ballydugan *Down* 33 P12
Ballyfarnan *Roscommon* 35 P7
Ballyferriter *Kerry* 38 T3
Ballyfin *Laois* 40 R9
Ballyforan *Roscommon* 35 R7
Ballygar *Galway* 35 Q7
Ballygarrett *Wexford* 40 S11
Ballygawley *Sligo* 32 P7
Ballygawley *Tyrone* 33 P9
Ballyglass *Mayo* 35 Q5
Ballygorman *Donegal* 32 M9
Ballygowan *Down* 33 N12
Ballygrant *Arg/Bute* 18 L11
Ballyhaght *Limerick* 39 T6
Ballyhahill *Limerick* 38 S5
Ballyhaise *Cavan* 36 P9
Ballyhalbert *Down* 33 P13
Ballyhale *Galway* 35 R5
Ballyhaunis *Mayo* 35 Q6
Ballyhean *Mayo* 34 Q5
Ballyheige *Kerry* 38 T4
Ballyhooly *Cork* 39 T7
Ballyhornan *Down* 33 P12
Ballyjamesduff *Cavan* 36 Q9
Ballykelly *Londonderry* 33 M9
Ballykillin *Donegal* 32 M9
Ballylanders *Limerick* 39 T7
Ballylaneen *Waterford* 40 T9
Ballyliffin *Donegal* 32 M9
Ballylongford *Kerry* 38 S5
Ballylooby *Tipperary* 39 T8
Ballylynan *Laois* 40 S9
Ballymacarbry *Waterford* 39 T8
Ballymacoda *Cork* 39 U8
Ballymagorry *Tyrone* 32 N9
Ballymahon *Longford* 36 Q8
Ballymakenny *Louth* 37 Q11
Ballymartin *Down* 37 P12
Ballymena *Antrim* 33 N11
Ballymoe *Galway* 35 Q7
Ballymoney *Antrim* 33 M10
Ballymore *Westmeath* 36 R8
Ballymore Eustace *Kildare* 37 R10
Ballymote *Sligo* 35 P6
Ballymullakill *Roscommon* 36 R7
Ballymurphy *Carlow* 40 S10
Ballymurray *Roscommon* 36 Q7
Ballynabola *Wexford* 40 T10
Ballynacally *Clare* 38 S5
Ballynacarrigy *Westmeath* 36 Q8
Ballynacorra *Cork* 39 U7
Ballynagore *Westmeath* 36 R9
Ballynahinch *Down* 33 P12
Ballynahown *Westmeath* 36 R8
Ballynamona *Cork* 39 T6
Ballynamult *Waterford* 39 T8
Ballyneety *Limerick* 39 S6
Ballynure *Antrim* 33 N12

Ballyporeen *Tipperary* 39 T7
Ballyragget *Kilkenny* 40 S9
Ballyroan *Laois* 40 S9
Ballyroe *Cork* 39 T7
Ballyronan *Londonderry* 33 N10
Ballyroney *Down* 33 P11
Ballysadare *Sligo* 32 P6
Ballyshannon *Donegal* 32 P7
Ballyshannon *Kildare* 37 R10
Ballyshrule *Galway* 35 R7
Ballysloe *Tipperary* 39 S8
Ballysteen *Limerick* 39 S6
Ballyvaghan *Clare* 35 R5
Ballyvourney *Cork* 38 U5
Ballyvoy *Antrim* 33 M11
Ballywalter *Down* 33 N13
Ballyward *Down* 33 P11
Ballywilliam *Wexford* 40 T10
Balmaclellan *Dumf/Gal* 19 M15
Balmedie *Aberds* 25 H19
Balnapaling *H'land* 28 G15
Balquhidder *Stirl* 24 K15
Balrath *Meath* 37 Q11
Balrothery *Dublin* 37 Q11
Balsall *W Midlands* 11 T20
Balsham *Cambs* 12 T24
Baltasound *Shetl'd* 31 A22
Baltimore *Cork* 39 V5
Baltinglass *Wicklow* 40 S10
Baltracey *Kildare* 37 R10
Baltray *Louth* 37 Q11
Balvicar *Arg/Bute* 23 K12
Bamber Bridge *Lancs* 15 Q18
Bamburgh *Northum* 21 L20
Bamford *Derby* 16 R20
Bampton *Devon* 4 W17
Bampton *Oxon* 5 U20
Banagher *Offaly* 36 R8
Banbridge *Down* 33 P11
Banbury *Oxon* 11 T21
Banchory *Aberds* 25 H18
Bandon *Cork* 39 U6
Banff *Aberds* 29 G18
Bangor *Mayo* 34 P4
Bangor *Down* 33 N12
Bangor *Gwyn* 8 R15
Bangor-is-y-coed *Wrex* 10 S18
Banham *Norfolk* 13 T26
Bankend *Dumf/Gal* 20 M16
Bankfoot *Perth/Kinr* 24 J16
Bankhead *Aberd C* 25 H19
Banks *Lancs* 15 Q18
Bannockburn *Stirl* 24 K16
Bannow *Wexford* 40 T10
Banstead *Surrey* 6 V23
Banteer *Cork* 39 T6
Bantry *Cork* 38 U5
Banwell *N Som'set* 4 V18
Bar Hill *Cambs* 12 T24
Barabhas *W Isles* 26 F10
Baranailt *Londonderry* 33 M9
Barassie *S Ayrs* 19 L14
Barbon *Cumb* 15 P18
Bardney *Lincs* 17 R23
Barefield *Clare* 39 S6
Barford *Warwick* 11 T20
Bargoed *Caerph* 4 U17
Bargrennan *Dumf/Gal* 19 M14
Barham *Kent* 7 V26
Barkway *Herts* 12 U24
Barlborough *Derby* 16 R21
Barley *N Yorks* 16 Q21
Barley *Herts* 12 T24
Barmby Moor *E Riding Yorks* 17 Q22
Barmoor Castle *Northum* 21 L19
Barmouth *Gwyn* 8 S15
Barna *Galway* 35 R5
Barnaderg *Galway* 35 R6
Barnard Castle *Durham* 21 N20
Barnesmore *Donegal* 32 N7
Barnet *Gtr Lon* 6 U23
Barnetby le Wold *N Lincs* 17 Q23
Barnham *Suffolk* 13 T25
Barnhill *Moray* 28 G17
Barnoldswick *Lancs* 15 Q19
Barnsley *S Yorks* 16 Q21
Barnstaple *Devon* 3 V15
Barnt Green *Heref/Worcs* 11 T20
Barr *S Ayrs* 19 M14
Barraduff *Kerry* 38 T5

Barran *Cavan* 32 P8
Barrhead *E Renf* 19 L15
Barrhill *S Ayrs* 18 M14
Barrow-in-Furness *Cumb* 15 P17
Barrow upon Humber *N Lincs* 17 Q23
Barrowford *Lancs* 15 Q19
Barry *Angus* 25 K18
Barry *V of Glam* 4 V17
Barton *N Yorks* 16 P20
Barton-le-Clay *Beds* 12 U23
Barton upon Humber *N Lincs* 17 Q23
Barwell *Leics* 11 S21
Baschurch *Shrops* 10 S18
Basildon *Essex* 7 U25
Basingstoke *Hants* 5 V21
Baslow *Derby* 10 R20
Bassingham *Lincs* 12 S23
Bath *Bath/NE Som'set* 5 V19
Bathford *Bath/NE Som'set* 5 V19
Bathgate *W Loth* 24 L16
Batley *W Yorks* 16 Q20
Batterstown *Meath* 37 R10
Battle *E Sussex* 7 W24
Bawdeswell *Norfolk* 13 S26
Bawdsey *Suffolk* 13 T26
Bawnboy *Cavan* 36 P8
Bawtry *S Yorks* 16 R21
Bayston Hill *Shrops* 10 S18
Beachley *Glos* 4 U18
Beaconsfield *Bucks* 6 U22
Beadnell *Northum* 21 L20
Bealin *Westmeath* 36 R8
Bealnablath *Cork* 39 U6
Beaminster *Dorset* 4 W18
Bearsden *E Dunb* 19 L15
Bearsted *Kent* 7 V25
Beattock *Dumf/Gal* 20 M17
Beaufort *Kerry* 38 T4
Beaufort *Bl Gwent* 4 U17
Beaulieu *Hants* 5 W21
Beauly *H'land* 28 H15
Beaumaris *Angl* 8 R15
Bebington *Mersey* 15 R17
Beccles *Suffolk* 13 T27
Beck Row *Suffolk* 12 T24
Beckermet *Cumb* 14 P16
Beckfoot *Cumb* 20 N17
Beckhampton *Wilts* 5 V20
Beckingham *Notts* 17 R22
Beckington *Som'set* 5 V19
Bedale *N Yorks* 16 P20
Beddgelert *Gwyn* 8 R15
Bedford *Beds* 12 T23
Bedlington *Northum* 21 M20
Bedwas *Caerph* 4 U17
Bedworth *Warwick* 11 T21
Beech Hill *Down* 33 P11
Beeford *E Riding Yorks* 17 Q23
Beelaha *Clare* 38 S4
Beer *Devon* 4 W17
Beeston *Notts* 11 S21
Beeswing *Dumf/Gal* 19 M16
Begelly *Pembs* 9 U14
Beguildy *Powys* 10 T17
Beighton *S Yorks* 16 R21
Beith *N Ayrs* 19 L14
Belbroughton *Heref/Worcs* 10 T19
Belchford *Lincs* 17 R23
Belclare *Galway* 35 R6
Belcoo *Fermanagh* 36 P8
Belderg *Mayo* 34 P4
Belfast *Antrim* 33 N12
Belford *Northum* 21 L20
Belgooly *Cork* 39 U7
Bellacorick *Mayo* 34 P4
Bellaghy *Londonderry* 33 N10
Bellahy *Sligo* 35 Q6
Bellanagare *Roscommon* 35 Q7
Bellanaleck *Fermanagh* 32 P8
Bellanamore *Donegal* 32 N7
Bellananagh *Cavan* 36 Q8
Bellavary *Mayo* 35 Q5
Belleek *Donegal* 32 N7
Belleek *Armagh* 33 P11
Belleville *Galway* 35 R6
Bellinamuck *Longford* 36 Q8
Bellingham *Northum* 21 M19
Bellsbank *E Ayrs* 19 M15
Bellshill *N Lanarks* 19 L15

Belmont *Lancs* 15 Q19
Belmont *Shetl'd* 31 A22
Belmullet *Mayo* 34 P4
Belper *Derby* 11 R21
Belsay *Northum* 21 M20
Beltinge *Kent* 7 V26
Belton *N Lincs* 17 Q22
Belton *Norfolk* 13 S27
Beltra *Mayo* 34 Q5
Beltra *Sligo* 32 P6
Belturbet *Cavan* 36 P9
Bembridge *I of Wight* 5 W21
Benburb *Tyrone* 33 P10
Benington *Lincs* 12 R24
Benllech *Angl* 8 R15
Bennettsbridge *Kilkenny* 40 S9
Benson *Oxon* 5 U21
Bentley *Hants* 6 V22
Bentley *S Yorks* 16 Q21
Benwick *Cambs* 12 T23
Beragh *Tyrone* 32 N9
Bere Alston *Devon* 3 X15
Bere Regis *Dorset* 5 W19
Berkeley *Glos* 5 U19
Berkhamsted *Herts* 6 U22
Berriedale *H'land* 28 F17
Berriew *Powys* 10 S17
Berrow *Som'set* 4 V17
Berwick *E Sussex* 6 W24
Berwick-upon-Tweed *Northum* 21 L19
Bessbrook *Armagh* 33 P11
Bethersden *Kent* 7 V25
Bethesda *Gwyn* 8 R15
Bettws Bledrws *Ceredig'n* 9 T15
Bettyhill *H'land* 28 E15
Bettystown *Meath* 37 Q11
Betws *Bridg* 9 U16
Betws-y-Coed *Conwy* 8 R16
Beulah *Powys* 9 T16
Beverley *E Riding Yorks* 17 Q23
Beville *Mayo* 34 P5
Bewcastle *Cumb* 21 M18
Bewdley *Heref/Worcs* 10 T19
Bexhill *E Sussex* 7 W24
Bexley *Gtr Lon* 6 V24
Bibury *Glos* 5 U20
Bicester *Oxon* 11 U21
Bickington *Devon* 4 W16
Bicton *Shrops* 10 S18
Biddenden *Kent* 7 V25
Biddulph *Staffs* 10 R19
Bideford *Devon* 3 V15
Bidford-on-Avon *Warwick* 11 T20
Bigbury *Devon* 3 X16
Biggar *S Lanarks* 20 L16
Biggin Hill *Gtr Lon* 6 V24
Biggleswade *Beds* 12 T23
Bildeston *Suffolk* 13 T25
Billericay *Essex* 7 U24
Billesdon *Leics* 11 S22
Billingborough *Lincs* 12 S23
Billingham *Stockton* 21 N21
Billinghay *Lincs* 12 R23
Billingshurst *W Sussex* 6 V23
Bilston *W Midlands* 10 S19
Binbrook *Lincs* 17 R23
Bingham *Notts* 11 S22
Bingley *W Yorks* 15 Q20
Birchgrove *Swan* 9 U16
Birchington *Kent* 7 V26
Birdhill *Tipperary* 39 S7
Birdlip *Glos* 5 U19
Birkdale *Mersey* 15 Q17
Birkenhead *Mersey* 15 R17
Birmingham *W Midlands* 11 T20
Birr *Offaly* 36 R8
Birtley *Northum* 21 M19
Birtley *Tyne/Wear* 21 N20
Bishop Auckland *Durham* 21 N20
Bishop Monkton *N Yorks* 16 P21
Bishopbriggs *E Dunb* 19 L15
Bishop's Castle *Shrops* 10 T18
Bishop's Cleeve *Glos* 10 U19
Bishop's Frome *Heref/Worcs* 10 T19
Bishops Lydeard *Som'set* 4 V17

Place	County	Map	Ref
Bishop's Nympton	Devon	3	W16
Bishop's Stortford	Herts	6	U24
Bishop's Tawton	Devon	3	V15
Bishop's Waltham	Hants	5	W21
Bishopsteignton	Devon	4	W16
Bishopstoke	Hants	5	W21
Bishopston	Swan	9	U15
Bitton	S Gloucs	5	V19
Blaby	Leics	11	S21
Black Rock	Louth	37	Q11
Blackburn	Lancs	15	Q19
Blackford	Cumb	20	N18
Blackford	Perth/Kinr	24	K16
Blackpool	Lancs	15	Q17
Blackridge	W Loth	19	L16
Blackrock	Dublin	37	R11
Blackwater	Wexford	40	T11
Blackwaterfoot	N Ayrs	18	L13
Blackwood	Caerph	4	U17
Blackwood	S Lanarks	19	L16
Blaenau Ffestiniog	Gwyn	8	S16
Blaenavon	Torf	4	U17
Blagdon	N Som'set	4	V18
Blaina	Bl Gwent	4	U17
Blair Atholl	Perth/Kinr	24	J16
Blairgowrie	Perth/Kinr	24	J17
Blakeney	Glos	5	U19
Blakeney	Norfolk	13	S26
Blanchland	Northum	21	N19
Blanchardstown	Dublin	37	R11
Blandford Forum	Dorset	5	W19
Blaney	Fermanagh	32	P8
Blarney	Cork	39	U6
Blaydon	Tyne/Wear	21	N20
Bleadon	N Som'set	4	V18
Blean	Kent	7	V26
Blessington	Wicklow	37	R10
Bletchingdon	Oxon	5	U21
Bletchley	M/Keynes	12	U22
Blewbury	Oxon	5	U21
Blidworth	Notts	11	R21
Blisworth	Northants	11	T22
Blockley	Gloucs	11	T20
Blofield	Norfolk	13	S26
Bloxham	Oxon	11	T21
Blubberhouses	N Yorks	16	Q20
Blundeston	Norfolk	13	S27
Blyth	Northum	21	M20
Blyth	Notts	16	R21
Blyth Bridge	Borders	20	L17
Blythburgh	Suffolk	13	T27
Blythe Bridge	Staffs	10	S19
Blyton	Lincs	17	R22
Boat of Garten	H'land	29	H20
Boddam	Aberds	29	H20
Boddam	Shetl'd	31	C21
Bodedern	Angl	8	R14
Bodenham	Heref/Worcs	10	T18
Bodiam	E Sussex	7	V25
Bodinnick	Cornw'l	2	X14
Bodmin	Cornw'l	2	X14
Bodyke	Clare	39	S6
Boggaun	Leitrim	32	P7
Bognor Regis	W Sussex	6	W22
Boheraphuca	Offaly	36	R8
Boherboy	Cork	38	T5
Boherlahan	Tipperary	39	S8
Boho	Fermanagh	32	P8
Bohola	Mayo	35	Q5
Boldon	Tyne/Wear	21	N21
Bolea	Londonderry	33	M10
Boley	Kildare	40	R10
Bollington	Ches	15	R19
Bolney	W Sussex	6	W23
Bolsover	Derby	16	R21
Bolton	Gtr Man	15	Q19
Bolton Abbey	N Yorks	15	Q20
Bolton Bridge	N Yorks	15	Q20
Bolton by Bowland	Lancs	15	Q19
Bolton le Sands	Lancs	15	P18
Bonarbridge	H'land	28	G15
Bonby	N Lincs	17	Q23
Bonchester Bridge	Borders	21	M18
Bonchurch	I of Wight	5	W21
Bo'ness	Falk	24	K16
Bonhill	W Dunb	24	L14
Bonnybridge	Falk	24	K16
Bonnyrigg	Midloth	20	L17
Bonvilston	V of Glam	4	V17
Boot	Cumb	15	P17
Bootle	Cumb	14	P17
Bootle	Mersey	15	R17
Bordon	Hants	6	V22
Borehamwood	Herts	6	U23
Boreland	Dumf/Gal	20	M17
Borgh	W Isles	26	F11
Borgue	Dumf/Gal	19	N15
Borough Green	Kent	7	V24
Boroughbridge	N Yorks	16	P21
Borris	Carlow	40	S10
Borris-in-Ossory	Laois	36	S8
Borrisokane	Tipperary	36	S7
Borrisoleigh	Tipperary	39	S8
Borrowdale	Cumb	15	N17
Borth	Ceredig'n	8	T15
Bosbury	Heref/Worcs	10	T19
Boscastle	Cornw'l	2	W14
Bosham	W Sussex	6	W22
Boston	Lincs	12	S23
Boston Spa	W Yorks	16	Q21
Botesdale	Suffolk	13	T25
Bothel	Cumb	20	N17
Bothenhampton	Dorset	4	W18
Botley	Oxon	5	U21
Bottesford	Leics	11	S22
Bottisham	Cambs	12	T24
Botwnnog	Gwyn	8	S14
Bouladuff	Tipperary	39	S8
Bourne	Lincs	12	S23
Bourne End	Bucks	6	U22
Bournemouth	Bournem'th	5	W20
Bourton-on-the-Water	Glos	11	U20
Bovey Tracey	Devon	4	W16
Bow	Devon	3	W16
Bowes	Durham	15	N20
Bowmore	Arg/Bute	18	L11
Bowness-on-Solway	Cumb	20	N17
Bowness-on-Windermere	Cumb	15	P18
Box	Wilts	5	V19
Boyle	Roscommon	35	Q7
Bozeat	Northants	12	T22
Brabourne	Kent	7	V25
Brabourne Lees	Kent	7	V25
Bracadale	H'land	26	H11
Bracebridge Heath	Lincs	12	R22
Bracklesham	W Sussex	6	W22
Brackley	Northants	11	T21
Bracklin	Cavan	37	Q10
Bracknagh	Offaly	36	R9
Bracknell	Berks	6	V22
Braco	Perth/Kinr	24	K16
Bradford	W Yorks	15	Q20
Bradford on Avon	Wilts	5	V19
Brading	I of Wight	5	W21
Bradpole	Dorset	4	W18
Bradwell-on-Sea	Essex	7	U25
Bradworthy	Devon	3	W15
Brae	Shetl'd	31	B21
Brae Roy Lodge	H'land	24	J14
Braemar	Aberds	24	H17
Braemore	H'land	27	G13
Braemore	H'land	28	F16
Brailsford	Derby	11	S20
Braintree	Essex	7	U25
Bramford	Suffolk	13	T26
Bramhall	Gtr Man	15	R19
Bramhope	W Yorks	16	Q20
Brampton	Cambs	12	T23
Brampton	Cumb	21	N18
Brancaster	Norfolk	13	S25
Branden	Kerry	38	T3
Branderburgh	Moray	28	G17
Brandon	Durham	21	N20
Brandon	Suffolk	13	T25
Branston	Lincs	17	R23
Brantham	Suffolk	13	U26
Bratton Fleming	Devon	3	V16
Braunston	Northants	11	T21
Braunton	Devon	3	V15
Bray	Wicklow	37	R11
Bray	Berks	6	U22
Breage	Cornw'l	2	X13
Breaghva	Clare	38	S4
Breakish	H'land	23	H12
Bream	Glos	4	U18
Breanais	W Isles	26	F9
Brechfa	Carms	9	U15
Brechin	Angus	25	J18
Brecon	Powys	9	U17
Brede	E Sussex	7	W25
Bredenbury	Heref/Worcs	10	T18
Breedoge	Roscommon	35	Q7
Breenagh	Donegal	32	N8
Brent	Gtr Lon	6	U23
Brentwood	Essex	7	U24
Bretforton	Heref/Worcs	11	T20
Brewood	Staffs	10	S19
Bride	I of Man	14	P15
Bridestowe	Devon	3	W15
Brideswell	Roscommon	36	R7
Bridge	Kent	7	V26
Bridge End	Donegal	32	M9
Bridge of Allan	Stirl	24	K16
Bridge of Balgie	Perth/Kinr	24	J15
Bridge of Cally	Perth/Kinr	24	J17
Bridge of Don	Aberd C	25	H19
Bridge of Earn	Perth/Kinr	24	K17
Bridge of Orchy	Arg/Bute	24	J14
Bridge of Weir	Renf	19	L14
Bridgend	Arg/Bute	18	L11
Bridgend	Bridg	4	U16
Bridgetown	Wexford	40	T10
Bridgnorth	Shrops	10	S19
Bridgwater	Som'set	4	V18
Bridlington	E Riding Yorks	17	P23
Bridport	Dorset	4	W18
Brierfield	Lancs	15	Q19
Brierley Hill	W Midlands	10	T19
Brigg	N Lincs	17	Q23
Brighouse	W Yorks	15	Q20
Brighstone	I of Wight	5	W21
Brightlingsea	Essex	7	U26
Brighton	Brighton/Hove	6	W23
Brigstock	Northants	12	T22
Brill	Bucks	6	U21
Brimfield	Heref/Worcs	10	T18
Brinklow	Warwick	11	T21
Brinkworth	Wilts	5	U20
Brinyan	Orkney	30	D17
Bristol	Bristol	4	V18
Briston	Norfolk	13	S26
Briton Ferry	Neath P Talb	9	U16
Brittas	Dublin	37	R11
Brixham	Devon	3	X16
Brixton	Devon	3	X15
Brixworth	Northants	11	T22
Brize Norton	Oxon	5	U20
Broad Chalke	Wilts	5	V20
Broad Haven	Pembs	9	U13
Broad Hinton	Wilts	5	V20
Broadclyst	Devon	4	W17
Broadford	Clare	39	S6
Broadford	Limerick	39	S6
Broadford	H'land	23	H12
Broadhembury	Devon	4	W17
Broadmayne	Dorset	5	W19
Broadstairs	Kent	7	V26
Broadstone	Poole	5	W19
Broadwas	Heref/Worcs	10	T19
Broadway	Wexford	40	T11
Broadway	Heref/Worcs	11	T20
Broadwey	Dorset	5	W19
Broadwindsor	Dorset	4	W18
Brochel	H'land	27	H11
Brockenhurst	Hants	5	W20
Brockworth	Glos	5	U19
Brocton	Staffs	10	S19
Brodick	N Ayrs	18	L13
Bromfield	Shrops	10	T18
Bromham	Beds	12	T22
Bromham	Wilts	5	V19
Bromley	Gtr Lon	6	V24
Bromley Green	Kent	7	V25
Brompton	N Yorks	16	P21
Brompton Regis	Som'set	4	V16
Bromsgrove	Heref/Worcs	10	T19
Bromyard	Heref/Worcs	10	T19
Brooke	Norfolk	13	S26
Brookeborough	Fermanagh	32	P9
Broomfield	Monaghan	37	P10
Broomfield	Essex	7	U24
Broomhaugh	Northum	21	N20
Broomhill	Northum	21	M20
Brora	H'land	28	F16
Broseley	Shrops	10	S19
Brothertoft	Lincs	12	R23
Brotton	Redcar/Clevel'd	17	N22
Brough	Cumb	15	N19
Brough	E Riding Yorks	17	Q22
Brough	H'land	28	E17
Broughderg	Tyrone	33	N10
Broughshane	Antrim	33	N11
Broughton	Cumb	20	N17
Broughton	Hants	5	V20
Broughton	Lancs	15	Q18
Broughton	N Lincs	17	Q22
Broughton	Northants	11	T22
Broughton	Borders	20	L17
Broughton Astley	Leics	11	S21
Broughton-in-Furness	Cumb	15	P17
Broughty Ferry	Dundee C	25	K18
Brownhills	W Midlands	11	S20
Broxburn	W Loth	24	L17
Broxton	Ches	10	R18
Bruff	Limerick	39	T6
Bruichladdich	Arg/Bute	18	L11
Brundall	Norfolk	13	S26
Brunton	Northum	21	L20
Brunton	Northum	21	M19
Bruree	Limerick	39	T6
Bruton	Som'set	5	V19
Brymbo	Wrex	10	R17
Brynamman	Carms	9	U16
Bryncrug	Gwyn	8	S15
Brynmawr	Bl Gwent	4	U17
Brynsiencyn	Angl	8	R15
Bubwith	E Riding Yorks	17	Q22
Buchlyvie	Stirl	24	K15
Buckden	Cambs	12	T23
Buckden	N Yorks	15	P19
Buckfast	Devon	3	X16
Buckfastleigh	Devon	3	X16
Buckhaven	Fife	25	K17
Buckie	Moray	29	G18
Buckingham	Bucks	11	T22
Buckland	Oxon	5	U21
Buckland Brewer	Devon	3	W15
Buckland Newton	Dorset	5	W19
Buckley	Flints	10	R17
Buck's Cross	Devon	3	W15
Bucksburn	Aberd C	25	H19
Bude	Cornw'l	2	W14
Budleigh Salterton	Devon	4	W17
Bugbrooke	Northants	11	T22
Buggan	Fermanagh	32	P8
Bugle	Cornw'l	2	X14
Builth Wells	Powys	9	T17
Bulford	Wilts	5	V20
Bulkington	Warwick	11	T21
Bullaun	Galway	35	R6
Bulwell	Notts	11	R21
Bunahowen	Mayo	34	P4
Bunalunn	Cork	38	U5
Bunaw	Kerry	38	U4
Bunbeg	Donegal	32	M7
Bunbrosna	Westmeath	36	Q9
Bunbury	Ches	10	R18
Bunclody	Wexford	40	S10
Buncrana	Donegal	32	M9
Bundoran	Donegal	32	P7
Bunessan	Arg/Bute	22	K11
Bungay	Suffolk	13	T26
Bunmahon	Waterford	40	T9
Bunnaglass	Galway	35	R6
Bunnahabhain	Arg/Bute	18	L11
Bunnanaddan	Sligo	35	P6
Bunnyconnellan	Mayo	35	P5
Bunratty	Clare	39	S6
Buntingford	Herts	12	U23
Bunwell	Norfolk	13	S26
Burbage	Derby	15	R20
Burbage	Leics	11	S21
Burbage	Wilts	5	V20
Bures	Suffolk	13	U25
Burford	Oxon	5	U20
Burgess Hill	W Sussex	6	W23
Burgh-by-Sands	Cumb	20	N17
Burgh le Marsh	Lincs	12	R24
Burghclere	Hants	5	V21
Burghead	Moray	28	G17
Burghfield Common	Berks	6	V21
Burley	Hants	5	W20
Burley	W Yorks	15	Q20
Burlton	Shrops	10	S18
Burneside	Cumb	15	P18
Burness	Orkney	30	D18
Burnfoot	Cork	39	T6
Burnfoot	Donegal	32	M9
Burnham	Bucks	6	U22
Burnham Market	Norfolk	13	S25
Burnham-on-Crouch	Essex	7	U25
Burnham-on-Sea	Som'set	4	V18
Burniston	N Yorks	17	P23
Burnley	Lancs	15	Q19
Burnmouth	Borders	21	L19
Burntisland	Fife	25	K17
Burntwood	Staffs	11	S20
Burravoe	Shetl'd	31	A21
Burrelton	Perth/Kinr	24	J17
Burren	Clare	35	R5
Burren	Down	37	P11
Burry Port	Carms	9	U15
Burscough Bridge	Lancs	15	Q18
Burstwick	E Riding Yorks	17	Q23
Burton	Cumb	15	P18
Burton Agnes	E Riding Yorks	17	P23
Burton Bradstock	Dorset	4	W18
Burton Fleming	E Riding Yorks	17	P23
Burton in Lonsdale	N Yorks	15	P18
Burton Latimer	Northants	12	T22
Burton upon Stather	N Lincs	17	Q22
Burton upon Trent	Staffs	11	S20
Burtonport	Donegal	32	N7
Burwash	E Sussex	7	W24
Burwell	Cambs	12	T24
Burwick	Orkney	30	E18
Bury	Gtr Man	15	Q19
Bury St. Edmunds	Suffolk	13	T25
Bushey	Herts	6	U23
Bushmills	Antrim	33	M10
Butler's Bridge	Cavan	36	P9
Butlerstown	Cork	39	U6
Buttermere	Cumb	20	N17
Buttevant	Cork	39	T6
Buxted	E Sussex	6	W24
Buxton	Derby	15	R20
Bweeng	Cork	39	T6
Byfield	Northants	11	T21
Byfleet	Surrey	6	V23
Bylchau	Conwy	8	R16

C

Place	County	Map	Ref
Cabinteely	Dublin	37	R11
Cabrach	Moray	29	H17
Cabragh	Tyrone	33	P10
Cadamstown	Offaly	36	R8
Caenby Corner	Lincs	17	R22
Caergwrle	Flints	10	R17

Place			Place			Place			Place			Place		
Caerleon *Newp*	4	U18	Carlow *Carlow*	40	S10	Castlegregory *Kerry*	38	T3	Charmouth *Dorset*	4	W18	Clady Milltown *Armagh*	33	P10
Caernarfon *Gwyn*	8	R15	Carlton *N Yorks*	16	Q21	Castlehill *Mayo*	34	P4	Chartham *Kent*	7	V26	Claggan *H'land*	23	J12
Caerphilly *Caerph*	4	U17	Carlton *Notts*	11	S21	Castleisland *Kerry*	38	T5	Chasel *Mayo*	34	Q4	Claigan *H'land*	26	H10
Caersws *Powys*	8	S17	Carlton Colville *Suffolk*	13	T27	Castlelyons *Cork*	39	T7	Chatham *Kent*	7	V25	Clanabogan *Tyrone*	32	N9
Caerwent *Monmouths*	4	U18	Carlton-in-Lindrick *Notts*	16	R21	Castlemaine *Kerry*	38	T4	Chathill *Northum*	21	L20	Clane *Kildare*	37	R10
Caher *Clare*	35	S6	Carlton Miniott *N Yorks*	16	P21	Castlemartin *Pembs*	9	U13	Chatteris *Cambs*	12	T24	Clanfield *Hants*	6	W22
Caher *Galway*	34	R5	Carluke *S Lanarks*	19	L16	Castlemartyr *Cork*	39	U7	Chatton *Northum*	21	L20	Claonaig *Arg/Bute*	18	L13
Caher *Tipperary*	39	T8	Carmarthen *Carms*	9	U15	Castleplunket *Roscommon*	35	Q7	Chawleigh *Devon*	3	W16	Clapham *Beds*	12	T23
Caherciveen *Kerry*	38	U3	Carmyllie *Angus*	25	J18	Castlepollard *Westmeath*	36	Q9	Cheadle *Gtr Man*	15	R19	Clapham *N Yorks*	15	P19
Caherconlish *Limerick*	39	S7	Carna *Galway*	34	R4	Castlerea *Roscommon*	35	Q7	Cheadle *Staffs*	11	S20	Clara *Offaly*	36	R8
Caherdaniel *Kerry*	38	U3	Carnachuin *H'land*	24	H16	Castlerock *Londonderry*	33	M10	Chedburgh *Suffolk*	13	T25	Clarahill *Laois*	36	R9
Cahermore *Cork*	38	U3	Carnaross *Meath*	37	Q10	Castleside *Durham*	21	N20	Cheddar *Som'set*	4	V18	Clare *Suffolk*	13	T25
Cahermurphy *Clare*	38	S5	Carncastle *Antrim*	33	N12	Castleton *Derby*	15	R20	Cheddleton *Staffs*	10	S19	Clarecastle *Clare*	39	S6
Cairinis *W Isles*	26	G9	Carndonagh *Donegal*	32	M9	Castleton *N Yorks*	17	P22	Chellaston *Derby C*	11	S21	Clareen *Offaly*	36	R8
Cairndow *Arg/Bute*	23	K14	Carnew *Wicklow*	40	S11	Castletown *Laois*	36	S9	Chelmarsh *Shrops*	10	T19	Claregalway *Galway*	35	R6
Cairnryan *Dumf/Gal*	18	N13	Carney *Sligo*	32	P6	Castletown *Meath*	37	Q10	Chelmsford *Essex*	7	U24	Claremorris *Mayo*	35	Q5
Caister-on-Sea *Norfolk*	13	S27	Carnforth *Lancs*	15	P18	Castletown *H'land*	28	E17	Cheltenham *Glos*	10	U19	Claretuam *Galway*	35	R6
Caistor *Lincs*	17	R23	Carnlough *Antrim*	33	N12	Castletown *I of Man*	14	P14	Chepstow *Monmouths*	4	U18	Clarina *Limerick*	39	S6
Calanais *W Isles*	26	F10	Carno *Powys*	8	S16	Castletown Bearhaven *Cork*	38	U4	Cherhill *Wilts*	5	V20	Clarinbridge *Galway*	35	R6
Caldbeck *Cumb*	20	N17	Carnoustie *Angus*	25	J18	Castletown Geoghegan *Westmeath*	36	R9	Cheriton *Hants*	5	V21	Clash *Cork*	39	U7
Calder Bridge *Cumb*	14	P17	Carnwath *S Lanarks*	20	L16	Castletownroche *Cork*	39	T7	Cheriton Fitzpaine *Devon*	4	W16	Clashmore *Waterford*	39	T8
Caldercruix *N Lanarks*	19	L16	Carracastle *Mayo*	35	Q6	Castletownshend *Cork*	38	U5	Chertsey *Surrey*	6	V23	Clashmore *H'land*	28	G15
Caldicot *Monmouths*	4	U18	Carradale *Arg/Bute*	18	L13	Castlewellan *Down*	33	P12	Chesham *Bucks*	6	U22	Claudy *Londonderry*	32	N9
Caledon *Tyrone*	33	P10	Carragh *Kildare*	37	R10	Caston *Norfolk*	13	S25	Cheshunt *Herts*	6	U23	Clavering *Essex*	12	U24
Calfsound *Orkney*	30	D18	Carran *Clare*	35	R5	Castor *Cambs*	12	S23	Chester *Ches*	10	R18	Claverley *Shrops*	10	S19
Calgary *Arg/Bute*	22	J11	Carraroe *Galway*	34	R4	Catcleugh *Northum*	21	M19	Chester-le-Street *Durham*	21	N20	Clawton *Devon*	3	W15
Callan *Kilkenny*	40	S9	Carrbridge *H'land*	28	H16	Caterham *Surrey*	6	V23	Chesterfield *Derby*	16	R21	Clay Cross *Derby*	11	R21
Callander *Stirl*	24	K15	Carrick *Donegal*	32	N6	Caton *Lancs*	15	P18	Chew Magna *Bath/NE Som'set*	4	V18	Claydon *Suffolk*	13	T26
Callington *Cornw'l*	3	X15	Carrick *Arg/Bute*	23	K14	Catrine *E Ayrs*	19	L15	Chewton Mendip *Som'set*	4	V18	Claypole *Lincs*	12	R22
Callow *Galway*	34	R3	Carrick-on-Shannon *Roscommon*	36	Q7	Catsfield *E Sussex*	7	W24	Chichester *W Sussex*	6	W22	Cleadale *H'land*	22	J11
Callow *Mayo*	35	Q5	Carrick-on-Suir *Tipperary*	40	T9	Catterall *Lancs*	15	Q18	Chiddingfold *Surrey*	6	V22	Cleady *Kerry*	38	U4
Calne *Wilts*	5	V20	Carrickart *Donegal*	32	M8	Catterick *N Yorks*	16	P20	Chideock *Dorset*	4	W18	Cleat *Orkney*	30	E18
Calshot *Hants*	5	W21	Carrickbeg *Waterford*	40	T9	Catterick Camp *N Yorks*	16	P20	Chigwell *Essex*	6	U24	Cleator Moor *Cumb*	14	N16
Calstock *Cornw'l*	3	X15	Carrickboy *Longford*	36	Q8	Catton *Northum*	21	N19	Chilcompton *Som'set*	4	V18	Cleethorpes *NE Lincs*	17	Q23
Calta *Galway*	35	R7	Carrickfergus *Antrim*	33	N12	Caulkerbush *Dumf/Gal*	20	N16	Chilham *Kent*	7	V25	Cleeve Prior *Warwick*	11	T20
Calverton *Notts*	11	R21	Carrickmacross *Monaghan*	37	Q10	Causeway *Kerry*	38	T4	Chillingham *Devon*	3	X16	Cleggan *Galway*	34	Q3
Cam *Glos*	5	U19	Carrickmore *Tyrone*	33	N9	Cavan *Cavan*	36	Q9	Chilton *Durham*	21	N20	Clehonger *Heref/Worcs*	10	T18
Camber *E Sussex*	7	W25	Carrigaholt *Clare*	38	S4	Cavangarden *Donegal*	32	N7	Chingford *Gtr Lon*	6	U24	Cleobury Mortimer *Shrops*	10	T19
Camberley *Surrey*	6	V22	Carrigahorig *Tipperary*	36	R7	Cawdor *H'land*	28	G16	Chinnor *Oxon*	6	U22	Clevedon *N Som'set*	4	V18
Cambo *Northum*	21	M20	Carrigaline *Cork*	39	U7	Cawood *N Yorks*	16	Q21	Chippenham *Wilts*	5	V19	Cleveleys *Lancs*	15	Q17
Camborne *Cornw'l*	2	X13	Carrigallen *Leitrim*	36	Q8	Cawston *Norfolk*	13	S26	Chipping Campden *Glos*	11	T20	Cley *Norfolk*	13	S26
Cambridge *Cambs*	12	T24	Carriganimmy *Cork*	38	U5	Caythorpe *Lincs*	12	R22	Chipping Norton *Oxon*	11	U20	Clifden *Galway*	34	R3
Camden *Gtr Lon*	6	U23	Carrigfadda *Cork*	38	U5	Cefn-mawr *Wrex*	10	S17	Chipping Ongar *Essex*	7	U24	Cliffe *Kent*	7	V25
Camelford *Cornw'l*	2	W14	Carrigkerry *Limerick*	38	T5	Celbridge *Kildare*	37	R10	Chipping Sodbury *S Gloucs*	5	U19	Cliffony *Sligo*	32	P7
Camlough *Armagh*	33	P11	Carrignavar *Cork*	39	U7	Cemaes *Angl*	8	R15	Chirbury *Shrops*	10	S17	Clifford *Heref/Worcs*	10	T17
Cammachmore *Aberds*	25	H19	Carrigtohill *Cork*	39	U7	Cemmaes Road *Powys*	8	S16	Chirk *Wrex*	10	S17	Clipston *Northants*	11	T22
Camolin *Wexford*	40	S11	Carronbridge *Dumf/Gal*	19	M16	Cenarth *Carms*	9	T14	Chirnside *Borders*	21	L19	Clitheroe *Lancs*	15	Q19
Camp *Kerry*	38	T4	Carrowbehy *Roscommon*	35	Q6	Ceres *Fife*	25	K18	Chiseldon *Thamesd'n*	5	U20	Clive *Shrops*	10	S18
Campbeltown *Arg/Bute*	18	M12	Carrowkeel *Donegal*	32	M8	Cerne Abbas *Dorset*	5	W19	Chitterne *Wilts*	5	V19	Clogh *Kilkenny*	40	S9
Campile *Wexford*	40	T10	Carrowkeel *Donegal*	32	M9	Cerrigydrudion *Conwy*	8	R16	Chobham *Surrey*	6	V22	Clogh *Antrim*	33	N11
Camrose *Pembs*	9	U13	Carrowkeel *Galway*	35	R7	Chacewater *Cornw'l*	2	X13	Chollerton *Northum*	21	M19	Cloghan *Donegal*	32	N8
Camross *Wexford*	40	T10	Carrowkennedy *Mayo*	34	Q4	Chaddesley Corbet *Heref/Worcs*	10	T19	Cholsey *Oxon*	5	U21	Cloghan *Offaly*	36	R8
Canisbay *H'land*	29	E17	Carrowreagh *Antrim*	33	M11	Chadwell St. Mary *Essex*	7	V24	Chorley *Lancs*	15	Q18	Cloghan *Westmeath*	36	Q9
Cannich *H'land*	27	H14	Carrowreilly *Sligo*	35	P6	Chagford *Devon*	3	W16	Chorleywood *Herts*	6	U22	Cloghane *Kerry*	38	T3
Canningstown *Cavan*	36	Q9	Carrowroe *Longford*	36	Q8	Chalfont St. Giles *Bucks*	6	U22	Christchurch *Cambs*	12	S24	Clogheneely *Donegal*	32	M7
Cannington *Som'set*	4	V17	Carryduff *Down*	33	N12	Chalford *Glos*	5	U19	Christchurch *Dorset*	5	W20	Cloghboy *Donegal*	32	N6
Cannock *Staffs*	10	S17	Carsaig *Arg/Bute*	23	K12	Chalgrove *Oxon*	6	U21	Christow *Devon*	4	W16	Clogheen *Tipperary*	39	T8
Canonbie *Dumf/Gal*	20	M18	Carsphairn *Dumf/Gal*	19	M15	Challacombe *Devon*	3	V16	Chudleigh *Devon*	4	W16	Clogher *Roscommon*	36	Q7
Canterbury *Kent*	7	V26	Carstairs *S Lanarks*	20	L16	Challock *Kent*	7	V25	Chulmleigh *Devon*	3	W16	Clogher *Tyrone*	32	P9
Canvey *Essex*	7	U25	Carterton *Oxon*	5	U20	Chandler's Ford *Hants*	5	W21	Church Hill *Donegal*	32	N8	Clogher Head *Louth*	37	Q11
Caol *H'land*	23	J13	Cartmel *Cumb*	15	P18	Chanonrock *Louth*	37	Q10	Church Hill *Fermanagh*	32	P8	Cloghjordan *Tipperary*	36	S7
Caolas Stocinis *W Isles*	26	G10	Cashel *Galway*	35	Q6	Chapel en le Frith *Derby*	15	R20	Church Stretton *Shrops*	10	S18	Cloghran *Dublin*	37	R11
Caoles *Arg/Bute*	22	J10	Cashel *Tipperary*	39	S8	Chapel St. Leonards *Lincs*	17	R24	Church Village *Rh Cyn Taff*	9	U17	Cloghy *Down*	33	N12
Capel *Surrey*	6	V23	Castle Acre *Norfolk*	13	S25	Chapeltown *S Lanarks*	19	L15	Churchdown *Glos*	10	U19	Clomantagh *Kilkenny*	40	S9
Capel Curig *Conwy*	8	R16	Castle Cary *Som'set*	4	V18	Chapeltown *S Yorks*	16	R21	Churchill *Oxon*	11	U20	Clonakilty *Cork*	39	U6
Capel St. Mary *Suffolk*	13	T26	Castle Donington *Leics*	11	S21	Chard *Som'set*	4	W18	Churchstow *Devon*	3	X16	Clonaslee *Laois*	36	R8
Cappagh *Cork*	39	T7	Castle Douglas *Dumf/Gal*	19	N16	Charing *Kent*	7	V25	Churchtown *Cork*	39	U6	Clonbulloge *Offaly*	36	R9
Cappagh *Galway*	35	R7	Castlebar *Mayo*	34	Q5	Charlbury *Oxon*	11	U21	Churchtown *Wexford*	40	T11	Clonbur *Galway*	34	Q5
Cappagh White *Tipperary*	39	S7	Castlebay = Bagh a Chaisteil *W Isles*	22	J8	Charlemont *Armagh*	33	P10	Chwilog *Gwyn*	8	S15	Cloncurry *Kildare*	37	R10
Cappamore *Limerick*	39	S7	Castlebellingham *Louth*	37	Q11	Charlestown *Mayo*	35	Q6	Cilgerran *Pembs*	9	T14	Clondalkin *Dublin*	37	R11
Cappeen *Cork*	39	U6	Castleblakeney *Galway*	35	R7	Charlestown of Aberlour *Moray*	29	H17	Cille Bhrighde *W Isles*	22	H9	Clonea *Waterford*	40	T9
Cappoquin *Waterford*	39	T8	Castleblaney *Monaghan*	37	P10	Charleville *Cork*	39	T6	Cilycwm *Carms*	9	T16	Clonee *Meath*	37	R11
Carbis Bay *Cornw'l*	2	X13	Castlebridge *Wexford*	40	T11	Charlton *Wilts*	5	U19	Cinderford *Glos*	5	U19	Cloneen *Tipperary*	39	T8
Carbost *H'land*	26	H11	Castlecomer *Kilkenny*	40	S9	Charlton Horethorne *Som'set*	5	W19	Cirencester *Glos*	5	U20	Clonelly *Fermanagh*	32	N8
Carbost *H'land*	26	H11	Castleconnell *Limerick*	39	S7	Charlton Kings *Glos*	10	U19	Clabby *Fermanagh*	32	P9	Clones *Monaghan*	32	P9
Carbury *Kildare*	37	R10	Castlecor *Cork*	39	T6	Charlwood *Surrey*	6	V23	Clabhach *Arg/Bute*	22	J10	Cloney *Kildare*	40	R9
Cardiff *Card*	4	U17	Castledawson *Londonderry*	33	N10	Charminster *Dorset*	5	W19	Clachan *Arg/Bute*	18	L12	Clonfert *Galway*	36	R7
Cardigan *Ceredig'n*	9	T14	Castlederg *Tyrone*	32	N8				Clachan *H'land*	27	H11	Clonlee *Mayo*	35	Q6
Cardington *Beds*	12	T22	Castledermot *Kildare*	40	S10				Clachan na Luib *W Isles*	26	G9	Clonmacnoise *Offaly*	36	R8
Cardross *Arg/Bute*	19	L14	Castlefinn *Donegal*	32	N8				Clackmannan *Clack*	24	K16	Clonmany *Donegal*	32	M9
Cargill *Perth/Kinr*	24	J17	Castleford *W Yorks*	16	Q21				Clacton-on-Sea *Essex*	7	U26	Clonmel *Tipperary*	39	T8
Carhampton *Som'set*	4	V17							Cladich *Arg/Bute*	23	K13	Clonmellon *Westmeath*	36	Q9
Carisbrooke *I of Wight*	5	W21							Clady *Tyrone*	32	N8	Clonmore *Carlow*	40	S10
Cark *Cumb*	15	P18										Clonmore *Offaly*	36	R9
Carlabhagh *W Isles*	26	F10										Clonmore *Tipperary*	39	S8
Carlanstown *Meath*	37	Q10										Clonord *Meath*	36	R9
Carleton Rode *Norfolk*	13	S26										Clonroche *Wexford*	40	T10
Carlingford *Louth*	37	P11										Clontarf *Dublin*	37	R11
Carlisle *Cumb*	20	N18										Cloodara *Longford*	36	Q8
Carlops *Borders*	20	L17										Cloonacool *Sligo*	35	P6
												Cloonart *Longford*	36	Q8
												Cloonbannin *Cork*	38	T5
												Cloonboo *Galway*	35	R5
												Cloone *Leitrim*	36	Q8

Cloonfad		
Roscommon	35	Q6
Cloonkeen _Kerry_	38	U5
Cloonlara _Clare_	39	S6
Cloonloogh _Sligo_	35	Q7
Cloonmore _Mayo_	35	Q6
Clophill _Beds_	12	T23
Clorbern _Galway_	35	Q6
Closeburn _Dumf/Gal_	19	M16
Clough _Down_	33	P12
Cloughton _N Yorks_	17	P23
Clova _Angus_	25	J17
Clovelly _Devon_	3	W15
Clovenfords _Borders_	20	L18
Clowne _Derby_	16	R21
Cloyne _Cork_	39	U7
Clun _Shrops_	10	T17
Clunbury _Shrops_	10	T18
Clunes _H'land_	23	J14
Clungunford _Shrops_	10	T18
Clutton		
Bath/NE Som'set	4	V18
Clydach _Swan_	9	U16
Clydebank _W Dunb_	19	L15
Clynnog-fawr _Gwyn_	8	R15
Clyro _Powys_	10	T17
Coachford _Cork_	39	U6
Coagh _Tyrone_	33	N10
Coalbrookdale		
Shrops	10	S18
Coalburn _S Lanarks_	19	L16
Coalisland _Tyrone_	33	N10
Coalville _Leics_	11	S21
Coatbridge _N Lanarks_	19	L15
Cóbh _Cork_	39	U7
Cobham _Kent_	7	V24
Cobham _Surrey_	6	V23
Cock Bridge _Aberds_	25	H17
Cockburnspath		
Borders	25	L19
Cockenzie _E Loth_	25	L18
Cockerham _Lancs_	15	Q18
Cockermouth _Cumb_	20	N17
Cockfield _Durham_	21	N20
Cockfield _Suffolk_	13	T25
Cockshutt _Shrops_	10	S18
Coddenham _Suffolk_	13	T26
Codford St. Mary		
Wilts	5	V19
Coggeshall _Essex_	7	U25
Coignafearn Lodge		
H'land	24	H15
Coille Mhorgil _H'land_	23	H13
Coillore _H'land_	26	H11
Colby _I of Man_	14	P14
Colchester _Essex_	13	U25
Cold Ashton _S Gloucs_	5	V19
Coldingham _Borders_	21	L19
Coldstream _Borders_	21	L19
Colebrooke _Devon_	4	W16
Coleford _Glos_	4	U18
Colehill _Longford_	36	Q8
Coleraine		
Londonderry	33	M10
Coleshill _Warwick_	11	T20
Colinton _C of Edinb_	25	L17
Colintraive _Arg/Bute_	18	L13
Collin _Dumf/Gal_	20	M16
Collingbourne		
Kingston _Wilts_	5	V20
Collingham _Notts_	11	R22
Collingham _W Yorks_	16	Q21
Collinstown		
Westmeath	36	Q9
Collon _Louth_	37	Q11
Collooney _Sligo_	32	P7
Colmonel _S Ayrs_	18	M14
Colne _Lancs_	15	Q19
Colpy _Aberds_	29	H18
Colsterworth _Lincs_	12	S22
Coltishall _Norfolk_	13	S26
Colwell _Northum_	21	M19
Colwich _Staffs_	11	S20
Colwyn Bay _Conwy_	8	R16
Colyton _Devon_	4	W17
Combe Martin _Devon_	3	V15
Comber _Down_	33	N12
Comberton _Cambs_	12	T24
Combwich _Som'set_	4	V17
Commeen _Donegal_	32	N8
Compton _Berks_	5	U21
Compton _W Sussex_	6	W22
Compton Martin		
Bath/NE Som'set	4	V18
Comrie _Perth/Kinr_	24	K16
Condover _Shrops_	10	S18
Cong _Mayo_	34	Q5
Congleton _Ches_	10	R19
Congresbury		
N Som'set	4	V18
Coningsby _Lincs_	12	R23
Conisbrough _S Yorks_	16	R21
Coniston _Cumb_	15	P17
Conlig _Down_	33	N12
Conna _Cork_	39	T7
Connagh _Galway_	35	S7
Connah's Quay _Flints_	15	P17
Connel _Arg/Bute_	23	K13
Connel Park _E Ayrs_	19	M15
Connonagh _Cork_	38	U5
Connor _Antrim_	33	N11
Cononbridge _H'land_	28	G15
Consett _Durham_	21	N20
Contin _H'land_	28	G14
Convoy _Donegal_	32	N8
Conwy _Conwy_	8	R16
Cookham _Berks_	6	U22
Cookstown _Tyrone_	33	N10
Coola _Sligo_	35	P7
Coolaney _Sligo_	32	P6
Coolbaun _Tipperary_	35	S7
Coolderg _Galway_	35	Q6
Coole _Westmeath_	36	Q9
Coolgreany _Wexford_	40	S11
Coolham _W Sussex_	6	W23
Coolmore _Donegal_	32	N7
Coolrain _Laois_	36	S8
Coombe Bissett _Wilts_	5	V20
Cooneen _Fermanagh_	32	P9
Cooraclare _Clare_	38	S5
Cootehill _Cavan_	36	P9
Copplestone _Devon_	4	W16
Coppull _Lancs_	15	Q18
Copthorne _W Sussex_	6	V23
Corbally _Laois_	40	S9
Corbally _Sligo_	35	P5
Corbridge _Northum_	21	N19
Corby _Northants_	12	T22
Corby Glen _Lincs_	12	S22
Cordal _Kerry_	38	T5
Corfe Castle _Dorset_	5	W19
Corfe Mullen _Dorset_	5	W19
Corgary _Tyrone_	32	N8
Cork _Cork_	39	U7
Corlea _Longford_	36	Q8
Corlogh _Mayo_	34	P3
Cornafulla		
Roscommon	35	P7
Corringham _Essex_	7	U25
Corringham _Lincs_	17	R22
Corris _Gwyn_	8	S16
Corrofin _Clare_	35	S5
Corsham _Wilts_	5	V19
Corsley _Wilts_	5	V19
Corsock _Dumf/Gal_	19	M16
Corton _Norfolk_	13	S27
Corvally _Monaghan_	37	Q10
Corvoy _Monaghan_	37	P10
Corwen _Denbs_	8	S17
Coseley _W Midlands_	10	S19
Cosham _Portsm'th_	5	W21
Costelloe _Galway_	34	R4
Costessey _Norfolk_	13	S26
Cotgrave _Notts_	11	S21
Cotherstone _Durham_	21	N20
Cottenham _Cambs_	12	T24
Cottered _Herts_	12	U23
Cottesmore _Rutl'd_	12	S22
Cottingham		
E Riding Yorks	17	Q23
Coulags _H'land_	27	H13
Coulport _Arg/Bute_	23	K14
Countesthorpe _Leics_	11	S21
Coupar Angus		
Perth/Kinr	24	J17
Courtmacsherry _Cork_	39	U6
Courtown _Wexford_	40	S11
Cove _Arg/Bute_	23	L14
Cove _H'land_	27	G12
Cove Bay _Aberd C_	25	H19
Coventry _W Midlands_	11	T21
Coverack _Cornw'l_	2	X13
Cowbit _Lincs_	12	S23
Cowbridge _V of Glam_	4	V17
Cowdenbeath _Fife_	24	K17
Cowes _I of Wight_	5	W21
Cowfold _W Sussex_	6	W23
Cowpen _Northum_	21	M20
Cowplain _Hants_	6	W21
Coxheath _Kent_	7	V25
Coylton _S Ayrs_	19	M14
Craanford _Wexford_	40	S11
Craggie _H'land_	28	H15
Crai _Powys_	9	U16
Craibstone _Moray_	29	G18
Craigavon _Armagh_	33	P11
Craigellachie _Moray_	29	H17
Craighouse _Arg/Bute_	18	L12
Craigmore _Arg/Bute_	18	L13
Craignure _Arg/Bute_	23	K12
Craigtown _H'land_	28	F16
Crail _Fife_	25	K18
Cramlington _Northum_	21	M20
Cranagh _Tyrone_	33	N9
Cranborne _Dorset_	5	W20
Cranbrook _Kent_	7	V25
Cranleigh _Surrey_	6	V23
Cranmore _Som'set_	5	V19
Cranwell _Lincs_	12	R23
Crataloe _Limerick_	38	T5
Crathie _Aberds_	25	H17
Craughwell _Galway_	35	R6
Craven Arms _Shrops_	10	T18
Crawford _S Lanarks_	20	M16
Crawfordjohn		
S Lanarks	19	L16
Crawley _W Sussex_	6	V23
Creag Ghoraidh		
W Isles	26	H9
Creaghanroe		
Monaghan	33	P10
Creake _Norfolk_	13	S25
Credenhill		
Heref/Worcs	10	T18
Crediton _Devon_	4	W16
Creegh _Clare_	38	S5
Creeragh _Mayo_	34	P5
Creeslough _Donegal_	32	M8
Creetown _Dumf/Gal_	19	N15
Creeve _Tyrone_	33	N10
Creeves _Limerick_	38	S5
Creggan _Tyrone_	33	N9
Cregganbaun _Mayo_	34	Q4
Creggs _Galway_	35	Q7
Cressage _Shrops_	10	S18
Cresselly _Pembs_	9	U14
Crewe _Ches_	10	R19
Crewkerne _Som'set_	4	W18
Crianlarich _Stirl_	24	K14
Criccieth _Gwyn_	8	S15
Crick _Northants_	11	T21
Crickhowell _Powys_	4	U17
Cricklade _Wilts_	5	U20
Crieff _Perth/Kinr_	24	K16
Crimond _Aberds_	29	G20
Crinan _Arg/Bute_	23	K12
Crindle _Londonderry_	33	M10
Crinkill _Offaly_	36	R8
Croagh _Limerick_	39	S6
Crocketford _Dumf/Gal_	19	M16
Crockets Town _Mayo_	35	P5
Croggan _Arg/Bute_	23	K12
Croghan _Offaly_	36	R9
Croghan _Roscommon_	35	Q7
Croglin _Cumb_	21	N18
Croick _H'land_	28	G14
Crolly _Donegal_	32	M7
Cromarty _H'land_	28	G15
Cromer _Norfolk_	13	S26
Cromor _W Isles_	26	F11
Crondall _Hants_	6	V22
Crook _Durham_	21	N20
Crookedwood		
Westmeath	36	Q9
Crookham _Northum_	21	L19
Crookhaven _Cork_	39	V4
Crooklands _Cumb_	15	P18
Crookstown _Cork_	39	U6
Crosbost _W Isles_	26	F11
Crosby _Cumb_	20	N17
Crosby _Mersey_	15	R17
Crosby Ravensworth		
Cumb	21	N18
Cross Barry _Cork_	39	U6
Cross-Hands _Carms_	9	U15
Cross Keys _Meath_	37	Q10
Crossakiel _Meath_	36	Q9
Crossdoney _Cavan_	36	Q9
Crossgar _Down_	33	P12
Crosshaven _Cork_	39	U7
Crosshill _S Ayrs_	19	M14
Crossmaglen _Armagh_	37	P10
Crossmichael		
Dumf/Gal	19	N16
Crossmolina _Mayo_	34	P5
Croston _Lancs_	15	Q18
Crowborough		
E Sussex	6	V24
Crowland _Lincs_	12	S23
Crowle _N Lincs_	17	Q22
Crowthorne _Berks_	6	V22
Croxton Kerrial _Leics_	11	S22
Croyde _Devon_	3	V15
Croydon _Gtr Lon_	6	V23
Cruden Bay _Aberds_	29	H20
Crudgington _Shrops_	10	S18
Crumlin _Dublin_	37	R11
Crumlin _Antrim_	33	N11
Crusheen _Clare_	35	S6
Crymych _Pembs_	9	U14
Cuckfield _W Sussex_	6	V23
Cuddington _Bucks_	6	U22
Cuddington _Ches_	15	R18
Cudworth _S Yorks_	16	Q21
Cuffley _Herts_	6	U23
Culdaff _Donegal_	32	M9
Culgaith _Cumb_	21	N18
Culkein _H'land_	27	F13
Cullaville _Armagh_	37	P10
Cullen _Tipperary_	39	S7
Cullen _Moray_	29	G18
Cullicudden _H'land_	28	G15
Cullinane _Antrim_	33	N11
Cullion _Tyrone_	32	N9
Cullivoe _Shetl'd_	31	A21
Culloden _H'land_	28	H15
Cullompton _Devon_	4	W17
Cullyhanna _Armagh_	37	P10
Culmazie _Dumf/Gal_	19	N14
Culmington _Shrops_	10	T18
Culmstock _Devon_	4	W17
Culrain _H'land_	28	G15
Culross _Fife_	24	K16
Cults _Aberd C_	25	H19
Cumbernauld		
N Lanarks	19	L16
Cuminestown _Aberds_	29	G19
Cummertrees		
Dumf/Gal	20	N17
Cumnock _E Ayrs_	19	M15
Cumnor _Oxon_	5	U21
Cumwhinton _Cumb_	20	N18
Cupar _Fife_	25	K17
Curraglass _Cork_	39	T7
Currie _C of Edinb_	24	L17
Curry _Sligo_	35	Q6
Curry Rivel _Som'set_	4	V18
Curryglass _Cork_	38	U4
Cushendall _Antrim_	33	M11
Cushendun _Antrim_	33	M11
Cushina _Offaly_	36	R9
Cwmafan		
Neath P Talb	9	U16
Cwmann _Carms_	9	T15
Cwmbran _Torf_	4	U17
Cwrt _Gwyn_	8	S16
Cymmer _Neath P Talb_	9	U16
Cynwyl Elfed _Carms_	9	U15
D		
Dacklin _Roscommon_	36	Q7
Dagenham _Gtr Lon_	6	U24
Dail bho Dheas		
W Isles	26	F11
Dailly _S Ayrs_	19	M14
Daingean _Offaly_	36	R9
Dalabrog _W Isles_	22	H9
Dalbeattie _Dumf/Gal_	19	N16
Dale _Pembs_	9	U13
Dale _Shetl'd_	31	B20
Dalguise _Perth/Kinr_	24	J16
Dalhalvaig _H'land_	28	F16
Dalkeith _Midloth_	25	L17
Dalkey _Dublin_	37	R11
Dallas _Moray_	28	G17
Dalleagles _E Ayrs_	19	M15
Dalmally _Arg/Bute_	23	K14
Dalmellington _E Ayrs_	19	M15
Dalnaspidal _Perth/Kinr_	24	J15
Dalnessie _H'land_	28	F15
Dalry _Dumf/Gal_	19	M15
Dalry _N Ayrs_	19	L14
Dalrymple _E Ayrs_	19	M14
Dalston _Cumb_	20	N18
Dalton _Dumf/Gal_	20	M17
Dalton _N Yorks_	16	P20
Dalton-in-Furness		
Cumb	15	P17
Dalwhinnie _H'land_	24	J15
Dalystown _Galway_	35	R7
Damerham _Hants_	5	W20
Damerstown _Kilkenny_	40	S9
Danbury _Essex_	7	U25
Darkley _Armagh_	33	P10
Darlington _D'lington_	16	N20
Darragh _Clare_	38	S5
Dartford _Kent_	6	V24
Dartington _Devon_	3	X16
Dartmouth _Devon_	3	X16
Darton _S Yorks_	16	Q20
Darvel _E Ayrs_	19	L15
Darwen _Lancs_	15	Q19
Daventry _Northants_	11	T21
Davington _Dumf/Gal_	20	M17
Dawlish _Devon_	4	W17
Deal _Kent_	7	V26
Dearham _Cumb_	20	N17
Dearne _S Yorks_	16	Q21
Debenham _Suffolk_	13	T26
Deddington _Oxon_	11	U21
Deelish _Cork_	38	U5
Deeping St. Nicholas		
Lincs	12	S23
Deerness _Orkney_	30	E18
Deganwy _Conwy_	8	R16
Delabole _Cornw'l_	2	W14
Delchirach _Moray_	28	H17
Delves _Durham_	21	N20
Delvin _Westmeath_	36	Q9
Denbigh _Denbs_	8	R17
Denby Dale _W Yorks_	16	Q20
Denholm _Borders_	21	M18
Denny _Falk_	24	K16
Dent _Cumb_	15	P19
Denton _Gtr Man_	15	R19
Denton _Lincs_	12	S22
Derby _Derby C_	11	S21
Derry _Sligo_	35	P7
Derrybeg _Donegal_	32	M7
Derryboy _Down_	33	P12
Derrybrien _Galway_	35	R6
Derrycoosh _Mayo_	34	Q5
Derrygonnelly		
Fermanagh	32	P8
Derrygorry _Monaghan_	33	P9
Derrygrogan _Offaly_	36	R9
Derrykeighan _Antrim_	33	M10
Derrylin _Fermanagh_	32	P8
Derry _C of York_	32	BD
Derrymore _Kerry_	38	T4
Derrynacreeve _Cavan_	36	P8
Derrynane _Kerry_	38	U3
Derryrush _Galway_	34	R4
Derrytrasna _Armagh_	33	N11
Dersingham _Norfolk_	13	S25
Dervaig _Arg/Bute_	22	J11
Dervock _Antrim_	33	M11
Desborough		
Northants	11	T22
Desertmartin		
Londonderry	33	N10
Desford _Leics_	11	S21
Devil's Bridge		
Ceredig'n	9	T16
Devizes _Wilts_	5	V20
Devonport _Devon_	3	X15
Dewsbury _W Yorks_	16	Q20
Diabaig _H'land_	27	G12
Diamond _Down_	33	P11
Dibden Purlieu _Hants_	5	W21
Dickleborough		
Norfolk	13	T26
Didcot _Oxon_	5	U21
Digby _Lincs_	12	R23
Dinas Mawddwy		
Gwyn	8	S16
Dinas Powis		
V of Glam	4	V17
Dingle _Kerry_	38	T3
Dingwall _H'land_	28	G15
Dinnington _S Yorks_	16	R21
Dinton _Wilts_	5	V20
Dippen _N Ayrs_	18	M13
Dirleton _E Loth_	25	K18
Dirtagh _Londonderry_	33	M10
Diss _Norfolk_	13	T26
Distington _Cumb_	20	N16
Ditchingham _Norfolk_	13	T26
Ditchling _E Sussex_	6	W23
Dittisham _Devon_	3	X16
Ditton Priors _Shrops_	10	T18
Doagh _Antrim_	33	N11
Dobwalls _Cornw'l_	2	X14

Docking *Norfolk* 13 S25
Dockray *Cumb* 20 N18
Doddinghurst *Essex* 7 U24
Doddington *Cambs* 12 S24
Doddington *Northum* 21 L19
Dolanog *Powys* 8 S17
Dolfor *Powys* 8 T17
Dolgarrog *Conwy* 8 R16
Dolgellau *Gwyn* 8 S16
Dolla *Tipperary* 39 S7
Dollar *Clack* 24 K16
Dolphinton *S Lanarks* 20 L17
Dolton *Devon* 3 W15
Dolwyddelan *Conwy* 8 R16
Donabate *Dublin* 37 R11
Donadea *Kildare* 37 R10
Donagh *Fermanagh* 32 P9
Donaghadee *Down* 33 N12
Donaghmore *Laois* 39 S8
Donaghmore *Tyrone* 33 N10
Donard *Wicklow* 40 R10
Doncaster *S Yorks* 16 Q21
Donegal *Donegal* 32 N7
Doneraile *Cork* 39 T6
Donhead St.Andrew *Wilts* 5 V19
Donington *Lincs* 12 S23
Donnington *Shrops* 10 S19
Donohill *Tipperary* 39 S7
Donore *Meath* 37 Q10
Donoughmore *Cork* 39 U6
Dooagh *Mayo* 34 Q3
Doocharry *Donegal* 32 N7
Doogary *Cavan* 36 P8
Doogort *Mayo* 34 P3
Dooish *Tyrone* 32 N9
Doolin *Clare* 34 R5
Doon *Limerick* 39 S7
Doonaha *Clare* 38 S4
Doonbeg *Clare* 38 S4
Dorchester *Dorset* 5 W19
Dorchester *Oxon* 5 U21
Dores *H'land* 28 H15
Dorking *Surrey* 6 V23
Dornie *H'land* 27 H12
Dornoch *H'land* 28 G15
Dorridge *W Midlands* 11 T20
Dorstone *Heref/Worcs* 10 T18
Douglas *Cork* 39 U7
Douglas *I of Man* 14 P15
Douglas *S Lanarks* 19 L16
Dounby *Orkney* 30 D17
Doune *Stirl* 24 K15
Dounreay *H'land* 28 E16
Dove Holes *Derby* 15 R20
Dover *Kent* 7 V26
Doveridge *Derby* 11 S20
Downham *Cambs* 12 T24
Downham Market *Norfolk* 12 S24
Downhill *Londonderry* 33 M10
Downies *Donegal* 32 M8
Downpatrick *Down* 33 P12
Downton *Wilts* 5 W20
Dowra *Cavan* 32 P7
Drangan *Tipperary* 39 S8
Draperstown *Londonderry* 33 N10
Drayton *Norfolk* 13 S26
Dreenagh *Kerry* 38 T4
Dreghorn *N Ayrs* 19 L14
Drem *E Loth* 25 K18
Driffield *E Riding Yorks* 17 P23
Drigg *Cumb* 14 P17
Drimnin *H'land* 23 J12
Drimoleague *Cork* 38 U5
Drinagh *Cork* 38 U5
Dripsey *Cork* 39 U6
Drogheda *Louth* 37 Q11
Droitwich *Heref/Worcs* 10 T19
Dromahair *Leitrim* 32 P7
Dromara *Down* 33 P11
Dromard *Sligo* 32 P6
Dromcolliher *Limerick* 39 T6
Dromin *Louth* 37 Q11
Dromina *Cork* 39 T6
Dromineer *Tipperary* 35 S7
Dromiskin *Louth* 37 Q11
Dromkeen *Limerick* 39 S7
Dromod *Leitrim* 36 Q8
Dromore *Down* 33 P11
Dromore *Tyrone* 32 N9
Dromore West *Sligo* 35 P6
Dronfield *Derby* 16 R21
Drongan *E Ayrs* 19 M15
Druid *Denbs* 8 S17

Drum *Monaghan* 36 P9
Drumaduff *Londonderry* 33 N10
Drumahoe *Londonderry* 32 N9
Drumakilly *Tyrone* 32 N9
Drumbad *Longford* 36 Q8
Drumbadmeen *Fermanagh* 32 P8
Drumbear *Monaghan* 33 P10
Drumbeg *Donegal* 32 N8
Drumbeg *Down* 33 N12
Drumbeg *H'land* 27 F13
Drumbilla *Louth* 37 P11
Drumbo *Monaghan* 37 Q10
Drumcard *Fermanagh* 32 P8
Drumcliff *Sligo* 32 P6
Drumcondra *Dublin* 37 R11
Drumcondra *Meath* 37 Q10
Drumcoo *Monaghan* 32 P9
Drumcree *Westmeath* 36 Q9
Drumdallagh *Antrim* 33 M11
Drumfin *Sligo* 35 P7
Drumfree *Donegal* 32 M9
Drumgask *H'land* 24 H15
Drumjohn *Dumf/Gal* 19 M15
Drumkeeran *Leitrim* 36 P7
Drumlegagh *Tyrone* 32 N9
Drumlish *Longford* 36 Q8
Drummore *Dumf/Gal* 18 N14
Drumnacross *Donegal* 32 N8
Drumnadrochit *H'land* 28 H15
Drumquin *Tyrone* 32 N9
Drumramer *Londonderry* 33 M10
Drumsallan *Armagh* 33 P10
Drumsaragh *Londonderry* 33 N10
Drumshanbo *Leitrim* 36 P7
Drumskinny *Fermanagh* 32 N8
Drumsna *Leitrim* 36 Q7
Drumsurn *Londonderry* 33 M10
Drymen *Stirl* 24 K15
Drynoch *H'land* 26 H11
Dublin *Dublin* 37 R11
Duchally *H'land* 27 F14
Duddington *Northants* 12 S22
Dudley *W Midlands* 10 S19
Duffield *Derby* 11 S21
Dufftown *Moray* 29 H17
Dukinfield *Gtr Man* 37 Q11
Duleek *Meath* 37 Q11
Dullingham *Cambs* 12 T24
Dulnain Bridge *H'land* 28 H16
Duloe *Cornw'l* 3 X15
Dulverton *Som'set* 4 V16
Dumbarton *W Dunb* 19 L14
Dumfries *Dumf/Gal* 20 M16
Dun Laoghaire *Dublin* 37 R11
Dunaff *Donegal* 32 M9
Dunans *Arg/Bute* 23 K13
Dunbar *E Loth* 25 K18
Dunbeath *H'land* 28 F17
Dunblane *Stirl* 24 K16
Dunboyne *Meath* 37 R11
Duncansby *H'land* 29 E17
Dunchurch *Warwick* 11 T21
Duncormick *Wexford* 40 T10
Dundalk *Louth* 37 P11
Dundee *Dundee C* 25 J17
Dunderrow *Cork* 39 U6
Dunderry *Meath* 37 Q10
Dundonald *Down* 33 N12
Dundonald *S Ayrs* 19 L14
Dundrennan *Dumf/Gal* 19 N16
Dundrod *Antrim* 33 N11
Dundrum *Dublin* 37 R11
Dundrum *Tipperary* 39 S7
Dundrum *Down* 33 P12
Dunecht *Aberds* 25 H19
Dunfanaghy *Donegal* 32 M8
Dunfermline *Fife* 24 K17
Dungannon *Tyrone* 33 N10
Dungarvan *Waterford* 39 T8
Dungiven *Londonderry* 33 N10
Dunglow *Donegal* 32 N7
Dungourney *Cork* 39 U7
Dunheeda *Meath* 37 Q10
Dunino *Fife* 25 K18
Dunipace *Falk* 24 K16
Dunkeld *Perth/Kinr* 24 J16
Dunkerrin *Offaly* 39 S8
Dunkineely *Donegal* 32 N7
Dunlavin *Wicklow* 40 R10

Dunleer *Louth* 37 Q11
Dunlop *E Ayrs* 19 L14
Dunloy *Antrim* 33 M11
Dunmanway *Cork* 38 U5
Dunmore *Galway* 35 Q6
Dunmore East *Waterford* 40 T10
Dunmurry *Antrim* 33 N11
Dunnamanagh *Tyrone* 32 N9
Dunnet *H'land* 28 E17
Dunning *Perth/Kinr* 24 K16
Dunnington *C of York* 17 Q22
Dunoon *Arg/Bute* 18 L14
Dunragit *Dumf/Gal* 18 N14
Duns *Borders* 21 L19
Dunsany *Meath* 37 Q10
Dunsby *Lincs* 12 S23
Dunscore *Dumf/Gal* 19 M16
Dunsford *Devon* 4 W16
Dunshaughlin *Meath* 37 Q10
Dunstable *Beds* 6 U22
Dunster *Som'set* 4 V17
Dunston *Staffs* 10 S19
Dunsyre *S Lanarks* 20 L17
Dunure *S Ayrs* 19 M14
Dunvegan *H'land* 26 H10
Durham *Durham* 21 N20
Durness *H'land* 27 E14
Durrington *Wilts* 5 V20
Durrow *Laois* 40 S9
Durrow Abbey *Offaly* 36 R8
Durrus *Cork* 38 U4
Dursley *Glos* 5 U19
Dyan *Tyrone* 33 P10
Dyce *Aberd C* 25 H19
Dykehead *Angus* 25 J17
Dymchurch *Kent* 7 V26
Dymock *Glos* 10 U19
Dysart *Westmeath* 36 R9
Dysart *Fife* 25 K17
Dyserth *Denbs* 8 R17

E

Eaglescliffe *Stockton* 16 N21
Eaglesfield *Dumf/Gal* 20 M17
Eaglesham *E Renf* 19 L15
Eakring *Notts* 11 R22
Ealing *Gtr Lon* 6 U23
Earby *Lancs* 15 Q19
Eardisley *Heref/Worcs* 10 T17
Eargantea *Londonderry* 33 M10
Earith *Cambs* 12 T24
Earl Shilton *Leics* 11 S21
Earl Soham *Suffolk* 13 T26
Earls Barton *Northants* 12 T22
Earl's Colne *Essex* 13 U25
Earlsferry *Fife* 25 K18
Earlston *Borders* 21 L18
Earlstown *Galway* 35 R7
Earsdon *Tyne/Wear* 21 M21
Easebourne *W Sussex* 6 W22
Easington *Durham* 21 N21
Easington *E Riding Yorks* 17 Q24
Easington Colliery *Durham* 21 N21
Easingwold *N Yorks* 16 P21
Easky *Sligo* 35 P6
East Bergholt *Suffolk* 13 U26
East Boldre *Hants* 5 W21
East Brent *Som'set* 4 V18
East Bridgford *Notts* 11 S22
East Calder *W Loth* 20 L17
East Cowes *I of Wight* 5 W21
East Cowton *N Yorks* 16 P20
East Dean *E Sussex* 6 W23
East Dereham *Norfolk* 13 S25
East Grinstead *W Sussex* 6 V24
East Harling *Norfolk* 13 T25
East Horsley *Surrey* 6 V23
East Ilsley *Berks* 5 U21
East Kilbride *S Lanarks* 19 L15
East Leake *Notts* 11 S21
East Linton *E Loth* 25 L18
East Looe *Cornw'l* 3 X15
East Markham *Notts* 17 R22
East Norton *Leics* 11 S22
East Oakley *Hants* 5 V21

East Wemyss *Fife* 25 K17
East Wittering *W Sussex* 6 W22
East Witton *N Yorks* 15 P20
East Woodhay *Hants* 5 V21
Eastbourne *E Sussex* 7 W24
Eastchurch *Kent* 7 V25
Easter Skeld *Shetl'd* 31 B21
Eastfield *N Yorks* 17 P23
Eastleigh *Hants* 5 W21
Eastnor *Heref/Worcs* 10 T19
Easton *Dorset* 5 W19
Easton *Northants* 12 S22
Easton-in-Gordano *N Som'set* 4 V18
Eastry *Kent* 7 V26
Eastwood *Notts* 11 R21
Eaton *Leics* 11 S22
Eaton Socon *Cambs* 12 T23
Ebberston *N Yorks* 17 P22
Ebbw Vale *Bl Gwent* 4 U17
Ecclaw *Borders* 25 L19
Ecclefechan *Dumf/Gal* 20 M17
Eccleshall *Staffs* 10 S19
Echt *Aberds* 25 H19
Eckington *Derby* 16 R21
Eckington *Heref/Worcs* 10 T19
Edderton *H'land* 28 G15
Eden *Antrim* 33 N12
Edenaveagh *Fermanagh* 32 N8
Edenbridge *Kent* 6 V24
Edenderry *Offaly* 36 R9
Ederny *Fermanagh* 32 N8
Edgeworthstown *Longford* 36 Q8
Edgmond *Shrops* 10 S19
Edinburgh *C of Edinb* 25 L17
Edington *Wilts* 5 V19
Edmondstown *Louth* 37 Q10
Edmundbyers *Durham* 21 N20
Edwinstowe *Notts* 11 R21
Edzell *Angus* 25 J18
Egham *Surrey* 6 V22
Eglinton *Londonderry* 32 M9
Eglish *Tyrone* 33 P10
Eglwyswrw *Pembs* 9 T14
Egremont *Cumb* 14 P16
Egton *N Yorks* 17 P22
Eighter *Cavan* 36 Q9
Eilean Iarmain *H'land* 23 H12
Elan Village *Powys* 9 T16
Elgin *Moray* 28 G17
Elgol *H'land* 22 H11
Elham *Kent* 7 V26
Elie *Fife* 25 K18
Elishaw *Northum* 21 M19
Elland *W Yorks* 15 Q20
Ellesmere *Shrops* 10 S18
Ellesmere Port *Ches* 15 R18
Ellington *Northum* 21 M20
Ellistrin *Donegal* 32 N8
Ellon *Aberds* 29 H19
Elmswell *Suffolk* 13 T25
Elphin *Roscommon* 35 Q7
Elphin *H'land* 27 F13
Elsdon *Northum* 21 M19
Elsenham *Essex* 12 U24
Elstead *Surrey* 6 V22
Elston *Notts* 11 R22
Elvanfoot *S Lanarks* 20 M16
Elveden *Suffolk* 13 T25
Elvington *C of York* 17 Q22
Elworth *Ches* 10 R19
Ely *Cambs* 12 T24
Embleton *Northum* 21 M20
Embo *H'land* 28 G15
Emly *Tipperary* 39 T7
Emmoo *Roscommon* 36 Q7
Empingham *Rutl'd* 12 S22
Emsworth *Hants* 6 W22
Emyvale *Monaghan* 33 N10
Enderby *Leics* 11 S21
Endon *Staffs* 10 R19
Enfield *Gtr Lon* 6 U23
Ennis *Clare* 39 S6
Enniscorthy *Wexford* 40 S10
Enniskean *Cork* 39 U6
Enniskerry *Wicklow* 37 R11
Enniskillen *Fermanagh* 32 P8
Ennistimon *Clare* 34 S5
Enstone *Oxon* 11 U21
Enterkinfoot *Dumf/Gal* 19 M16
Epping *Essex* 6 U24
Epsom *Surrey* 6 V23

Epworth *N Lincs* 17 Q22
Eriboll *H'land* 28 F14
Errill *Laois* 39 S8
Errogie *H'land* 28 H15
Errol *Perth/Kinr* 25 K17
Erskine *Renf* 19 L15
Escrick *N Yorks* 16 Q21
Esh Winning *Durham* 21 N20
Esher *Surrey* 6 V23
Eskdalemuir *Dumf/Gal* 20 M17
Essexford *Monaghan* 37 Q10
Eston *Redcar/Clevel'd* 21 N21
Etchingham *E Sussex* 7 V24
Eton *Berks* 6 V22
Ettington *Warwick* 11 T20
Etwall *Derby* 11 S20
Euxton *Lancs* 15 Q18
Evanton *H'land* 28 G15
Evercreech *Som'set* 5 V19
Everleigh *Wilts* 5 V20
Evershot *Dorset* 4 W18
Evesham *Heref/Worcs* 11 T20
Ewell *Surrey* 6 V23
Ewhurst *Surrey* 6 V23
Ewyas Harold *Heref/Worcs* 10 U18
Exbourne *Devon* 3 W16
Exeter *Devon* 4 W16
Exford *Som'set* 4 V16
Exminster *Devon* 4 W17
Exmouth *Devon* 4 W17
Exton *Rutl'd* 12 S22
Eyam *Derby* 16 R20
Eye *Cambs* 12 S23
Eye *Suffolk* 13 T26
Eyemouth *Borders* 21 L19
Eynsford *Kent* 6 V24
Eynsham *Oxon* 5 U21
Eyrecourt *Galway* 36 R7

F

Faddiley *Ches* 10 R18
Fairbourne *Gwyn* 8 S15
Fairford *Glos* 5 U20
Fairlie *N Ayrs* 18 L14
Fairlight *E Sussex* 7 W25
Fakenham *Norfolk* 13 S25
Fala *Midloth* 20 L18
Falcarragh *Donegal* 32 M7
Faldingworth *Lincs* 17 R23
Falkirk *Falk* 24 K16
Falkland *Fife* 25 K17
Fallmore *Mayo* 34 P3
Falmer *E Sussex* 6 W23
Falmouth *Cornw'l* 2 X13
Falstone *Northum* 21 M19
Fardrum *Westmeath* 36 R8
Fareham *Hants* 5 W21
Faringdon *Oxon* 5 U20
Farnborough *Berks* 5 U21
Farnborough *Hants* 6 V22
Farndon *Ches* 10 R18
Farnham *Surrey* 6 V22
Farnworth *Gtr Man* 15 Q19
Farr *H'land* 28 H15
Farranfore *Kerry* 38 T4
Fasag *H'land* 27 G12
Faslane *Arg/Bute* 23 K14
Fauldhouse *W Loth* 20 L16
Faversham *Kent* 7 V25
Fawley *Hants* 5 W21
Fazeley *Staffs* 11 S20
Feakle *Clare* 35 S6
Fearn *H'land* 28 G16
Fearnan *Perth/Kinr* 24 J15
Feckenham *Heref/Worcs* 11 T20
Fedamore *Limerick* 39 S6
Feeard *Clare* 38 S4
Feenhanagh *Limerick* 39 T6
Feeny *Londonderry* 33 N9
Felinheli *Gwyn* 8 R15
Felixstowe *Suffolk* 13 U26
Felton *Northum* 21 M20
Feltwell *Norfolk* 13 T25
Fenagh *Leitrim* 36 P8
Fenit *Kerry* 38 T4
Fennagh *Carlow* 40 S10
Fenny Bentley *Derby* 11 R20
Fenny Compton *Warwick* 11 T21
Fenny Stratford *M/Keynes* 12 U22

Fenwick *E Ayrs*	19	L15
Feock *Cornw'l*	2	X13
Feolin Ferry *Arg/Bute*	18	L11
Ferbane *Offaly*	36	R8
Fermoy *Cork*	39	T7
Ferndown *Dorset*	5	W20
Ferness *H'land*	28	H16
Fernhurst *W Sussex*	6	V22
Fernilea *H'land*	26	H11
Ferns *Wexford*	40	S11
Ferryhill *Durham*	21	N20
Ferryside *Carms*	9	U15
Fethard *Tipperary*	39	T8
Fethard *Wexford*	40	T10
Fettercairn *Aberds*	25	J18
Ffestiniog *Gwyn*	8	S16
Fiddown *Kilkenny*	40	T9
Filby *Norfolk*	13	S27
Filey *N Yorks*	17	P23
Fillongley *Warwick*	11	T20
Filton *S Gloucs*	4	U18
Fincarn *Londonderry*	33	N10
Fincham *Norfolk*	12	S24
Finchingfield *Essex*	12	U24
Finchley *Gtr Lon*	6	U23
Findhorn *Moray*	28	G16
Findochty *Moray*	29	G18
Findon *W Sussex*	6	W23
Finedon *Northants*	12	T22
Finglas *Dublin*	37	R11
Finnea *Westmeath*	36	Q9
Finningley *S Yorks*	17	R22
Finnis *Down*	33	P11
Finstown *Orkney*	30	D17
Fintona *Tyrone*	32	P9
Fintown *Donegal*	32	N7
Fintry *Stirl*	24	K15
Finvoy *Antrim*	33	M11
Fishbourne *I of Wight*	5	W21
Fishguard *Pembs*	9	U14
Fishnish *Arg/Bute*	23	J12
Fishtoft *Lincs*	12	S24
Five Alley *Offaly*	36	R8
Fivemiletown *Tyrone*	32	P9
Flagmount *Clare*	35	R6
Flamborough		
E Riding Yorks	17	P23
Fleet *Hants*	6	V22
Fleetwood *Lancs*	15	Q17
Flimby *Cumb*	20	N17
Flint *Flints*	15	R17
Flitwick *Beds*	12	U22
Flodden *Northum*	21	L19
Flookburgh *Cumb*	15	P18
Fochabers *Moray*	29	G17
Foel *Powys*	8	S17
Folkestone *Kent*	7	V26
Fontmell Magna		
Dorset	5	W19
Fontstown *Kildare*	40	R10
Ford *Wexford*	40	S11
Ford *Arg/Bute*	23	K13
Forden *Powys*	10	S17
Fordham *Cambs*	12	T24
Fordingbridge *Hants*	5	W20
Fordstown *Meath*	37	Q10
Fordyce *Aberds*	29	G18
Fore *Westmeath*	36	Q9
Forest Row *E Sussex*	6	V24
Forfar *Angus*	25	J18
Forgney *Longford*	36	Q8
Forkill *Armagh*	37	P11
Formby *Mersey*	15	Q17
Forres *Moray*	28	G16
Forsinain *H'land*	28	F16
Forsinard *H'land*	28	F16
Fort Augustus *H'land*	24	H14
Fort William *H'land*	23	J13
Forth *S Lanarks*	20	L16
Fortrie *Aberds*	29	G18
Fortrose *H'land*	28	G15
Fortuneswell *Dorset*	5	W19
Fothergill *Cumb*	20	N17
Fotheringhay		
Northants	12	S23
Foulden *Borders*	21	L19
Foulkesmill *Wexford*	40	T10
Foulsham *Norfolk*	13	S26
Fountain Cross *Clare*	38	S5
Fountainhall *Borders*	20	L18
Four Mile House		
Roscommon	35	Q7
Fovant *Wilts*	5	V20
Fowey *Cornw'l*	2	X14
Fownhope		
Heref/Worcs	10	T18
Foxdale *I of Man*	14	P14
Foxford *Mayo*	35	Q5
Foyers *H'land*	24	H15
Foygh *Longford*	36	Q8
Foynes *Limerick*	38	S5
Fraddon *Cornw'l*	2	X14
Framlingham *Suffolk*	13	T26
Frampton on Severn		
Glos	5	U19
Frankville *Down*	33	P12
Frant *E Sussex*	7	V24
Fraserburgh *Aberds*	29	G19
Freckleton *Lancs*	15	Q18
Freemount *Cork*	39	T6
Freethorpe *Norfolk*	13	S27
Fremington *Devon*	3	V15
Frenchpark		
Roscommon	35	Q7
Frensham *Surrey*	6	V22
Freshford *Kilkenny*	40	S9
Freshwater *I of Wight*	5	W20
Fressingfield *Suffolk*	13	T26
Freswick *H'land*	29	E17
Freuchie *Fife*	25	K17
Friday Bridge *Cambs*	12	S24
Fridaythorpe		
E Riding Yorks	17	P22
Frimley *Surrey*	6	V22
Frinton-on-Sea *Essex*	7	U26
Friockheim *Angus*	25	J18
Frizington *Cumb*	20	N17
Frodsham *Ches*	15	R18
Frome *Som'set*	5	V19
Frongoch *Gwyn*	8	S16
Froxfield *Wilts*	5	V20
Fuerty *Roscommon*	35	Q7
Fulbourn *Cambs*	12	T24
Fulford *C of York*	16	Q21
Fulwood *Lancs*	15	Q18
Funzie *Shetl'd*	31	A22
Furnace *Arg/Bute*	23	K13
Fybagh *Kerry*	38	T4
Fyfield *Essex*	7	U24
Fyvie *Aberds*	29	H19

G

Gaerwen *Angl*	8	R15
Gaick Lodge *H'land*	24	J15
Gailey *Staffs*	10	S19
Gainford *Durham*	21	N20
Gainsborough *Lincs*	17	R22
Gairloch *H'land*	27	G12
Gairlochy *H'land*	23	J14
Galashiels *Borders*	20	L18
Galbally *Limerick*	39	T7
Galgate *Lancs*	15	Q18
Galmisdale *H'land*	22	J11
Galmoy *Kilkenny*	39	S8
Galmpton *Devon*	3	X16
Galston *E Ayrs*	19	L15
Galway *Galway*	35	R5
Gamlingay *Cambs*	12	T23
Garbally *Galway*	35	R7
Garbhallt *Arg/Bute*	23	K13
Garboldisham *Norfolk*	13	T25
Gardenstown *Aberds*	29	G19
Garelochhead		
Arg/Bute	23	K14
Garforth *W Yorks*	16	Q21
Gargrave *N Yorks*	15	Q19
Gargunnock *Stirl*	24	K15
Garlieston *Dumf/Gal*	19	N15
Garmouth *Moray*	29	G17
Garrane *Cork*	38	U5
Garrison *Fermanagh*	32	P7
Garristown *Dublin*	37	Q10
Garrow *Perth/Kinr*	24	J16
Garryvoe *Cork*	39	U7
Garsdale Head *Cumb*	15	P19
Garstang *Lancs*	15	Q18
Garston *Mersey*	15	R18
Garton-on-the-Wolds		
E Riding Yorks	17	P22
Garvagh *Londonderry*	33	N10
Garvaghy *Down*	33	P11
Garvaghy *Tyrone*	32	P9
Garvald *E Loth*	25	L18
Garvary *Fermanagh*	32	P8
Garve *H'land*	27	G13
Gatehouse of Fleet		
Dumf/Gal	19	N15
Gateshead *Tyne/Wear*	21	N20
Gatley *Gtr Man*	15	R19
Gattabaun *Kilkenny*	40	S9
Gawthwaite *Cumb*	15	P17
Gay Brook		
Westmeath	36	R9
Gaydon *Warwick*	11	T21
Gayton *Norfolk*	13	S25
Gaywood *Norfolk*	12	S24
Gearraidh na h-		
Aibhne *W Isles*	26	F10
Geary *H'land*	26	G10
Geashill *Offaly*	36	R9
Geddington *Northants*	12	T22
Gedney *Lincs*	12	S24
Georgeham *Devon*	3	V15
Gerrards Cross *Bucks*	6	U22
Gifford *E Loth*	25	L18
Giggleswick *N Yorks*	15	P19
Gilford *Down*	33	P11
Gillingham *Dorset*	5	V19
Gillingham *Kent*	7	V25
Gilmerton *Perth/Kinr*	24	K16
Gilsland *Northum*	21	N18
Gilwern *Monmouths*	4	U17
Giosla *W Isles*	26	F10
Girton *Cambs*	12	T24
Girvan *S Ayrs*	18	M14
Gisburn *Lancs*	15	Q19
Gladestry *Powys*	10	T17
Glamis *Angus*	25	J17
Glanaman *Carms*	9	U16
Glandore *Cork*	38	U5
Glanton *Northum*	21	M20
Glanworth *Cork*	39	T7
Glasbury *Powys*	10	T17
Glasdrumman *Down*	37	P12
Glasgow *C of Glasg*	19	L15
Glaslough *Monaghan*	33	P10
Glasnevin *Dublin*	37	R11
Glassan *Westmeath*	36	R8
Glasserton *Dumf/Gal*	19	N15
Glasson *Lancs*	15	Q18
Glastonbury *Som'set*	4	V18
Glastry *Down*	33	P13
Glemsford *Suffolk*	13	T25
Glen *Donegal*	32	M8
Glen *Fermanagh*	32	P7
Glenade *Leitrim*	32	P7
Glenamoy *Mayo*	34	P4
Glenariff *Antrim*	33	M11
Glenarm *Antrim*	33	N12
Glenavy *Antrim*	33	N11
Glenbar *Arg/Bute*	18	L12
Glenbeigh *Kerry*	38	T4
Glenborrodale *H'land*	23	J12
Glenbrittle *H'land*	22	H11
Glencaple *Dumf/Gal*	20	N16
Glencar *Kerry*	38	T4
Glencarse *Perth/Kinr*	24	K17
Glencoe *H'land*	23	J13
Glencolumbkille		
Donegal	32	N6
Glendalough *Wicklow*	40	R11
Glendoll Lodge *Angus*	25	J17
Glendree *Clare*	39	S6
Gleneagles *Perth/Kinr*	24	K16
Glenealy *Wicklow*	40	S11
Gleneely *Donegal*	32	M9
Glenelg *H'land*	23	H12
Glenfarn *Leitrim*	32	P8
Glenfesk *Kerry*	38	T5
Glenfinnan *H'land*	23	J13
Glengarriff *Cork*	38	U4
Glengavlen *Cavan*	32	P8
Glengormly *Antrim*	33	N12
Glenluce *Dumf/Gal*	18	N13
Glenmaye *I of Man*	14	P14
Glenmore Lodge		
H'land	24	H16
Glennamaddy *Galway*	35	Q6
Glenoe *Antrim*	33	N12
Glenprosen Lodge		
Angus	25	J17
Glenrothes *Fife*	25	K17
Glenstal Abbey		
Limerick	39	S7
Glenstriven *Arg/Bute*	18	L13
Glentane *Galway*	35	R6
Glenties *Donegal*	32	N7
Glentrool Village		
Dumf/Gal	19	M14
Glenville *Cork*	39	T7
Glenwhilly *Dumf/Gal*	18	M14
Glin *Limerick*	38	S5
Glinsk *Galway*	34	R4
Glinsk *Galway*	35	Q7
Glinton *Cambs*	12	S23
Glossop *Derby*	15	R20
Gloucester *Glos*	10	U19
Glusburn *N Yorks*	15	Q20
Glyn Ceiriog *Wrex*	10	S17
Glyn Neath		
Neath P Talb	9	U16
Glyncorrwg		
Neath P Talb	9	U16
Glynde *E Sussex*	6	W24
Glyndyfrdwy *Denbs*	10	S17
Glynn *Carlow*	40	S10
Glynn *Antrim*	33	N12
Gnosall *Staffs*	10	S19
Goathland *N Yorks*	17	P22
Gobowen *Shrops*	10	S17
Godalming *Surrey*	6	V22
Godmanchester		
Cambs	12	T23
Godshill *I of Wight*	5	W21
Godstone *Surrey*	6	V23
Golden *Tipperary*	39	T8
Goldhanger *Essex*	7	U25
Goleen *Cork*	39	V4
Golspie *H'land*	28	G16
Goodrich		
Heref/Worcs	10	U18
Goodwick *Pembs*	9	T13
Goodwood *W Sussex*	6	W22
Goole *E Riding Yorks*	17	Q22
Goonhavern *Cornw'l*	2	X13
Gordon *Borders*	21	L18
Gorebridge *Midloth*	20	L17
Goresbridge *Kilkenny*	40	S10
Gorey *Wexford*	40	S11
Gorey *Chan Is*	2	Z19
Goring *Oxon*	5	U21
Goring-by-Sea		
W Sussex	6	W23
Gorleston *Norfolk*	13	S27
Gormanstown *Meath*	37	Q11
Gorran Haven *Cornw'l*	2	X14
Gorseinon *Swan*	9	U15
Gorslas *Carms*	9	U15
Gort *Galway*	35	R6
Gortahork *Donegal*	32	M7
Gorteen *Galway*	35	Q6
Gorteen *Galway*	35	R6
Gorteen *Sligo*	35	Q6
Gorteen *Waterford*	39	T8
Gorteeng *Galway*	35	R7
Gortin *Tyrone*	32	N9
Gortnacross		
Londonderry	33	N10
Gortroe *Cork*	39	T6
Gortymadden *Galway*	35	R7
Gosberton *Lincs*	12	S23
Gosforth *Cumb*	14	P17
Gosforth *Tyne/Wear*	21	N20
Gosport *Hants*	5	W21
Goswick *Northum*	21	L20
Gotham *Notts*	11	S21
Goudhurst *Kent*	7	V24
Gourdon *Aberds*	25	J19
Gourock *Invercl*	18	L14
Gowerton *Swan*	9	U15
Gowlaun *Galway*	34	Q4
Gowran *Kilkenny*	40	S9
Grabhair *W Isles*	26	F11
Graghil *Mayo*	34	P4
Graigue *Laois*	40	S10
Graiguenamanagh		
Kilkenny	40	S10
Grain *Kent*	7	V25
Grainthorpe *Lincs*	17	R24
Grampound *Cornw'l*	2	X14
Gramsdal *W Isles*	26	H9
Granard *Longford*	36	Q9
Grange *Kilkenny*	40	S9
Grange *Roscommon*	36	Q7
Grange *Sligo*	32	P6
Grange-over-Sands		
Cumb	15	P18
Grangebellew *Louth*	37	Q11
Grangemouth *Falk*	24	K16
Grantham *Lincs*	12	S22
Grantown-on-Spey		
H'land	28	H16
Grantshouse *Borders*	21	L19
Granville *Tyrone*	33	P10
Grasby *Lincs*	17	R23
Grasmere *Cumb*	15	P17
Grassington *N Yorks*	15	P20
Grateley *Hants*	5	V20
Gravesend *Kent*	7	V24
Grayrigg *Cumb*	15	P18
Grays *Essex*	7	V24
Grayshott *Hants*	6	V22
Great Ayton *N Yorks*	16	N21
Great Baddow *Essex*	7	U25
Great Badminton		
S Gloucs	5	U19
Great Barford *Beds*	12	T23
Great Bentley *Essex*	7	U26
Great Bridgeford		
Staffs	10	S19
Great Broughton		
N Yorks	16	P21
Great Chesterford		
Essex	12	T24
Great Clifton *Cumb*	20	N17
Great Dunmow *Essex*	7	U24
Great Eccleston		
Lancs	15	Q18
Great Ellingham		
Norfolk	13	S25
Great Gidding *Cambs*	12	T23
Gretna Harwood *Lancs*	15	Q19
Great Horwood		
Bucks	11	U22
Great Malvern		
Heref/Worcs	10	T19
Great Massingham		
Norfolk	13	S25
Great Missenden		
Bucks	6	U22
Great Oakley *Essex*	7	U26
Great Sampford		
Essex	12	U24
Great Shefford *Berks*	5	V21
Great Shelford		
Cambs	12	T24
Great Somerford		
Wilts	5	U19
Great Staunton		
Cambs	12	T23
Great Torrington		
Devon	3	W15
Great Wakering *Essex*	7	U25
Great Waltham *Essex*	7	U24
Great Witley		
Heref/Worcs	10	T19
Great Yarmouth		
Norfolk	13	S27
Greatham *Hartlep'l*	21	N21
Greatstone-on-Sea		
Kent	7	W25
Green Hammerton		
N Yorks	16	P21
Greencastle *Donegal*	32	M10
Greencastle *Down*	37	P11
Greencastle *Tyrone*	33	N9
Greenhead *Northum*	21	N18
Greenholm *E Ayrs*	19	L15
Greenisland *Antrim*	33	N12
Greenlaw *Borders*	21	L19
Greenloaning		
Perth/Kinr	24	K16
Greenock *Invercl*	18	L14
Greenodd *Cumb*	15	P17
Greenore *Louth*	37	P11
Greenway *Pembs*	9	U14
Greenwich *Gtr Lon*	6	V24
Greevagh *Sligo*	35	P7
Gretna *Dumf/Gal*	20	N17
Gretna Green		
Dumf/Gal	20	M17
Gretton *Northants*	12	S22
Greyabbey *Down*	33	N12
Greysteel		
Londonderry	33	M9
Greystoke *Cumb*	20	N18
Greystones *Wicklow*	37	R11
Grimsby *NE Lincs*	17	Q23
Gritley *Orkney*	30	E18
Grizebeck *Cumb*	15	P17
Groby *Leics*	11	S21
Groomsport *Down*	33	N12
Grove *Oxon*	5	U21
Grundisburgh *Suffolk*	13	T26
Guard Bridge *Fife*	25	K18
Gubaveeny *Cavan*	32	P8
Gudderstown *Louth*	37	Q10
Guestling Green		
E Sussex	7	W25
Guildford *Surrey*	6	V22
Guildtown *Perth/Kinr*	24	K17
Guilsfield *Powys*	10	S17
Guisborough		
Redcar/Clevel'd	16	N21
Guiseley *W Yorks*	16	Q20
Gulladuff		
Londonderry	33	N10
Gullane *E Loth*	25	K18
Gunnerside *N Yorks*	15	P19
Gunnislake *Cornw'l*	3	W15
Gunnista *Shetl'd*	31	B21
Gutcher *Shetl'd*	31	A21
Gwalchmai *Angl*	8	R15
Gwaun-Cae-Gurwen		
Neath P Talb	9	U16

Gwbert-on-Sea *Ceredig'n* 9 T14
Gweedore *Donegal* 32 M7
Gweek *Cornw'l* 2 X13
Gwennap *Cornw'l* 2 X13
Gwesalia *Mayo* 34 P4
Gwyddelwern *Denbs* 8 R17
Gwytherin *Conwy* 8 R16

H

Hacketstown *Carlow* 40 S10
Hackney *Gtr Lon* 6 U23
Hackthorpe *Cumb* 21 N18
Haddenham *Bucks* 6 U22
Haddenham *Cambs* 12 T24
Haddington *E Loth* 25 L18
Haddiscoe *Norfolk* 13 S27
Hadleigh *Essex* 7 U25
Hadleigh *Suffolk* 13 T25
Hadlow *Kent* 7 V24
Hadnall *Shrops* 10 S18
Hagworthingham *Lincs* 17 R24
Hailsham *E Sussex* 7 W24
Hainton *Lincs* 17 R23
Halberton *Devon* 4 W17
Halesowen *W Midlands* 10 T19
Halesworth *Suffolk* 13 T27
Halford *Warwick* 11 T20
Halifax *W Yorks* 15 Q20
Halkirk *H'land* 28 E16
Halland *E Sussex* 6 W24
Hallow *Heref/Worcs* 10 T19
Hallworthy *Cornw'l* 2 W14
Halstead *Essex* 13 U25
Halton *Lancs* 15 P18
Haltwhistle *Northum* 21 N19
Halwill Junction *Devon* 3 W15
Hamble-le-Rice *Hants* 5 W21
Hambledon *Hants* 5 W21
Hambleton *Lancs* 15 Q18
Hambleton *N Yorks* 16 Q21
Hamerton *Cambs* 12 T23
Hamilstownbawn *Armagh* 33 P10
Hamilton *S Lanarks* 19 L15
Hammersmith & Fulham *Gtr Lon* 6 V23
Hamnavoe *Shetl'd* 31 B21
Hamnavoe *Shetl'd* 31 B21
Hampstead Norris *Berks* 5 V21
Hampton in Arden *W Midlands* 11 T20
Hamstreet *Kent* 7 V25
Handcross *W Sussex* 6 V23
Hannington *Hants* 5 V21
Harbury *Warwick* 11 T21
Harby *Leics* 11 S22
Hardingstone *Northants* 11 T22
Harewood *W Yorks* 16 Q20
Haringey *Gtr Lon* 6 U23
Harlech *Gwyn* 8 S15
Harleston *Norfolk* 13 T26
Harlow *Essex* 6 U24
Haroldswick *Shetl'd* 31 A22
Harpenden *Herts* 6 U22
Harrietfield *Perth/Kinr* 24 K16
Harrietsham *Kent* 7 V25
Harrington *Cumb* 20 N16
Harris *H'land* 22 J11
Harrogate *N Yorks* 16 P20
Harrold *Beds* 12 T22
Harrow *Gtr Lon* 6 U23
Harston *Cambs* 12 T24
Hartburn *Northum* 21 M20
Hartest *Suffolk* 13 T25
Hartfield *E Sussex* 6 V24
Harthill *N Lanarks* 19 L16
Hartington *Derby* 11 R20
Hartland *Devon* 3 W15
Hartlebury *Heref/Worcs* 10 T19
Hartlepool *Hartlep'l* 21 N21
Hartley *Kent* 7 V24
Hartley *Northum* 21 M21
Hartley Wintney *Hants* 6 V22
Hartpury *Glos* 10 U19
Hartshill *Warwick* 11 S20
Harvington *Heref/Worcs* 11 T20

Harwell *Oxon* 5 U21
Harwich *Essex* 13 U26
Harworth *Notts* 16 R21
Haselbury Plucknett *Som'set* 4 W18
Haslemere *Surrey* 6 V22
Haslingden *Lancs* 15 Q19
Hassocks *W Sussex* 6 W23
Hastigrow *H'land* 29 E17
Hastings *E Sussex* 7 W25
Haswell *Durham* 21 N21
Hatch Beauchamp *Som'set* 4 W18
Hatfield *Herts* 6 U23
Hatfield *S Yorks* 17 Q22
Hatfield Heath *Essex* 6 U24
Hatfield Peverel *Essex* 7 U25
Hatherleigh *Devon* 3 W15
Hathersage *Derby* 16 R20
Hatton *Aberds* 29 H20
Hatton *Derby* 11 S20
Haugh of Urr *Dumf/Gal* 19 N16
Haughley *Suffolk* 13 T25
Haughton *Staffs* 10 S19
Havant *Hants* 6 W22
Haverfordwest *Pembs* 9 U14
Haverhill *Suffolk* 12 T24
Haverigg *Cumb* 14 P17
Havering *Gtr Lon* 6 U24
Hawarden *Flints* 15 R17
Hawes *N Yorks* 15 P19
Hawick *Borders* 20 M18
Hawkchurch *Devon* 4 W18
Hawkesbury Upton *S Gloucs* 5 U19
Hawkhurst *Kent* 7 V25
Hawkinge *Kent* 7 V26
Hawkshead *Cumb* 15 P18
Hawnby *N Yorks* 16 P21
Haworth *W Yorks* 15 Q20
Hawkser *N Yorks* 17 P22
Haxby *C of York* 16 P21
Haxey *N Lincs* 17 R22
Haydon Bridge *Northum* 21 N19
Hayfield *Derby* 15 R20
Hayle *Cornw'l* 2 X13
Hayton *Cumb* 20 N18
Hayton *E Riding Yorks* 17 Q22
Haywards Heath *W Sussex* 6 W23
Hazel Grove *Gtr Man* 15 R19
Hazlemere *Bucks* 6 U22
Heacham *Norfolk* 12 S24
Headcorn *Kent* 7 V25
Headford *Galway* 35 R5
Headley *Hants* 6 V22
Heanor *Derby* 11 R21
Heath End *Hants* 5 V21
Heathfield *E Sussex* 7 W24
Hebburn *Tyne/Wear* 21 N20
Hebden Bridge *W Yorks* 15 Q19
Heckington *Lincs* 12 S23
Hedge End *Hants* 5 W21
Hednesford *Staffs* 11 S20
Hedon *E Riding Yorks* 17 Q23
Heighington *Durham* 21 N20
Heilam *H'land* 28 E14
Helensburgh *Arg/Bute* 24 K14
Hellifield *N Yorks* 15 P19
Helmsdale *H'land* 28 F16
Helmsley *N Yorks* 16 P21
Helperby *N Yorks* 16 P21
Helpringham *Lincs* 12 S23
Helsby *Ches* 15 R18
Helston *Cornw'l* 2 X13
Hemel Hempstead *Herts* 6 U23
Hemingbrough *N Yorks* 17 Q22
Hempnall *Norfolk* 13 S26
Hempton *Norfolk* 13 S25
Hemsby *Norfolk* 13 S27
Hemsworth *W Yorks* 16 Q21
Hemyock *Devon* 4 W17
Henfield *W Sussex* 6 W23
Hengoed *Caerph* 4 U17
Henley-in-Arden *Warwick* 11 T20
Henley-on-Thames *Oxon* 6 U22
Henllan *Denbs* 8 R17
Henlow *Beds* 12 T23
Henstridge *Som'set* 5 W19

Herbertstown *Limerick* 39 S7
Herbrandston *Pembs* 9 U13
Hereford *Heref/Worcs* 10 T18
Heriot *Borders* 20 L18
Hermitage *Berks* 5 V21
Herne Bay *Kent* 7 V26
Herstmonceux *E Sussex* 7 W24
Hertford *Herts* 6 U23
Hessle *Kingston/Hull* 17 Q23
Heswall *Mersey* 15 R17
Hethersett *Norfolk* 13 S26
Hetton-le-Hole *Tyne/Wear* 21 N21
Hexham *Northum* 21 N19
Heybridge *Essex* 7 U25
Heysham *Lancs* 15 P18
Heytesbury *Wilts* 5 V19
Heywood *Gtr Man* 15 Q19
Hibaldstow *N Lincs* 17 Q22
High Bentham *N Yorks* 15 P19
High Bickington *Devon* 3 W15
High Ercall *Shrops* 10 S18
High Hesket *Cumb* 20 N18
High Legh *Ches* 15 R19
Highley *Shrops* 10 T19
Hightae *Dumf/Gal* 20 M17
Highworth *Thamesd'n* 5 U20
Hilborough *Norfolk* 13 S25
Hildenborough *Kent* 6 V24
Hilgay *Norfolk* 12 S24
Hillingdon *Gtr Lon* 6 U23
Hillington *Norfolk* 13 S25
Hillsborough *Down* 33 P11
Hillswick *Shetl'd* 31 B21
Hilltown *Down* 33 P11
Hilmarton *Wilts* 5 V20
Hilton *Derby* 11 S20
Hinckley *Leics* 11 S21
Hinderwell *N Yorks* 17 N22
Hindhead *Surrey* 6 V22
Hindley *Gtr Man* 15 Q18
Hindon *Wilts* 5 V19
Hingham *Norfolk* 13 S25
Hinstock *Shrops* 10 S19
Hirwaun *Rh Cyn Taff* 9 U17
Histon *Cambs* 12 T24
Hitchin *Herts* 12 U23
Hockley *Essex* 7 U25
Hockliffe *Beds* 12 U22
Hoddesdon *Herts* 6 U23
Hodnet *Shrops* 10 S18
Hoff *Cumb* 21 N18
Holbeach *Lincs* 12 S24
Holbrook *Suffolk* 13 U26
Holbury *Hants* 5 W21
Holford *Som'set* 4 V17
Holkham *Norfolk* 13 S25
Holland on Sea *Essex* 7 U26
Hollandstoun *Orkney* 30 D19
Hollym *E Riding Yorks* 17 Q24
Hollymount *Mayo* 35 Q5
Hollywood *Wicklow* 37 R10
Holme-on-Spalding-moor *E Riding Yorks* 17 Q23
Holmer *Heref/Worcs* 10 T18
Holmes Chapel *Ches* 10 R19
Holmfirth *W Yorks* 15 Q20
Holsworthy *Devon* 3 W15
Holt *Norfolk* 13 S26
Holt *Wrex* 10 R18
Holycross *Limerick* 39 S6
Holycross *Tipperary* 39 S8
Holyhead *Angl* 8 R14
Holywell *Flints* 15 R17
Holywood *Down* 33 N12
Honington *Lincs* 12 S22
Honiton *Devon* 4 W17
Hoo *Kent* 7 V25
Hook *Hants* 5 V22
Hook Norton *Oxon* 11 U21
Hope *Flints* 10 R17
Hope under Dinmore *Heref/Worcs* 10 T18
Hopeman *Moray* 28 G17
Horam *E Sussex* 7 W24
Horden *Durham* 21 N21
Horley *Surrey* 6 V23

Horncastle *Lincs* 17 R23
Horndean *Hants* 6 W21
Horningsham *Wilts* 5 V19
Hornsea *E Riding Yorks* 17 Q23
Horrabridge *Devon* 3 X15
Horringer *Suffolk* 13 T25
Horseleap *Offaly* 36 R8
Horseleap Crossroads *Galway* 35 R6
Horsey *Norfolk* 13 S27
Horsford *Norfolk* 13 S26
Horsforth *W Yorks* 16 Q20
Horsham *W Sussex* 6 V23
Horsham St. Faith *Norfolk* 13 S26
Horsted Keynes *W Sussex* 6 V23
Horton *Northants* 11 T22
Horton *Som'set* 4 W18
Horton in Ribblesdale *N Yorks* 15 P19
Horwich *Gtr Man* 15 Q18
Hospital *Limerick* 39 T7
Hoswick *Shetl'd* 31 C21
Houghton *Cumb* 20 N18
Houghton-le-Spring *Tyne/Wear* 21 N21
Houghton Regis *Beds* 12 U22
Hounslow *Gtr Lon* 6 V23
Hove *Brighton/Hove* 6 W23
Hoveton *Norfolk* 13 S26
Hovingham *N Yorks* 17 P22
Howden *E Riding Yorks* 17 Q22
Howpasley *Borders* 20 M17
Howth *Dublin* 37 R11
Hoxne *Suffolk* 13 T26
Hoylake *Mersey* 15 R17
Hucknall *Notts* 11 R21
Huddersfield *W Yorks* 15 Q20
Hugh Town *I of Scilly* 2 Y11
Hulland Ward *Derby* 11 R20
Hullavington *Wilts* 5 U19
Hullbridge *Essex* 7 U25
Hulme End *Staffs* 11 R20
Humberston *NE Lincs* 17 Q23
Humshaugh *Northum* 21 M19
Hundred House *Powys* 9 T17
Hungerford *Berks* 5 V20
Hunmanby *N Yorks* 17 P23
Hunstanton *Norfolk* 12 S24
Hunterston *N Ayrs* 18 L14
Huntford *Borders* 21 M19
Huntingdon *Cambs* 12 T23
Huntley *Glos* 10 U19
Huntly *Aberds* 29 H18
Hurlers Cross *Clare* 39 S6
Hurlford *E Ayrs* 19 L15
Hurliness *Orkney* 30 E17
Hurn *Dorset* 5 W20
Hursley *Hants* 5 V21
Hurstbourne Tarrant *Hants* 5 V21
Hurstpierpoint *W Sussex* 6 W23
Hurworth-on-Tees *Durham* 16 P20
Husbands Bosworth *Leics* 11 T21
Husinish *W Isles* 26 G9
Huttoft *Lincs* 17 R24
Hutton Cranswick *E Riding Yorks* 17 Q23
Hutton-le-Hole *N Yorks* 17 P22
Hutton Rudby *N Yorks* 16 P21
Huyton *Mersey* 15 R18
Hyde *Gtr Man* 15 R19
Hynish *Arg/Bute* 22 K10
Hythe *Hants* 5 W21
Hythe *Kent* 7 V26

I

Ibsey *Hants* 5 W20
Ibstock *Leics* 11 S21
Icklingham *Suffolk* 13 T25
Idmiston *Wilts* 5 V20
Ilchester *Som'set* 4 W18
Ilderton *Northum* 21 M20
Ilfracombe *Devon* 3 V15
Ilkeston *Derby* 11 S21
Ilkley *W Yorks* 15 Q20

Illogan *Cornw'l* 2 X13
Ilminster *Som'set* 4 W18
Immingham *NE Lincs* 17 Q23
Inagh *Clare* 38 S5
Inch *Cork* 39 U8
Inch *Kerry* 38 T4
Inchigeelagh *Cork* 38 U5
Inchnadamph *H'land* 27 F14
Inchture *Perth/Kinr* 25 K17
Ingatestone *Essex* 7 U24
Ingleton *N Yorks* 15 P19
Ingoldmells *Lincs* 12 R24
Ingram *Northum* 21 M20
Ingrave *Essex* 7 U24
Inishannon *Cork* 39 U6
Inishcrone *Sligo* 35 P5
Inishkeen *Monaghan* 37 P10
Inishrush *Londonderry* 33 N10
Inistioge *Kilkenny* 40 T9
Inkberrow *Heref/Worcs* 11 T20
Innellan *Arg/Bute* 18 L14
Innerleithen *Borders* 20 L17
Innermessan *Dumf/Gal* 18 N14
Innfield *Meath* 37 R10
Insch *Aberds* 29 H18
Instow *Devon* 3 V15
Inver *Donegal* 32 N7
Inverallochy *Aberds* 29 G20
Inveran *Galway* 34 R5
Inveran *H'land* 28 G15
Inveraray *Arg/Bute* 23 K13
Inverarity *Angus* 25 J18
Inverbervie *Aberds* 25 J19
Invergarry *H'land* 24 H14
Invergordon *H'land* 28 G15
Invergowrie *Dundee C* 25 K17
Inverie *H'land* 23 H12
Inverinate *H'land* 23 H13
Inverkeilor *Angus* 25 J18
Inverkeithing *Fife* 24 K17
Inverkirkaig *H'land* 27 F13
Inverlochlarig *Stirl* 24 K14
Invermoriston *H'land* 24 H14
Inverness *H'land* 28 H15
Inversnaid *Stirl* 24 K14
Inverurie *Aberds* 29 H19
Ipswich *Suffolk* 13 T26
Irchester *Northants* 12 T22
Irlam *Gtr Man* 15 R19
Ironbridge *Shrops* 10 S19
Irthlingborough *Northants* 12 T22
Irvine *N Ayrs* 19 L14
Irvinestown *Fermanagh* 32 P8
Isbister *Shetl'd* 31 A21
Islandtown *Antrim* 33 N11
Isle of Whithorn *Dumf/Gal* 19 N15
Isleham *Cambs* 12 T24
Islington *Gtr Lon* 6 U23
Islip *Oxon* 5 U21
Ivinghoe *Bucks* 6 U22
Iwerne Minster *Dorset* 5 W19
Ixworth *Suffolk* 13 T25

J

Jamestown *W Dunb* 24 K14
Jarrow *Tyne/Wear* 21 N21
Jaywick *Essex* 7 U26
Jedburgh *Borders* 21 M18
Jervaulx *N Yorks* 16 P20
John o' Groats *H'land* 29 E17
Johnshaven *Aberds* 25 J19
Johnston *Pembs* 9 U13
Johnstone *Renf* 19 L15
Johnstown *Kilkenny* 39 S8
Johnstown Bridge *Kildare* 37 R10
Julianstown *Meath* 37 Q11

K

Kames *Arg/Bute* 18 L13
Kanturk *Cork* 39 T6
Katesbridge *Down* 33 P11
Kea *Cornw'l* 2 X13
Keadow *Roscommon* 36 P7
Keady *Armagh* 33 P10

Kealkill Cork 38 U5
Kedington Suffolk 12 T24
Keel Mayo 34 Q3
Keelby Lincs 17 Q23
Keele Staffs 10 R19
Keenagh Longford 36 Q8
Kegworth Leics 11 S21
Keighley W Yorks 15 Q20
Keillmore Arg/Bute 18 L12
Keiss H'land 29 E17
Keith Moray 29 G18
Keld N Yorks 15 P19
Kellas Moray 28 G17
Kells Kilkenny 40 S9
Kells Meath 37 Q10
Kells Antrim 33 N11
Kellystown Louth 37 Q11
Kelsale Suffolk 13 T27
Kelsall Ches 10 R18
Kelso Borders 21 L19
Keltneyburn Perth/Kinr 24 J15
Kelty Fife 24 K17
Kelvedon Essex 7 U25
Kelynack Cornw'l 2 X12
Kemble Glos 5 U20
Kemnay Aberds 25 H19
Kempsey Heref/Worcs 10 T19
Kempston Beds 12 T22
Kemsing Kent 6 V24
Kendal Cumb 15 P18
Kenilworth Warwick 11 T20
Kenmare Kerry 38 U4
Kenmore Perth/Kinr 24 J16
Kennacraig Arg/Bute 18 L13
Kennethmont Aberds 29 H18
Kennford Devon 4 W16
Kenninghall Norfolk 13 T25
Kennington Oxon 5 U21
Kensington & Chelsea Gtr Lon 6 V23
Kentford Suffolk 13 T25
Kentisbeare Devon 4 W17
Kentstown Meath 37 Q10
Kerry Powys 10 S17
Kerrysdale H'land 27 G12
Kershopefoot Borders 20 M18
Kesgrave Suffolk 13 T26
Kesh Fermanagh 32 N8
Keshcarrigan Leitrim 36 P8
Kessingland Suffolk 13 T27
Keswick Cumb 20 N17
Kettering Northants 12 T22
Kettletoft Orkney 30 D18
Kettlewell N Yorks 15 P19
Ketton Rutl'd 12 S22
Kexby Lincs 17 R22
Keyingham E Riding Yorks 17 Q23
Keymer W Sussex 6 W23
Keynsham Bath/NE Som'set 4 V18
Keysoe Beds 12 T23
Keyworth Notts 11 S21
Kibworth Beauchamp Leics 11 S22
Kidderminster Heref/Worcs 10 T19
Kidlington Oxon 5 U21
Kidsgrove Staffs 10 R19
Kidstones N Yorks 15 P19
Kidwelly Carms 9 U15
Kielder Northum 21 M18
Kilamery Kilkenny 40 T9
Kilbaha Clare 38 S4
Kilbeggan Westmeath 36 R9
Kilbeheny Limerick 39 T7
Kilbennan Church Galway 35 Q6
Kilberry Meath 37 Q10
Kilberry Arg/Bute 18 L12
Kilbirnie N Ayrs 19 L14
Kilbrickan Galway 34 R4
Kilbride Wicklow 40 S11
Kilbride Arg/Bute 23 K13
Kilbrien Waterford 39 T8
Kilbrittain Cork 39 U6
Kilcadzow S Lanarks 19 L16
Kilcar Donegal 32 N6
Kilchattan Arg/Bute 18 L13
Kilchenzie Arg/Bute 18 M12
Kilchiaran Arg/Bute 18 L11
Kilchoan H'land 22 J11
Kilchreest Galway 35 R6
Kilchrenan Arg/Bute 23 K13
Kilclooney Donegal 32 N7
Kilcock Kildare 37 R10
Kilcoe Cork 38 U5
Kilcogy Cavan 36 Q9
Kilcolgan Galway 35 R6
Kilconly Galway 35 Q5
Kilconnell Galway 35 R7
Kilcoo Down 33 P11
Kilcoole Wicklow 37 R11
Kilcormac Offaly 36 R8
Kilcornan Limerick 39 S6
Kilcreggan Arg/Bute 23 L14
Kilcrohane Cork 38 U4
Kilcullen Kildare 37 R10
Kilcurry Louth 37 P11
Kildalkey Meath 37 Q10
Kildare Kildare 37 R10
Kildavin Carlow 40 S10
Kildimo Limerick 39 S6
Kildonan H'land 28 F16
Kildorrery Cork 39 T7
Kilfane Kilkenny 40 S9
Kilfeakle Tipperary 39 T7
Kilfearagh Clare 38 S4
Kilfenora Clare 35 S5
Kilfinan Arg/Bute 18 L13
Kilfinnane Limerick 39 T7
Kilflynn Kerry 38 T4
Kilgarrif Galway 35 R5
Kilgarvan Kerry 38 U5
Kilglass Galway 35 R7
Kilglass Sligo 35 P5
Kilgobnet Kerry 38 T4
Kilgolagh Cavan 36 Q9
Kilham E Riding Yorks 17 P23
Kilkea Kildare 40 S10
Kilkee Clare 38 S4
Kilkeel Down 37 P11
Kilkelly Mayo 35 Q6
Kilkenny Kilkenny 40 S9
Kilkerrin Galway 35 Q6
Kilkhampton Cornw'l 2 W14
Kilkieran Galway 34 R4
Kilkinlea Kerry 38 T5
Kilkishen Clare 39 S6
Kill Kildare 37 R10
Kill Waterford 40 T9
Killadangan Mayo 34 Q4
Killadeas Fermanagh 32 P8
Killadoon Mayo 34 Q4
Killadysert Clare 38 S5
Killala Mayo 35 P5
Killaloe Clare 39 S7
Killaloo Londonderry 32 N9
Killamarsh Derby 16 R21
Killane Offaly 36 R9
Killarbran Fermanagh 32 P9
Killarga Leitrim 32 P7
Killargue Leitrim 32 P7
Killarney Kerry 38 T4
Killashandra Cavan 36 P8
Killashee Longford 36 Q8
Killavally Mayo 34 Q5
Killavullen Cork 39 T6
Killeagh Cork 39 U8
Killean Arg/Bute 18 L12
Killearn Stirl 24 K15
Killeen Tipperary 36 R8
Killeen Tyrone 33 N10
Killeevan Monaghan 36 P9
Killeglan Roscommon 36 R7
Killeigh Offaly 36 R9
Killen Tyrone 32 N8
Killenagh Wexford 40 S11
Killenaule Tipperary 39 S8
Killerig Carlow 40 S10
Killeter Tyrone 32 N8
Killimor Galway 35 R7
Killin Stirl 24 K15
Killinaboy Clare 35 S5
Killinaspick Kilkenny 40 T9
Killiney Dublin 37 R11
Killinghall N Yorks 16 P20
Killinick Wexford 40 T11
Killorglin Kerry 38 T4
Killough Down 33 P12
Killowen Down 37 P11
Killsaran Louth 37 Q11
Killtullagh Galway 35 R6
Killucan Westmeath 36 Q9
Killurin Wexford 40 T10
Killybegs Donegal 32 N7
Killyfassy Cavan 36 Q9
Killygordon Donegal 32 N8
Killykergan Londonderry 33 M10
Killylea Armagh 33 P10
Killyleagh Down 33 P12
Killyon Offaly 36 R8
Kilmacolm Invercl 19 L14
Kilmacow Kilkenny 40 T9
Kilmacrenan Donegal 32 M8
Kilmacthomas Waterford 40 T9
Kilmaganny Kilkenny 40 T9
Kilmaine Mayo 35 Q5
Kilmaley Clare 38 S5
Kilmallock Limerick 39 T6
Kilmaluag H'land 26 G11
Kilmanagh Kilkenny 40 S9
Kilmany Fife 25 K18
Kilmarnock E Ayrs 19 L15
Kilmartin Arg/Bute 23 K13
Kilmaurs E Ayrs 19 L14
Kilmeadan Waterford 40 T9
Kilmeage Kildare 37 R10
Kilmeedy Limerick 39 T6
Kilmelford Arg/Bute 23 K13
Kilmichael Cork 38 U5
Kilmihil Clare 38 S5
Kilmore Wexford 40 T10
Kilmore Quay Wexford 40 T10
Kilmory Arg/Bute 18 L12
Kilmory H'land 22 H11
Kilmory H'land 22 J11
Kilmuckridge Wexford 40 S11
Kilmuir H'land 28 G15
Kilmurry Clare 38 S5
Kilmurry Clare 39 S6
Kilmurvy Galway 34 R4
Kilnaleck Cavan 36 Q9
Kilninver Arg/Bute 23 K12
Kilnsea E Riding Yorks 17 Q24
Kilpatrick Cork 39 U6
Kilrea Londonderry 33 N10
Kilreekil Galway 35 R7
Kilrenny Fife 25 K18
Kilronan Galway 34 R4
Kilronane Cork 38 U5
Kilross Tipperary 39 T7
Kilrush Clare 38 S5
Kilsallagh Galway 35 Q6
Kilsby Northants 11 T21
Kilshanny Clare 34 S5
Kilsheelan Tipperary 39 T8
Kilsyth N Lanarks 24 L15
Kiltamagh Mayo 35 Q5
Kiltartan Galway 35 R6
Kiltealy Wexford 40 S10
Kilteel Kildare 37 R10
Kilteely Limerick 39 S7
Kiltegan Wicklow 40 S10
Kiltiernan Dublin 37 R11
Kiltoom Roscommon 36 R7
Kiltormer Galway 35 R7
Kiltyclogher Leitrim 32 P7
Kilwinning N Ayrs 19 L14
Kilworth Cork 39 T7
Kimbolton Cambs 12 T23
Kimpton Herts 6 U23
Kinalag Galway 35 Q6
Kinawley Fermanagh 32 P8
Kinbrace H'land 28 F16
Kinbuck Stirl 24 K16
Kincardine Fife 24 K16
Kincardine H'land 28 G15
Kincaslough Donegal 32 M7
Kincraig H'land 24 H16
Kindrum Donegal 32 M8
Kineton Warwick 11 T20
Kingarrow Donegal 32 N7
Kingarth Arg/Bute 18 L13
Kinghorn Fife 25 K17
King's Cliffe Northants 12 S23
Kings Langley Herts 6 U23
King's Lynn Norfolk 12 S24
King's Somborne Hants 5 V21
King's Sutton Northants 11 T21
King's Thorn Heref/Worcs 10 U18
King's Worthy Hants 5 V21
Kingsbarns Fife 25 K18
Kingsbridge Devon 3 X16
Kingsbury Warwick 11 S20
Kingsclere Hants 5 V21
Kingscourt Cavan 37 Q10
Kingsdown Kent 7 V26
Kingskerswell Devon 3 X16
Kingsland Heref/Worcs 10 T18
Kingsley Hants 6 V22
Kingsley Staffs 11 R20
Kingsteignton Devon 4 W16
Kingston Devon 3 X16
Kingston Gtr Lon 6 V23
Kingston Bagpuize Oxon 5 U21
Kingston upon Hull Kingston/Hull 17 Q23
Kingswear Devon 3 X16
Kingswood S Gloucs 4 V18
Kington Heref/Worcs 10 T17
Kingussie H'land 24 H15
Kinloch H'land 22 H11
Kinloch H'land 27 F14
Kinloch Rannoch Perth/Kinr 24 J15
Kinlochbervie H'land 27 F13
Kinlocheil H'land 23 J13
Kinlochewe H'land 27 G13
Kinlochleven H'land 23 J14
Kinlochmoidart H'land 23 J12
Kinloss Moray 28 G16
Kinlough Leitrim 32 P7
Kinmel Bay Conwy 8 R16
Kinnegad Westmeath 36 R9
Kinnitty Offaly 36 R8
Kinross Perth/Kinr 24 K17
Kinsale Cork 39 U6
Kintarvie W Isles 26 F10
Kintore Aberds 25 H19
Kinuachdrachd Arg/Bute 23 K12
Kinvarra Galway 35 R6
Kinver Staffs 10 T19
Kippax W Yorks 16 Q21
Kippen Stirl 24 K15
Kircubbin Down 33 P12
Kirk Michael I of Man 14 P14
Kirkabister Shetl'd 31 B21
Kirkbean Dumf/Gal 20 N16
Kirkbride Cumb 20 N17
Kirkburton W Yorks 16 Q20
Kirkby Mersey 15 R18
Kirkby-in-Ashfield Notts 11 R21
Kirkby-in-Furness Cumb 15 P17
Kirkby Lonsdale Cumb 15 P18
Kirkby Malzeard N Yorks 16 P20
Kirkby Stephen Cumb 15 P19
Kirkby Thore Cumb 21 N18
Kirkbymoorside N Yorks 17 P22
Kirkcaldy Fife 25 K17
Kirkcolm Dumf/Gal 18 N13
Kirkconnel Dumf/Gal 19 M15
Kirkcowan Dumf/Gal 19 N14
Kirkcudbright Dumf/Gal 19 N15
Kirkham Lancs 15 Q18
Kirkinner Dumf/Gal 19 N15
Kirkintilloch E Dunb 19 L15
Kirkland Dumf/Gal 19 M16
Kirkliston C of Edinb 24 L17
Kirkmichael Perth/Kinr 24 J16
Kirkmichael S Ayrs 19 M14
Kirknewton Northum 21 L19
Kirkoswald Cumb 21 N18
Kirkoswald S Ayrs 18 M14
Kirkpatrick Durham Dumf/Gal 19 M16
Kirkpatrick Fleming Dumf/Gal 20 M17
Kirkton of Glenisla Angus 24 J17
Kirkton of Largo Fife 25 K18
Kirkwall Orkney 30 E18
Kirkwhelpington Northum 21 M20
Kirriemuir Angus 25 J18
Kirtling Cambs 12 T24
Kirtlington Oxon 11 U21
Kirton Lincs 12 S23
Kirton in Lindsey N Lincs 17 R22
Kishkeam Cork 38 T5
Knaresborough N Yorks 16 P21
Knayton N Yorks 16 P21
Knebworth Herts 6 U23
Knighton Powys 10 T17
Knock Clare 38 S5
Knock Mayo 35 Q6
Knockaderry Limerick 39 T6
Knockagree Cork 38 T5
Knockalina Mayo 34 P4
Knockalough Clare 38 S5
Knockananna Wicklow 40 S11
Knockatallan Monaghan 32 P9
Knockbrit Tipperary 39 T8
Knockcroghery Roscommon 36 Q7
Knockfold Donegal 32 M7
Knocklofty Tipperary 39 T8
Knocklong Limerick 39 T7
Knocktopher Kilkenny 40 T9
Knott End-on-Sea Lancs 15 Q18
Knottingley W Yorks 16 Q21
Knowle W Midlands 11 T20
Knowsley Mersey 15 R18
Knutsford Ches 15 R19
Kyle of Lochalsh H'land 27 H12
Kyleakin H'land 27 H12
Kylerhea H'land 23 H12
Kylesa Galway 34 R4
Kylestrome H'land 27 F13

L

Laban Galway 35 R6
Labasheeda Clare 38 S5
Labby Londonderry 33 N10
Laceby NE Lincs 17 Q23
Lack Fermanagh 32 N8
Lackamore Tipperary 39 S7
Lacock Wilts 5 V19
Ladock Cornw'l 2 X14
Ladybank Fife 25 K17
Ladysbridge Cork 39 U7
Lagg Arg/Bute 18 L12
Laggan H'land 24 H14
Laggan H'land 24 H15
Laggan Moray 29 H17
Laghtgeorge Galway 35 R6
Laghy Donegal 32 N7
Lahard Cavan 36 Q8
Lahardaun Mayo 34 P5
Laide H'land 27 G12
Lairg H'land 28 F15
Lakenheath Suffolk 13 T25
Lakyle Clare 38 S5
Lamberhurst Kent 7 V24
Lambeth Gtr Lon 6 V23
Lambley Northum 21 N18
Lambourn Berks 5 U20
Lamlash N Ayrs 18 L13
Lampeter Ceredig'n 9 T15
Lanark S Lanarks 19 L16
Lancaster Lancs 15 P18
Lanchester Durham 21 N20
Lancing W Sussex 6 W23
Landkey Devon 3 V15
Landrake Cornw'l 3 X15
Lanesborough Longford 36 Q8
Langford Budville Som'set 4 W17
Langham Rutl'd 11 S22
Langholm Dumf/Gal 20 M18
Langport Som'set 4 V18
Langsett S Yorks 16 Q20
Langtoft E Riding Yorks 17 P23
Langtoft Lincs 12 S23
Langton Matravers Dorset 5 W19
Langtree Devon 3 W15
Langwathby Cumb 21 N18
Langwell H'land 28 F15
Lanivet Cornw'l 2 X14
Lapford Devon 3 W16
Laracor Meath 37 Q10
Laragh Wicklow 40 R11
Larbert Falk 24 K16
Largan Mayo 34 P4
Largs N Ayrs 18 L14
Largy Donegal 32 N6
Larkhall S Lanarks 19 L16
Larkhill Wilts 5 V20
Larne Antrim 33 N12
Lasswade Midloth 20 L17
Latchingdon Essex 7 U25
Latheron H'land 28 F17
Lattin Tipperary 39 T7
Lauder Borders 21 L18
Laugharne Carms 9 U15
Launceston Cornw'l 3 W15
Lauragh Kerry 38 U4

Laurencekirk Aberds 25 J19
Laurencetown Galway 36 R7
Laurieston Dumf/Gal 19 N15
Lavendon M/Keynes 12 T22
Lavenham Suffolk 13 T25
Lavey Cavan 36 Q9
Lawers Perth/Kinr 24 J15
Lawrencetown Down 33 P11
Laxey I of Man 14 P15
Laxfield Suffolk 13 T26
Laxford Bridge H'land 27 F13
Laxton Notts 11 R22
Layer de la Haye
  Essex 7 U25
Laytown Meath 37 Q11
Lazonby Cumb 21 N18
Lea Lincs 17 R22
Leadburn Midloth 20 L17
Leaden Roding Essex 7 U24
Leadenham Lincs 12 R22
Leadgate Durham 21 N20
Leadhills S Lanarks 19 M16
Leap Cork 38 U5
Leasingham Lincs 12 R23
Leatherhead Surrey 6 V23
Lechlade Glos 5 U20
Leckanarainey Leitrim 32 P7
Leckaun Leitrim 32 P7
Leckemy Donegal 33 M9
Ledbury Heref/Worcs 10 T19
Ledmore H'land 27 F14
Lee-on-the-Solent
  Hants 5 W21
Leeds W Yorks 16 Q20
Leedstown Cornw'l 2 X13
Leek Staffs 10 R19
Leeming Bar N Yorks 16 P20
Leenaun Galway 34 Q4
Legbourne Lincs 17 R24
Legoniel Antrim 33 N12
Lehinch Clare 34 S5
Leicester Leics C 11 S21
Leigh Gtr Man 15 Q18
Leigh Heref/Worcs 10 T19
Leighlinbridge Carlow 40 S10
Leighton Buzzard
  Beds 12 U22
Leintwardine
  Heref/Worcs 10 T18
Leiston Suffolk 13 T27
Leith C of Edinb 25 L17
Leitholm Borders 21 L19
Leitrim Leitrim 36 Q7
Leixlip Kildare 37 R11
Lelant Cornw'l 2 X13
Lemanaghan Offaly 36 R8
Lemybrien Waterford 39 T8
Lendalfoot S Ayrs 18 M14
Lenham Kent 7 V25
Lennoxtown E Dunb 24 L15
Leominster
  Heref/Worcs 10 T18
Lephin H'land 26 H10
Lerrig Kerry 38 T4
Lerwick Shetl'd 31 B21
Lesbury Northum 21 M20
Leslie Fife 25 K17
Lesmahagow
  S Lanarks 19 L16
Leswalt Dumf/Gal 18 N13
Letchworth Herts 12 U23
Letterbreen
  Fermanagh 32 P8
Letterfrack Galway 34 Q4
Letterkenny Donegal 32 N8
Lettermacaward
  Donegal 32 N7
Lettermore Galway 34 R4
Lettermullan Galway 34 R4
Letterston Pembs 9 U14
Lettoch H'land 28 H17
Leuchars Fife 25 K18
Leumrabhagh W Isles 26 F11
Leven E Riding Yorks 17 Q23
Leven Fife 25 K18
Lewes E Sussex 6 W24
Lewisham Gtr Lon 6 V23
Lewiston H'land 28 H15
Leyburn N Yorks 15 P20
Leyland Lancs 15 Q18
Leysdown on Sea
  Kent 7 V25
Lhanbryde Moray 29 G17
Liatrie H'land 27 H14
Lichfield Staffs 11 S20
Lidgate Suffolk 13 T25
Lifford Donegal 32 N9
Lifton Devon 3 W15

Ligfordrum Tyrone 32 N9
Lilleshall Shrops 10 S19
Limavady
  Londonderry 33 M10
Limerick Limerick 39 S6
Limerick Junction
  Tipperary 39 T7
Lincoln Lincs 17 R22
Lindale Cumb 15 P18
Lingfield Surrey 6 V23
Linkinhorne Cornw'l 3 W15
Linksness Orkney 30 E17
Linlithgow W Loth 24 L16
Linslade Beds 12 U22
Linton Cambs 12 T24
Liphook Hants 6 V22
Lisacul Roscommon 35 Q6
Lisbane Down 33 N12
Lisbellaw Fermanagh 32 P8
Lisburn Antrim 00 N11
Liscannor Clare 34 S5
Liscarroll Cork 39 T6
Lisdoonvarna Clare 34 R5
Lisgall Monaghan 37 P10
Lisgarode Tipperary 39 S7
Lisheen Clare 38 S5
Liskeard Cornw'l 3 X15
Lislap Tyrone 32 N9
Lislea Armagh 37 P11
Lismore Waterford 39 T8
Lisnacree Down 37 P11
Lisnagry Limerick 39 S6
Lisnamusk
  Londonderry 33 N10
Lisnarrick Fermanagh 32 P8
Lisnaskea Fermanagh 32 P9
Lisnaveane
  Monaghan 36 P9
Lispole Kerry 38 T3
Lisronagh Tipperary 39 T8
Liss Hants 6 V22
Lissattinta Bridge
  Kerry 38 U4
Lisselton Kerry 38 T4
Lissett E Riding Yorks 17 P23
Lissinagroagh Leitrim 32 P7
Lissycasey Clare 38 S5
Listerlin Kilkenny 40 T9
Listowel Kerry 38 T5
Litcham Norfolk 13 S25
Litherland Mersey 15 R18
Little Shelford Cambs 12 T24
Little Stukeley Cambs 12 T23
Little Walsingham
  Norfolk 13 S25
Littleborough Gtr Man 15 Q19
Littlehampton
  W Sussex 6 W22
Littlemill H'land 28 G16
Littleport Cambs 12 T24
Littlestone-on-Sea
  Kent 7 W25
Littleton Tipperary 39 S8
Liverpool Mersey 15 R18
Livingston W Loth 24 L17
Lixnaw Kerry 38 T4
Lizard Cornw'l 2 Y13
Llanaber Gwyn 8 S15
Llanaelhaiarn Gwyn 8 S15
Llanafan-fawr Powys 9 T16
Llanarmon Denbs 10 R17
Llanarmon Dyffryn
  Ceiriog Wrex 10 S17
Llanarth Ceredig'n 9 T15
Llanarthney Carms 9 U15
Llanbadarn Fynydd
  Powys 9 T17
Llanbedr Gwyn 8 S15
Llanbedrog Gwyn 8 S15
Llanberis Gwyn 8 R15
Llanbister Powys 9 T17
Llanbrynmair Powys 8 S16
Llanddewi-Brefi
  Ceredig'n 9 T16
Llanddulas Conwy 8 R16
Llandeilo Carms 9 U16
Llandinam Powys 8 T17
Llandissilio Pembs 9 U14
Llandogo Monmouths 4 U18
Llandovery Carms 9 U16
Llandrillo Denbs 8 S17
Llandrindod Wells
  Powys 9 T17
Llandudno Conwy 8 R16
Llandybie Carms 9 U15
Llandyfriog Ceredig'n 9 T15
Llandygwydd
  Ceredig'n 9 T14

Llandyrnog Denbs 8 R17
Llandysul Ceredig'n 9 T15
Llanelidan Denbs 8 R17
Llanelli Carms 9 U15
Llanelltyd Gwyn 8 S16
Llanenddwyn Gwyn 8 S15
Llanerchymedd Angl 8 R15
Llanerfyl Powys 8 S17
Llanfaethlu Angl 8 R14
Llanfair Caereinion
  Powys 8 S17
Llanfair Talhaiarn
  Conwy 8 R16
Llanfairfechan Conwy 8 R16
Llanfairpwllgwngyll
  Angl 8 R15
Llanfechain Powys 10 S17
Llanfechell Angl 8 R15
Llanfihangel-ar-arth
  Carms 9 T15
Llanfrynach Powys 9 U17
Llanfyllin Powys 10 S17
Llangadfan Powys 8 S17
Llangadog Carms 9 U16
Llangammarch Wells
  Powys 9 T16
Llangefni Angl 8 R15
Llangeitho Ceredig'n 9 T15
Llangelynin Gwyn 8 S15
Llangennech Carms 9 U15
Llangernyw Conwy 8 R16
Llangoed Angl 8 R15
Llangollen Denbs 10 S17
Llangorse Powys 9 U17
Llangranog Ceredig'n 9 T15
Llangunllo Powys 10 T17
Llangurig Powys 9 T16
Llangwm Conwy 8 S16
Llangwm Monmouths 4 U18
Llangybi Ceredig'n 9 T15
Llangynidr Powys 10 U17
Llangynog Powys 8 S17
Llanharan
  Rh Cyn Taff 4 U17
Llanidloes Powys 8 T16
Llanilar Ceredig'n 9 T15
Llanllyfni Gwyn 8 R15
Llannor Gwyn 8 S15
Llanon Ceredig'n 9 T15
Llanpumsaint Carms 9 U15
Llanrhaeadr-ym-
  Mochnant Powys 8 S17
Llanrhian Pembs 9 U13
Llanrhidian Swan 9 U15
Llanrhystyd Ceredig'n 9 T15
Llanrug Gwyn 8 R15
Llanrwst Conwy 8 R16
Llansannan Conwy 8 R16
Llansawel Carms 9 T15
Llanstephan Carms 9 U15
Llanthony Monmouths 10 U17
Llantrisant
  Rh Cyn Taff 4 U17
Llantwit-Major
  V of Glam 4 V17
Llanuwchllyn Gwyn 8 S16
Llanvihangel
  Crucorney
  Monmouths 10 U18
Llanwddyn Powys 8 S17
Llanweog Ceredig'n 9 T15
Llanwrda Carms 9 U16
Llanwrtyd Wells
  Powys 9 T16
Llanyblodwel Shrops 10 S17
Llanybydder Carms 9 T15
Llanymynech Powys 10 S17
Llanystumdwy Gwyn 8 S15
Llay Wrex 10 R17
Lledrod Ceredig'n 9 T15
Llithfaen Gwyn 8 S15
Llwyngwril Gwyn 8 S15
Llyswen Powys 9 T17
Loanhead Midloth 20 L17
Lobinstown Meath 37 Q10
Loch Baghasdail
  W Isles 22 H9
Loch nam Madadh
  W Isles 26 G9
Lochailort H'land 23 J12
Lochaline H'land 23 J12
Lochans Dumf/Gal 18 N13
Locharbriggs
  Dumf/Gal 20 M16
Lochboisdale = Loch
  Baghasdail W Isles 22 H9
Lochbuie Arg/Bute 23 K12
Lochcarron H'land 27 H12

Lochdon Arg/Bute 23 K12
Lochearnhead Stirl 24 K15
Lochgair Arg/Bute 23 K13
Lochgelly Fife 24 K17
Lochgilphead
  Arg/Bute 23 K13
Lochgoilhead
  Arg/Bute 23 K14
Lochinver H'land 27 F13
Lochmaben Dumf/Gal 20 M17
Lochmaddy = Loch
  nam Madadh
  W Isles 26 G9
Lochranza N Ayrs 18 L13
Lochwinnoch Renf 19 L14
Lockerbie Dumf/Gal 20 M17
Lockton N Yorks 17 P22
Loddiswell Devon 3 X16
Loddon Norfolk 13 S27
Loftus
  Redcar/Clevel'd 17 N22
Logan E Ayrs 19 M15
Loghill Limerick 38 S5
London Gtr Lon 6 U23
London Colney Herts 6 U23
Long Ashton Bristol 4 V18
Long Bennington
  Lincs 11 S22
Long Clawson Leics 11 S22
Long Compton
  Warwick 11 T20
Long Crendon Bucks 6 U22
Long Eaton Derby 11 S21
Long Itchington
  Warwick 11 T21
Long Melford Suffolk 13 T25
Long Preston N Yorks 15 P19
Long Stratton Norfolk 13 T26
Long Sutton Lincs 12 S24
Longbenton
  Tyne/Wear 21 M20
Longbridge Deverill
  Wilts 5 V19
Longdon Heref/Worcs 10 T19
Longford Longford 36 Q8
Longford Glos 10 U19
Longforgan Perth/Kinr 25 K17
Longformacus
  Borders 21 L19
Longframlington
  Northum 21 M20
Longhope Orkney 30 E17
Longhorsley Northum 21 M20
Longhoughton
  Northum 21 M20
Longnor Staffs 11 R20
Longridge Lancs 15 Q18
Longside Aberds 29 G20
Longton Lancs 15 Q18
Longtown Cumb 20 M18
Longtown
  Heref/Worcs 10 U17
Longwood Meath 37 R10
Loose Kent 7 V25
Lossiemouth Moray 28 G17
Lostock Gralam Ches 15 R19
Lostwithiel Cornw'l 2 X14
Loughall Armagh 33 P10
Loughanavally
  Westmeath 36 R8
Loughanure Donegal 32 N7
Loughborough Leics 11 S21
Loughbrickland Down 33 P11
Loughglinn
  Roscommon 35 Q6
Loughguile Antrim 33 M11
Loughmoe Tipperary 39 S8
Loughor Swan 9 U15
Loughran Antrim 33 N11
Loughrea Galway 35 R6
Loughton Essex 6 U24
Louisburgh Mayo 34 Q4
Louth Louth 37 Q10
Louth Lincs 17 R23
Lowdham Notts 11 R22
Lower Beeding
  W Sussex 6 V23
Lower Killeany
  Arg/Bute 18 L11
Lower Langford
  N Som'set 4 V18
Lower Mayland Essex 7 U25
Lower Shiplake Oxon 6 U22
Lowestoft Suffolk 13 T27
Lowick Northum 21 L20
Loxwood W Sussex 6 V22
Lubcroy H'land 27 G14
Lucan Dublin 37 R11

Lucker Northum 21 L20
Ludborough Lincs 17 R23
Ludford Lincs 17 R23
Ludgershall Wilts 5 V20
Ludgvan Cornw'l 2 X12
Ludham Norfolk 13 S27
Ludlow Shrops 10 T18
Lugatemple Mayo 35 Q5
Lugton E Ayrs 19 L14
Lugwardine
  Heref/Worcs 10 T18
Lukeswell Kilkenny 40 T9
Lumphanan Aberds 25 H18
Lumsden Aberds 29 H18
Lurgan Armagh 33 P11
Lurgangreen Louth 37 Q11
Lusk Dublin 37 Q11
Luss Arg/Bute 24 K14
Lusta H'land 26 G10
Luton Luton 6 U23
Lutterworth Leics 11 T21
Lutton Northants 12 T23
Lybster H'land 28 F17
Lydd Kent 7 W25
Lydford Devon 3 W15
Lydham Shrops 10 S18
Lydney Glos 4 U18
Lyme Regis Dorset 4 W18
Lyminge Kent 7 V26
Lymington Hants 5 W20
Lymm Ches 15 R19
Lympne Kent 7 V26
Lympstone Devon 4 W17
Lyndhurst Hants 5 W20
Lyneham Wilts 5 U20
Lyness Orkney 30 E17
Lynmouth Devon 3 V16
Lynton Devon 3 V16
Lyracrumpane Kerry 38 T5
Lytchett Minster
  Dorset 5 W19
Lytham St. Anne's
  Lancs 15 Q17
Lythe N Yorks 17 N22

M

Maam Cross Galway 34 R4
Maas Donegal 32 N7
Mablethorpe Lincs 17 R24
Macclesfield Ches 15 R19
Macduff Aberds 29 G18
Machen Caerph 4 U17
Machrihanish
  Arg/Bute 18 M12
Machynlleth Powys 8 S16
Mackan Fermanagh 32 P8
Macmerry E Loth 25 L18
Macosquin
  Londonderry 33 M10
Macroom Cork 39 U6
Madeley Staffs 10 S19
Madley Heref/Worcs 10 T18
Maentwrog Gwyn 8 S16
Maesteg Bridg 9 U16
Maghera Londonderry 33 N10
Magherafelt
  Londonderry 33 N10
Magheragall Antrim 33 N11
Magheraveely
  Fermanagh 32 P9
Maghery Donegal 32 N7
Maghery Armagh 33 N10
Maghull Mersey 15 Q18
Magor Monmouths 4 U18
Maguiresbridge
  Fermanagh 32 P9
Maiden Bradley Wilts 5 V19
Maiden Newton
  Dorset 4 W18
Maidenhead Berks 6 U22
Maidstone Kent 7 V25
Malahide Dublin 37 R11
Maldon Essex 7 U25
Malham N Yorks 15 P19
Malin Donegal 32 M9
Malin More Donegal 32 N6
Mallaig H'land 23 H12
Mallaranny Mayo 34 Q4
Mallow Cork 39 T6
Mallwyd Gwyn 8 S16
Malmesbury Wilts 5 U19
Malpas Ches 10 R18
Maltby S Yorks 16 R21
Maltby le Marsh Lincs 17 R24

Place	County	Page	Grid
Malton	*N Yorks*	17	P22
Manafon	*Powys*	8	S17
Manby	*Lincs*	17	R24
Manchester	*Gtr Man*	15	R19
Manea	*Cambs*	12	T24
Manfieldstown	*Louth*	37	Q11
Mangotsfield	*S Gloucs*	5	V19
Manningtree	*Essex*	13	U26
Manorbier	*Pembs*	9	U14
Manorhamilton	*Leitrim*	32	P7
Manselstown	*Tipperary*	39	S8
Mansfield	*Notts*	11	R21
Mansfield Woodhouse	*Notts*	11	R21
Manton	*Rutl'd*	12	S22
Manulla	*Mayo*	35	Q5
Marazion	*Cornw'l*	2	X13
March	*Cambs*	12	S24
Marden	*Heref/Worcs*	10	T18
Marden	*Kent*	7	V24
Mareham le Fen	*Lincs*	12	R23
Maresfield	*E Sussex*	6	W24
Marfleet	*Kingston/Hull*	17	Q23
Margam	*Neath P Talb*	9	U16
Margate	*Kent*	7	V26
Marham	*Norfolk*	13	S25
Market Bosworth	*Leics*	11	S21
Market Deeping	*Lincs*	12	S23
Market Drayton	*Shrops*	10	S19
Market Harborough	*Leics*	11	T22
Market Lavington	*Wilts*	5	V20
Market Rasen	*Lincs*	17	R23
Market Weighton	*E Riding Yorks*	17	Q22
Markethill	*Armagh*	33	P10
Markfield	*Leics*	11	S21
Markinch	*Fife*	25	K17
Marks Tey	*Essex*	7	U25
Markyate	*Herts*	6	U23
Marlborough	*Devon*	3	X16
Marlborough	*Wilts*	5	V20
Marlow	*Bucks*	6	U22
Marnhull	*Dorset*	5	W19
Marple	*Gtr Man*	15	R19
Marshchapel	*Lincs*	17	R24
Marshfield	*S Gloucs*	5	V19
Marske by the Sea	*Redcar/Clevel'd*	16	N21
Marston Magna	*Som'set*	4	W18
Martham	*Norfolk*	13	S27
Martin	*Hants*	5	W20
Martley	*Heref/Worcs*	10	T19
Martock	*Som'set*	4	W18
Marton	*Lincs*	17	R22
Marykirk	*Aberds*	25	J18
Marypark	*Moray*	28	H17
Maryport	*Cumb*	20	N17
Marytavy	*Devon*	3	W15
Marywell	*Aberds*	25	H18
Marywell	*Angus*	25	J18
Masham	*N Yorks*	16	P20
Mathry	*Pembs*	9	U13
Matlock	*Derby*	11	R20
Mattishall	*Norfolk*	13	S26
Mauchline	*E Ayrs*	19	L15
Maud	*Aberds*	29	G19
Maughold	*I of Man*	14	P15
Maulyneill	*Kerry*	38	U4
Maum	*Galway*	34	Q4
Mawgan	*Cornw'l*	2	X13
Maxwellheugh	*Borders*	21	L19
Maybole	*S Ayrs*	19	M14
Mayfield	*E Sussex*	7	V24
Mayfield	*Staffs*	11	R20
Maylough	*Galway*	35	R6
Maynooth	*Kildare*	37	R10
Mayo	*Mayo*	35	Q5
Mayo Bridge	*Down*	33	P11
Mealabost	*W Isles*	26	F11
Mealsgate	*Cumb*	20	N17
Measham	*Leics*	11	S20
Medstead	*Hants*	6	V21
Meenaneary	*Donegal*	32	N6
Meidrim	*Carms*	9	U15
Meifod	*Powys*	10	S17
Meigh	*Armagh*	37	P11
Meigle	*Perth/Kinr*	25	J17
Melbourn	*Cambs*	12	T24
Melbourne	*Derby*	11	S21
Melksham	*Wilts*	5	V19
Mell	*Louth*	37	Q11
Mellon Charles	*H'land*	27	G12
Mellor	*Lancs*	15	Q18
Melmerby	*Cumb*	21	N18
Melsonby	*N Yorks*	16	P20
Meltham	*W Yorks*	15	Q20
Melton	*Suffolk*	13	T26
Melton Constable	*Norfolk*	13	S26
Melton Mowbray	*Leics*	11	S22
Melvaig	*H'land*	27	G12
Melvich	*H'land*	28	E16
Menai Bridge	*Angl*	8	R15
Mendlesham	*Suffolk*	13	T26
Menlough	*Galway*	35	R5
Mennock	*Dumf/Gal*	19	M16
Menston	*W Yorks*	15	Q20
Menstrie	*Clack*	24	K16
Meonstoke	*Hants*	5	W21
Meopham	*Kent*	7	V24
Mere	*Wilts*	5	V19
Mere Brow	*Lancs*	15	Q18
Meriden	*W Midlands*	11	T20
Merritt	*Som'set*	4	W18
Merthyr Tydfil	*Merth Tyd*	9	U17
Merton	*Gtr Lon*	6	V23
Meshaw	*Devon*	3	W16
Messingham	*N Lincs*	17	Q22
Metfield	*Suffolk*	13	T26
Metheringham	*Lincs*	12	R23
Methil	*Fife*	25	K17
Methlick	*Aberds*	29	H19
Methven	*Perth/Kinr*	24	K16
Methwold	*Norfolk*	13	S25
Mevagissey	*Cornw'l*	2	X14
Mexborough	*S Yorks*	16	R21
Mey	*H'land*	29	E17
Micheldever	*Hants*	5	V21
Michelmersh	*Hants*	5	W20
Mickleover	*Derby C*	11	S20
Mickleton	*Durham*	21	N19
Mickleton	*Glos*	11	T20
Mid Lavant	*W Sussex*	6	W22
Mid Yell	*Shetl'd*	31	A21
Midbea	*Orkney*	30	D18
Middle Barton	*Oxon*	11	U21
Middleham	*N Yorks*	15	P20
Middlemarsh	*Dorset*	5	W19
Middlesbrough	*Middlesbro'*	21	N21
Middleton	*Arg/Bute*	22	K10
Middleton	*Gtr Man*	15	Q19
Middleton	*Norfolk*	12	S24
Middleton Cheney	*Northants*	11	T21
Middleton in Teesdale	*Durham*	21	N19
Middleton-on-Sea	*W Sussex*	6	W22
Middleton	*Armagh*	33	P10
Middlewich	*Ches*	10	R19
Middlezoy	*Som'set*	4	V18
Midhurst	*W Sussex*	6	W22
Midleton	*Cork*	39	U7
Midsomer Norton	*Bath/NE Som'set*	5	V19
Milborne Port	*Som'set*	5	W19
Mildenhall	*Suffolk*	13	T25
Milestone	*Tipperary*	39	T8
Milford	*Cork*	39	T6
Milford	*Donegal*	32	M8
Milford	*Surrey*	6	V22
Milford Haven	*Pembs*	9	U13
Milford on Sea	*Hants*	5	W20
Millbrook	*Meath*	36	Q9
Millbrook	*Cornw'l*	3	X15
Millford	*Armagh*	33	P10
Millisle	*Down*	33	N12
Millom	*Cumb*	14	P17
Millport	*N Ayrs*	18	L14
Millstreet	*Cork*	38	T5
Millstreet	*Waterford*	39	T6
Milltown	*Cavan*	36	P9
Milltown	*Galway*	35	Q6
Milltown	*Kerry*	38	T3
Milltown	*Kerry*	38	T4
Milltown	*Monaghan*	33	P10
Milltown	*Antrim*	33	N12
Milltown	*Londonderry*	33	M10
Milltown Malbay	*Clare*	38	S5
Milnathort	*Perth/Kinr*	24	K17
Milngavie	*E Dunb*	19	L15
Milnthorpe	*Cumb*	15	P18
Milovaig	*H'land*	26	H10
Milton	*H'land*	27	G14
Milton Abbot	*Devon*	3	W15
Milton Keynes	*M/Keynes*	12	T22
Miltown	*Kildare*	37	R10
Milverton	*Som'set*	4	V17
Minane Bridge	*Cork*	39	U7
Minchinhampton	*Glos*	5	U19
Minehead	*Som'set*	4	V17
Minera	*Wrex*	10	R17
Minety	*Wilts*	5	U20
Mingary	*H'land*	22	J11
Minnigaff	*Dumf/Gal*	19	N15
Minstead	*Hants*	5	W20
Minster	*Kent*	7	V25
Minster	*Kent*	7	V26
Minsterley	*Shrops*	10	S18
Mintlaw	*Aberds*	29	G19
Mirfield	*W Yorks*	16	Q20
Misterton	*Notts*	17	R22
Misterton	*Som'set*	4	W18
Mistley	*Essex*	13	U26
Mitchel Troy	*Monmouths*	4	U18
Mitcheldean	*Glos*	5	U19
Mitchelstown	*Cork*	39	T7
Moate	*Westmeath*	36	R8
Modbury	*Devon*	3	X16
Modreeny	*Tipperary*	36	S7
Moelfre	*Angl*	8	R15
Moffat	*Dumf/Gal*	20	M17
Mohill	*Leitrim*	36	Q8
Moira	*Down*	33	P11
Mold	*Flints*	10	R17
Monaghan	*Monaghan*	33	P10
Monar Lodge	*H'land*	27	H14
Monasterevin	*Kildare*	36	R9
Moneygall	*Offaly*	39	S8
Moneyglass	*Antrim*	33	N11
Moneymore	*Londonderry*	33	N10
Moneyneany	*Londonderry*	33	N10
Moniaive	*Dumf/Gal*	19	M16
Monifieth	*Angus*	25	K18
Monikie	*Angus*	25	J18
Monivea	*Galway*	35	R6
Monkland	*Heref/Worcs*	10	T18
Monkokehampton	*Devon*	3	W15
Monkstown	*Cork*	39	U7
Monkton	*S Ayrs*	19	L14
Monmouth	*Monmouths*	4	U18
Montacute	*Som'set*	4	W18
Montgomery	*Powys*	10	S17
Montrose	*Angus*	25	J19
Monymusk	*Aberds*	25	H18
Mooncoin	*Kilkenny*	40	T9
Moone	*Kildare*	40	S10
Moorfields	*Antrim*	33	N11
Morar	*H'land*	23	J12
Morchard Bishop	*Devon*	4	W16
Mordiford	*Heref/Worcs*	10	T18
Morebattle	*Borders*	21	L19
Morecambe	*Lancs*	15	P18
Moreton-in-Marsh	*Glos*	11	U20
Moretonhampstead	*Devon*	3	W16
Morley	*W Yorks*	16	Q20
Mornington	*Meath*	37	Q11
Morpeth	*Northum*	21	M20
Mortehoe	*Devon*	3	V15
Mortimer's Cross	*Heref/Worcs*	10	T18
Morwenstow	*Cornw'l*	2	W14
Moss-side	*Antrim*	33	M11
Mossley	*Antrim*	33	N12
Mossley	*Gtr Man*	15	Q19
Mostyn	*Flints*	15	R17
Motcombe	*Dorset*	5	W19
Motherwell	*N Lanarks*	19	L16
Mottisfont	*Hants*	5	V20
Moulton	*Lincs*	12	S23
Moulton	*Northants*	11	T22
Moulton	*Suffolk*	13	T25
Mount Bellew Bridge	*Galway*	35	R7
Mount Ida	*Down*	33	P11
Mount Nugent	*Cavan*	36	Q9
Mount Talbot	*Roscommon*	35	Q7
Mountain Ash	*Rh Cyn Taff*	9	U17
Mountcharles	*Donegal*	32	N7
Mountfield	*Tyrone*	32	N9
Mountjoy	*Tyrone*	32	N9
Mountmellick	*Laois*	36	R9
Mountnorris	*Armagh*	33	P11
Mountrath	*Laois*	40	S9
Mountshannon	*Clare*	35	S7
Mountsorrel	*Leics*	11	S21
Mousehole	*Cornw'l*	2	X12
Mouswald	*Dumf/Gal*	20	M17
Moville	*Donegal*	33	M9
Moy	*H'land*	28	H15
Moy	*Tyrone*	33	P10
Moyard	*Galway*	34	Q3
Moyasta	*Clare*	38	S4
Moycullen	*Galway*	35	R5
Moymore	*Clare*	39	S6
Moynalty	*Meath*	37	Q10
Moyne	*Longford*	36	Q8
Moyne	*Tipperary*	39	S8
Moyroughly	*Westmeath*	36	R8
Moyvally	*Kildare*	37	R10
Moyvore	*Westmeath*	36	Q8
Much Dewchurch	*Heref/Worcs*	10	U18
Much Marcle	*Heref/Worcs*	10	U19
Much Wenlock	*Shrops*	10	S18
Muchalls	*Aberds*	25	H19
Muckross	*Kerry*	38	T5
Muff	*Donegal*	32	M9
Muine Bheag	*Carlow*	40	S10
Muineagh	*Donegal*	32	M8
Muir of Ord	*H'land*	28	G15
Muirdrum	*Angus*	25	J18
Muirhead	*N Lanarks*	19	L15
Muirkirk	*E Ayrs*	19	L15
Muker	*N Yorks*	15	P19
Mulben	*Moray*	29	G17
Mullagh	*Cavan*	37	Q10
Mullagh	*Galway*	35	R7
Mullagh	*Meath*	37	R10
Mullaghaneane	*Sligo*	32	P6
Mullan	*Fermanagh*	32	P8
Mullans Town	*Tyrone*	33	N9
Mullanys Cross	*Sligo*	35	P6
Mullarts	*Antrim*	33	M11
Mulldonagh	*Londonderry*	32	N9
Mullinahone	*Tipperary*	39	S8
Mullinavat	*Kilkenny*	40	T9
Mullingar	*Westmeath*	36	Q9
Mullion	*Cornw'l*	2	X13
Mullughmore	*Sligo*	32	P7
Mundesley	*Norfolk*	13	S26
Mundford	*Norfolk*	13	S25
Mungret	*Limerick*	39	S6
Munlochy	*H'land*	28	G15
Murlaggan	*H'land*	23	J13
Murroogh	*Clare*	34	R5
Murton	*Durham*	21	N21
Musbury	*Devon*	4	W17
Musselburgh	*E Loth*	25	L17
Muthill	*Perth/Kinr*	24	K16
Mybster	*H'land*	28	F17
Myddfai	*Carms*	9	U16
Myddle	*Shrops*	10	S18
Mydroilyn	*Ceredig'n*	9	T15
Mynydd Isa	*Flints*	10	R17
Myshall	*Carlow*	40	S10

N

Place	County	Page	Grid
Naas	*Kildare*	37	R10
Nad	*Cork*	39	T6
Nafferton	*E Riding Yorks*	17	P23
Nailsea	*N Som'set*	4	V18
Nailsworth	*Glos*	5	U19
Nairn	*H'land*	28	G16
Nannerch	*Flints*	14	R17
Nantwich	*Ches*	10	R18
Nappa	*N Yorks*	15	Q19
Naran	*Donegal*	32	N7
Narberth	*Pembs*	9	U14
Narborough	*Leics*	11	S21
Naseby	*Northants*	11	T22

Place	County	Page	Grid
Naul	*Dublin*	37	Q11
Navan	*Meath*	37	Q10
Navenby	*Lincs*	12	R22
Neale	*Mayo*	35	Q5
Neap	*Shetl'd*	31	B21
Neath	*Neath P Talb*	9	U16
Necton	*Norfolk*	13	S25
Needham Market	*Suffolk*	13	T26
Needingworth	*Cambs*	12	T23
Nefyn	*Gwyn*	8	S14
Neilston	*E Renf*	19	L15
Nelson	*Lancs*	15	Q19
Nenagh	*Tipperary*	39	S7
Nenthead	*Cumb*	21	N19
Neston	*Ches*	15	R17
Nether Stowey	*Som'set*	4	V17
Netheravon	*Wilts*	5	V20
Netherbury	*Dorset*	4	W18
Netherton	*Northum*	21	M19
Nethy Bridge	*H'land*	28	H16
Netley	*Hants*	5	W21
Nettlebed	*Oxon*	6	U22
Nettleham	*Lincs*	17	R23
Nettleton	*Lincs*	17	R23
Nevern	*Pembs*	9	T14
New Abbey	*Dumf/Gal*	20	N16
New Aberdour	*Aberds*	29	G19
New Alresford	*Hants*	5	V21
New Birmingham	*Tipperary*	39	S8
New Buckenham	*Norfolk*	13	T26
New Buildings	*Londonderry*	32	N9
New Chapel Cross	*Kerry*	38	U3
New Clipstone	*Notts*	11	R21
New Costessey	*Norfolk*	13	S26
New Cumnock	*E Ayrs*	19	M15
New Deer	*Aberds*	29	G19
New Earswick	*C of York*	16	Q21
New Edlington	*S Yorks*	16	R21
New Galloway	*Dumf/Gal*	19	M15
New Holland	*N Lincs*	17	Q23
New Inn	*Cavan*	36	Q9
New Inn	*Galway*	35	R7
New Inn	*Laois*	36	R9
New Luce	*Dumf/Gal*	18	N14
New Mills	*Derby*	15	R20
New Milton	*Hants*	5	W20
New Pitsligo	*Aberds*	29	G19
New Quay	*Ceredig'n*	9	T15
New Radnor	*Powys*	10	T17
New Romney	*Kent*	7	W25
New Ross	*Wexford*	40	T10
New Rossington	*S Yorks*	16	R23
New Scone	*Perth/Kinr*	24	K17
New Tredegar	*Caerph*	4	U17
New Waltham	*NE Lincs*	17	Q23
Newark-on-Trent	*Notts*	11	R22
Newbiggin-by-the-Sea	*Northum*	21	M20
Newbigging	*S Lanarks*	20	L16
Newbliss	*Monaghan*	36	P9
Newborough	*Angl*	8	R15
Newborough	*Galway*	35	Q7
Newbridge	*Kildare*	37	R10
Newbridge	*Limerick*	39	S6
Newbridge	*Caerph*	4	U17
Newbridge on Wye	*Powys*	9	T17
Newbrough	*Northum*	21	M19
Newburgh	*Aberds*	29	H19
Newburgh	*Fife*	25	K17
Newburn	*Tyne/Wear*	21	N20
Newbury	*Berks*	5	V21
Newby Bridge	*Cumb*	15	P18
Newbyth	*Aberds*	29	G19
Newcastle	*Tipperary*	39	T8
Newcastle	*Wicklow*	37	R11
Newcastle	*Down*	33	P12
Newcastle	*Shrops*	10	T17
Newcastle Emlyn	*Carms*	9	T15
Newcastle-under-Lyme	*Staffs*	10	R19
Newcastle-upon-Tyne	*Tyne/Wear*	21	N20

Newcastle West *Limerick* 38 T5
Newcastleton *Borders* 20 M18
Newchurch *Powys* 10 T17
Newdigate *Surrey* 6 V23
Newent *Glos* 10 U19
Newgale *Pembs* 9 U13
Newham *Gtr Lon* 6 U24
Newhaven *E Sussex* 6 W24
Newick *E Sussex* 6 W24
Newington *Kent* 7 V25
Newington *Kent* 7 V26
Newinn *Tipperary* 39 T8
Newlyn *Cornw'l* 2 X12
Newlyn East *Cornw'l* 2 X13
Newmachar *Aberds* 29 H19
Newmarket *Cork* 39 T6
Newmarket *Suffolk* 12 T24
Newmarket *W Isles* 26 F11
Newmarket-on-Fergus *Clare* 39 S6
Newmill *Moray* 29 G18
Newmills *Donegal* 32 N8
Newmilns *E Ayrs* 19 L15
Newnham *Glos* 5 U19
Newport *Mayo* 34 Q4
Newport *Tipperary* 39 S7
Newport *Essex* 12 U24
Newport *I of Wight* 5 W21
Newport *Newp* 4 U18
Newport *Pembs* 9 T14
Newport *Shrops* 10 S19
Newport-on-Tay *Fife* 25 K18
Newport Pagnell *M/Keynes* 12 T22
Newquay *Cornw'l* 2 X13
Newry *Down* 33 P11
Newton *Lancs* 15 Q19
Newton Abbot *Devon* 4 W16
Newton Arlosh *Cumb* 20 N17
Newton Aycliffe *Durham* 21 N20
Newton Ferrers *Devon* 3 X15
Newton le Willows *Mersey* 15 R18
Newton Mearns *E Renf* 19 L15
Newton Poppleford *Devon* 4 W17
Newton St. Cyres *Devon* 4 W16
Newton Stewart *Dumf/Gal* 19 N15
Newtongrange *Midloth* 20 L17
Newtonhill *Aberds* 25 H19
Newtonmore *H'land* 24 H15
Newtown *Laois* 40 S9
Newtown *Longford* 36 Q8
Newtown *Tipperary* 39 T7
Newtown *Heref/Worcs* 10 T18
Newtown *Powys* 8 S17
Newtown Crommelin *Antrim* 33 N11
Newtown Cunningham *Donegal* 32 N8
Newtown Forbes *Longford* 36 Q8
Newtown Gore *Leitrim* 36 P8
Newtown Hamilton *Armagh* 33 P10
Newtown Monasterboice *Louth* 37 Q11
Newtown Mount Kennedy *Wicklow* 37 R11
Newtown St. Boswells *Borders* 21 L18
Newtown Sands *Kerry* 38 S5
Newtownabbey *Antrim* 33 N12
Newtownards *Down* 33 N12
Newtownbreda *Down* 33 N12
Newtownbutler *Fermanagh* 32 P9
Newtownshandrum *Cork* 39 T6
Newtownstewart *Tyrone* 32 N9
Neyland *Pembs* 9 U14
Ninemilehouse *Tipperary* 40 T9
Ninfield *E Sussex* 7 W24
Niton *I of Wight* 5 W21
Nobber *Meath* 37 Q10
Nohaval *Cork* 39 U7
Nordelph *Norfolk* 12 S24
Norham *Northum* 21 L19
Normanby le Wold *Lincs* 17 R23
Normanton *W Yorks* 16 Q21
North Baddesley *Hants* 5 W21
North Berwick *E Loth* 25 K18
North Cerney *Glos* 5 U20
North Charlton *Northum* 21 M20
North Elmham *Norfolk* 13 S25
North Ferriby *E Riding Yorks* 17 Q22
North Frodingham *E Riding Yorks* 17 Q23
North Hill *Cornw'l* 3 W15
North Hykeham *Lincs* 12 R22
North Kessock *H'land* 28 G15
North Molton *Devon* 3 V16
North Newbald *E Riding Yorks* 17 Q22
North Petherton *Som'set* 4 V17
North Queensferry *Fife* 24 K17
North Somercotes *Lincs* 17 R24
North Sunderland *Northum* 21 L20
North Tawton *Devon* 3 W16
North Thoresby *Lincs* 17 R23
North Tidworth *Wilts* 5 V20
North Walsham *Norfolk* 13 S26
North Wingfield *Derby* 11 R21
Northallerton *N Yorks* 16 P21
Northam *Devon* 3 V15
Northampton *Northants* 11 T22
Northchapel *W Sussex* 6 V22
Northfleet *Kent* 7 V24
Northiam *E Sussex* 7 W25
Northleach *Glos* 5 U20
Northop *Flints* 10 R17
Northpunds *Shetl'd* 31 C21
Northrepps *Norfolk* 13 S26
Northwich *Ches* 15 R18
Northwold *Norfolk* 13 S25
Northwood *Gtr Lon* 6 U23
Northwood *I of Wight* 5 W21
Norton *Glos* 10 U19
Norton *Heref/Worcs* 10 T19
Norton *N Yorks* 17 P22
Norton *Suffolk* 13 T25
Norton Fitzwarren *Som'set* 4 V17
Norwich *Norfolk* 13 S26
Norwick *Shetl'd* 31 A22
Nottingham *Notts* 11 S21
Nuneaton *Warwick* 11 S21
Nunney *Som'set* 5 V19
Nurney *Carlow* 40 S10
Nutley *E Sussex* 6 V24
Nutts Corner *Antrim* 33 N11
Nybster *H'land* 29 E17

O

Oadby *Leics* 11 S21
Oakdale *Caerph* 4 U17
Oakengates *Shrops* 10 S19
Oakham *Rutl'd* 12 S22
Oban *Arg/Bute* 23 K13
O'Briensbridge *Clare* 39 S7
Ochiltree *E Ayrs* 19 M15
Ockley *Surrey* 6 V23
Odie *Orkney* 30 D18
Odiham *Hants* 6 V22
Offord D'Arcy *Cambs* 12 T23
Ogbourne St. George *Wilts* 5 V20
Oghill *Londonderry* 32 N9
Oilgate *Wexford* 40 T10
Okehampton *Devon* 3 W15
Old Basing *Hants* 6 V21
Old Bolingbroke *Lincs* 12 R24
Old Colwyn *Conwy* 8 R16
Old Deer *Aberds* 29 G19
Old Fletton *Cambs* 12 S23
Old Leake *Lincs* 12 R24
Old Radnor *Powys* 10 T17
Old Ross *Wexford* 40 T10
Oldbury *S Gloucs* 4 U18
Oldcastle *Meath* 36 Q9
Oldham *Gtr Man* 15 Q19
Oldleighlin *Carlow* 40 S9
Oldmeldrum *Aberds* 29 H19
Oldtown *Laois* 40 S9
Olgrinmore *H'land* 28 F16
Ollerton *Notts* 11 R21
Olney *M/Keynes* 12 T22
Omagh *Tyrone* 32 N9
Ombersley *Heref/Worcs* 10 T19
Omeath *Louth* 37 P11
Onchan *I of Man* 14 P15
Onich *H'land* 23 J13
Oola *Limerick* 39 S7
Oran *Roscommon* 35 Q7
Oranmore *Galway* 35 R6
Ordhead *Aberds* 25 H18
Ordie *Aberds* 25 H18
Orford *Suffolk* 13 T27
Oristown *Meath* 37 Q10
Orleton *Heref/Worcs* 10 T18
Ormesby St. Margaret *Norfolk* 13 S27
Ormiston *E Loth* 25 L18
Ormskirk *Lancs* 15 Q18
Orphir *Orkney* 30 E17
Orpington *Gtr Lon* 6 V24
Orton *Cumb* 15 P18
Osbournby *Lincs* 12 S23
Oskamull *Arg/Bute* 22 K11
Osmotherley *N Yorks* 16 P21
Ossett *W Yorks* 16 Q20
Oswaldtwistle *Lancs* 15 Q19
Oswestry *Shrops* 10 S17
Otford *Kent* 6 V24
Othery *Som'set* 4 V18
Otley *W Yorks* 16 Q20
Otter Ferry *Arg/Bute* 23 K13
Otterburn *Northum* 21 M19
Otterton *Devon* 4 W17
Ottery St. Mary *Devon* 4 W17
Oughterard *Galway* 34 R5
Oulton *Norfolk* 13 S27
Oulton Broad *Suffolk* 13 T27
Oundle *Northants* 12 T23
Ousdale *H'land* 28 F16
Outwell *Norfolk* 12 S24
Over *Cambs* 12 T24
Over Wallop *Hants* 5 V20
Overbister *Orkney* 30 D18
Overseal *Derby* 11 S20
Overstrand *Norfolk* 13 S26
Overton *Hants* 5 V21
Overton *Wrex* 10 S18
Owston Ferry *N Lincs* 17 R22
Oxenholme *Cumb* 15 P18
Oxford *Oxon* 5 U21
Oxnam *Borders* 21 M19
Oxted *Surrey* 6 V24
Oykel Bridge *H'land* 27 G14

P

Pabail *W Isles* 27 F11
Paddock Wood *Kent* 7 V24
Padiham *Lancs* 15 Q19
Padstow *Cornw'l* 2 W14
Paibeil *W Isles* 26 G9
Paignton *Devon* 3 X16
Pailton *Warwick* 11 T21
Painscastle *Powys* 10 T17
Painshawfield *Northum* 21 N20
Painswick *Glos* 5 U19
Paisley *Renf* 19 L15
Palgrave *Suffolk* 13 T26
Pallas Green *Limerick* 39 S7
Pallaskenry *Limerick* 39 S6
Palnackie *Dumf/Gal* 19 N16
Pangbourne *Berks* 5 V21
Papworth Everard *Cambs* 12 T23
Park *Galway* 35 R6
Park *Londonderry* 33 N9
Parkeston *Essex* 13 U26
Parkhurst *I of Wight* 5 W21
Parknasilla *Kerry* 38 U4
Parkview *Antrim* 33 N12
Parracombe *Devon* 3 V16
Partney *Lincs* 12 R24
Parton *Cumb* 20 N16
Partry *Mayo* 34 Q5
Passage East *Waterford* 40 T10
Passage West *Cork* 39 U7
Pateley Bridge *N Yorks* 15 P20
Pathhead *Midloth* 20 L18
Patna *E Ayrs* 19 M15
Patrick Brompton *N Yorks* 16 P20
Patrickswell *Limerick* 39 S6
Patrington *E Riding Yorks* 17 Q23
Patterdale *Cumb* 15 N18
Paull *E Riding Yorks* 17 Q23
Paulstown *Kilkenny* 40 S9
Paulton *Bath/NE Som'set* 4 V18
Peacehaven *E Sussex* 6 W23
Peak Forest *Derby* 15 R20
Peasedown St. John *Bath/NE Som'set* 5 V19
Peasenhall *Suffolk* 13 T26
Peasmarsh *E Sussex* 7 W25
Peebles *Borders* 20 L17
Peel *I of Man* 14 P14
Pegswood *Northum* 21 M20
Pembrey *Carms* 9 U15
Pembridge *Heref/Worcs* 10 T18
Pembroke *Pembs* 9 U14
Pembroke Dock *Pembs* 9 U14
Pembury *Kent* 7 V24
Penally *Pembs* 9 U14
Penarth *V of Glam* 4 V17
Pencader *Carms* 9 U15
Pencoed *Bridg* 4 U16
Pendeen *Cornw'l* 2 X12
Penderyn *Rh Cyn Taff* 9 U16
Pendine *Carms* 9 U14
Penicuik *Midloth* 20 L17
Penistone *S Yorks* 16 Q20
Penkridge *Staffs* 10 S19
Penmachno *Conwy* 8 R16
Penmaenmawr *Conwy* 8 R16
Pennan *Aberds* 29 G19
Pennyghael *Arg/Bute* 22 K11
Penpont *Dumf/Gal* 19 M16
Penrhyndeudraeth *Gwyn* 8 S15
Penrith *Cumb* 21 N18
Penryn *Cornw'l* 2 X13
Pensford *Bath/NE Som'set* 4 V18
Penshaw *Tyne/Wear* 21 N21
Penshurst *Kent* 6 V24
Pensilva *Cornw'l* 3 X15
Pentraeth *Angl* 8 R15
Pentrefoelas *Conwy* 8 R16
Penwortham *Lancs* 15 Q18
Penybont *Powys* 9 T17
Penybontfawr *Powys* 8 S17
Penygroes *Carms* 9 U15
Penygroes *Gwyn* 8 R15
Penysarn *Angl* 8 R15
Penzance *Cornw'l* 2 X12
Perranporth *Cornw'l* 2 X13
Perranzabuloe *Cornw'l* 2 X13
Pershore *Heref/Worcs* 10 T19
Perth *Perth/Kinr* 24 K17
Peterborough *Cambs* 12 S23
Peterchurch *Heref/Worcs* 10 T18
Peterculter *Aberd C* 25 H19
Peterhead *Aberds* 29 G20
Peterlee *Durham* 21 N21
Petersfield *Hants* 6 V22
Peterswell *Galway* 35 R6
Petham *Kent* 7 V26
Pettigo *Donegal* 32 N8
Petworth *W Sussex* 6 W22
Pevensey *E Sussex* 7 W24
Pewsey *Wilts* 5 V20
Pickering *N Yorks* 17 P22
Piddletrenthide *Dorset* 5 W19
Pidley *Cambs* 12 T23
Pierowall *Orkney* 30 D18
Pilling *Lancs* 15 Q18
Pilton *Som'set* 4 V18
Piltown *Kilkenny* 40 T9
Pinchbeck *Lincs* 12 S23
Pinhoe *Devon* 4 W17
Pinmore Mains *S Ayrs* 18 M14
Pinwherry *S Ayrs* 18 M14
Pirbright *Surrey* 6 V22
Pirnmill *N Ayrs* 18 L13
Pitlochry *Perth/Kinr* 24 J16
Pittenweem *Fife* 25 K18
Plean *Stirl* 24 K16
Plockton *H'land* 27 H12
Pluck *Donegal* 32 N8
Pluckley *Kent* 7 V25
Plumbridge *Tyrone* 32 N9
Plumpton *Cumb* 20 N18
Plymouth *Devon* 3 X15
Plympton *Devon* 3 X15
Plymstock *Devon* 3 X15
Pocklington *E Riding Yorks* 17 Q22
Polegate *E Sussex* 7 W24
Polesworth *Warwick* 11 S20
Polloch *H'land* 23 J12
Pollremon *Galway* 35 Q6
Polperro *Cornw'l* 2 X14
Polruan *Cornw'l* 2 X14
Polwarth *Borders* 21 L19
Polzeath *Cornw'l* 2 W14
Pomeroy *Tyrone* 33 N10
Pontardawe *Neath P Talb* 9 U16
Pontardulais *Swan* 9 U15
Pontefract *W Yorks* 16 Q21
Ponteland *Northum* 21 M20
Ponterwyd *Ceredig'n* 9 T16
Pontesbury *Shrops* 10 S18
Pontoon *Mayo* 35 Q5
Pontrhydfendigaid *Ceredig'n* 9 T16
Pontrilas *Heref/Worcs* 10 U18
Pontyates *Carms* 9 U15
Pontyberem *Carms* 9 U15
Pontycymer *Bridg* 9 U16
Pontypool *Torf* 4 U17
Pontypridd *Rh Cyn Taff* 9 U17
Pool *Cornw'l* 2 X13
Poole *Poole* 5 W20
Poolewe *H'land* 27 G12
Pooley Bridge *Cumb* 20 N18
Porlock *Som'set* 4 V16
Port Askaig *Arg/Bute* 18 L11
Port Bannatyne *Arg/Bute* 18 L13
Port Carlisle *Cumb* 20 N17
Port Charlotte *Arg/Bute* 18 L11
Port Ellen *Arg/Bute* 18 L11
Port Erin *I of Man* 14 P14
Port Eynon *Swan* 9 U15
Port Glasgow *Invercl* 19 L14
Port Henderson *H'land* 27 G12
Port Isaac *Cornw'l* 2 W14
Port Logan *Dumf/Gal* 18 N14
Port Nan Giuran *W Isles* 27 F11
Port Nis *W Isles* 27 F11
Port St. Mary *I of Man* 14 P14
Port Talbot *Neath P Talb* 9 U16
Port William *Dumf/Gal* 19 N14
Portacloy *Mayo* 34 P4
Portadown *Armagh* 33 P11
Portaferry *Down* 33 P12
Portarlington *Offaly* 36 R9
Portavadie *Arg/Bute* 18 L13
Portavogie *Down* 33 P13
Portballintrae *Antrim* 33 M10
Portglenone *Antrim* 33 N11
Portgordon *Moray* 29 G17
Porth *Rh Cyn Taff* 9 U17
Porthcawl *Bridg* 4 V16
Porthleven *Cornw'l* 2 X13
Porthmadog *Gwyn* 8 S15
Portishead *N Som'set* 4 V18
Portknockie *Moray* 29 G18
Portlaoise *Laois* 40 R9
Portlaw *Waterford* 40 T9
Portlethen *Aberds* 25 H19
Portmagee *Kerry* 38 U3
Portmahomack *H'land* 28 G16
Portmarnock *Dublin* 37 R11
Portnacroish *Arg/Bute* 23 J13
Portnahaven *Arg/Bute* 18 L10
Porton *Wilts* 5 V20
Portpatrick *Dumf/Gal* 18 N13
Portrane *Dublin* 37 R11

Portreath *Cornw'l* 2 X13
Portree *H'land* 27 H11
Portroe *Tipperary* 39 S7
Portrush *Antrim* 33 M10
Portsalon *Donegal* 32 M8
Portskerra *H'land* 28 E16
Portslade
  Brighton/Hove 6 W23
Portsmouth *Portsm'th* 5 W21
Portsoy *Aberds* 29 G18
Portstewart
  Londonderry 33 M10
Portumna *Galway* 35 R7
Postbridge *Devon* 3 W16
Potter Heigham
  Norfolk 13 S27
Potterne *Wilts* 5 V19
Potters Bar *Herts* 6 U23
Potterspury *Northants* 11 T22
Potton *Beds* 12 T23
Poulton-le-Fylde
  Lancs 15 Q18
Poundstock *Cornw'l* 2 W14
Powick *Heref/Worcs* 10 T19
Poynton *Ches* 15 R19
Poyntz Pass *Armagh* 33 P11
Praa Sands *Cornw'l* 2 X13
Prees *Shrops* 10 S18
Preesall *Lancs* 15 Q18
Presbury *Ches* 15 R19
Prescot *Mersey* 15 R18
Prestatyn *Denbs* 8 R17
Prestbury *Glos* 10 U19
Presteigne *Powys* 10 T17
Preston *Dorset* 5 W19
Preston
  E Riding Yorks 17 Q23
Preston *Kent* 7 V26
Preston *Lancs* 15 Q18
Preston *Borders* 21 L19
Preston Candover
  Hants 5 V21
Prestonpans *E Loth* 25 L18
Prestwich *Gtr Man* 15 Q19
Prestwick *S Ayrs* 19 M14
Prestwood *Bucks* 6 U22
Princes Risborough
  Bucks 6 U22
Princetown *Devon* 3 W15
Probus *Cornw'l* 2 X14
Prosperous *Kildare* 37 R10
Prudhoe *Northum* 21 N20
Puckaun *Tipperary* 35 S7
Pucklechurch
  S Gloucs 5 V19
Puddletown *Dorset* 5 W19
Pudsey *W Yorks* 16 Q20
Pulborough *W Sussex* 6 W22
Pulham Market
  Norfolk 13 T26
Pulham St. Mary
  Norfolk 13 T26
Pumpsaint *Carms* 9 T16
Purfleet *Essex* 7 V24
Purley *Berks* 6 V23
Purley *Gtr Lon* 6 V23
Purton *Wilts* 5 U20
Puttenham *Surrey* 6 V22
Pwllheli *Gwyn* 8 S15
Pyle *Bridg* 4 U16

Q

Quadring *Lincs* 12 S23
Quainton *Bucks* 6 U22
Quarryfield *Sligo* 35 P6
Quedgeley *Glos* 5 U19
Queenborough *Kent* 7 V25
Queensbury *W Yorks* 15 Q20
Queensferry *Flints* 10 R17
Quilty *Clare* 38 S5
Quin *Clare* 39 S6
Quorndon *Leics* 11 S21

R

Rackenford *Devon* 4 W16
Rackheath *Norfolk* 13 S26
Rackwick *Orkney* 30 E17
Radcliffe *Gtr Man* 15 Q19
Radcliffe-on-Trent
  Notts 11 S21

Radlett *Herts* 6 U23
Radley *Oxon* 5 U21
Radstock
  Bath/NE Som'set 5 V19
Radyr *Card* 4 U17
Raglan *Monmouths* 4 U18
Rahan *Offaly* 36 R8
Rahara *Roscommon* 36 Q7
Raharney *Westmeath* 36 Q9
Raheen *Tipperary* 39 T8
Rainham *Kent* 7 V25
Rainworth *Notts* 11 R21
Rampark *Louth* 37 P11
Rampside *Cumb* 15 P17
Ramsbottom *Gtr Man* 15 Q19
Ramsbury *Wilts* 5 V20
Ramsey *Cambs* 12 T23
Ramsey *Essex* 13 U26
Ramsey *I of Man* 14 P15
Ramseycleuch
  Borders 20 M17
Ramsgate *Kent* 7 V26
Randalstown *Antrim* 33 N11
Rannoch Station
  Perth/Kinr 24 J14
Raphoe *Donegal* 32 N8
Rasharkin *Antrim* 33 N11
Rath *Offaly* 36 R8
Rathangan *Kildare* 37 R10
Ratharney *Longford* 36 Q8
Rathclogh *Tipperary* 39 S8
Rathconrath
  Westmeath 36 Q8
Rathcool *Cork* 39 T6
Rathcoole *Dublin* 37 R11
Rathcor *Louth* 37 Q11
Rathcormack *Cork* 39 T7
Rathdowney *Laois* 39 S8
Rathdrum *Wicklow* 40 S11
Rathduff *Cork* 39 T6
Rathen *Aberds* 29 G20
Rathfriland *Down* 33 P11
Rathgormuck
  Waterford 39 T9
Rathkeale *Limerick* 39 S6
Rathkenny *Meath* 37 Q10
Rathlackan *Mayo* 34 P5
Rathmelton *Donegal* 32 M8
Rathmolyon *Meath* 37 R10
Rathmore *Kerry* 38 T5
Rathmore *Kildare* 37 R10
Rathmore *Longford* 36 Q8
Rathmullan *Donegal* 32 M8
Rathnew *Wicklow* 40 S11
Rathnure *Wexford* 40 T10
Rathowen *Westmeath* 36 Q8
Rathvilla *Offaly* 36 R9
Rathvilly *Carlow* 40 S10
Ratoath *Meath* 37 Q11
Rattray *Perth/Kinr* 24 J17
Raunds *Northants* 12 T22
Ravenglass *Cumb* 14 P17
Ravensthorpe *Louth* 37 P11
Ravenshead *Notts* 11 R21
Ravenstonedale
  Cumb 15 P19
Rawcliffe *C of York* 16 Q21
Rawmarsh *S Yorks* 16 R21
Rawtenstall *Lancs* 15 Q19
Rayleigh *Essex* 7 U25
Reading *Berks* 6 V22
Rear Cross *Tipperary* 39 S7
Reay *H'land* 28 E16
Recess *Galway* 34 R4
Red Castle *Donegal* 32 M9
Red Dial *Cumb* 20 N17
Red Point *H'land* 27 G12
Redbourn *Herts* 6 U23
Redbridge *Gtr Lon* 6 U24
Redcar
  Redcar/Clevel'd 16 N21
Redditch *Heref/Worcs* 11 T20
Redesmouth *Northum* 21 M19
Redhill *Surrey* 6 V23
Redland *Orkney* 30 D17
Redlynch *Wilts* 5 W20
Redmile *Leics* 11 S22
Redmire *N Yorks* 15 P20
Redruth *Cornw'l* 2 X13
Reedham *Norfolk* 13 S27
Reens *Limerick* 39 S6
Reepham *Norfolk* 13 S26
Reeth *N Yorks* 15 P20
Reiff *H'land* 27 F13
Reigate *Surrey* 6 V23
Reiss *H'land* 29 F17

Renfrew *Renf* 19 L15
Rennington *Northum* 21 M20
Repton *Derby* 11 S20
Resolven
  Neath P Talb 9 U16
Reston *Borders* 21 L19
Retford *Notts* 17 R22
Reydon *Suffolk* 13 T27
Rhayader *Powys* 9 T17
Rhewl *Denbs* 8 R17
Rhiconich *H'land* 27 F14
Rhiw *Gwyn* 8 S14
Rhode *Offaly* 36 R9
Rhondda *Rh Cyn Taff* 9 U17
Rhoose *V of Glam* 4 V17
Rhos-on-Sea *Conwy* 8 R16
Rhoslan *Gwyn* 8 S15
Rhosllanerchrugog
  Wrex 10 R17
Rhosneigr *Angl* 8 R14
Rhossili *Swan* 9 U15
Rhostryfan *Gwyn* 8 R15
Rhubodach *Arg/Bute* 18 L13
Rhuddlan *Denbs* 8 R17
Rhyd-Ddu *Gwyn* 8 R15
Rhyl *Denbs* 8 R17
Rhymney *Caerph* 9 U17
Rhynie *Aberds* 29 H18
Riccall *N Yorks* 16 Q21
Rich Hill *Armagh* 33 P10
Richmond *Gtr Lon* 6 V23
Richmond *N Yorks* 16 P20
Rickmansworth *Herts* 6 U23
Ridsdale *Northum* 21 M19
Rievaulx *N Yorks* 16 P21
Rigside *S Lanarks* 19 L16
Rillington *N Yorks* 17 P22
Ringaskiddy *Cork* 39 U7
Ringford *Dumf/Gal* 19 N15
Ringmer *E Sussex* 6 W24
Ringsend
  Londonderry 33 M10
Ringville *Waterford* 39 T8
Ringwood *Hants* 5 W20
Ripley *Derby* 11 R21
Ripley *N Yorks* 16 P20
Ripley *Surrey* 6 V23
Ripon *N Yorks* 16 P20
Ripponden *W Yorks* 15 Q20
Risca *Caerph* 4 U17
Rishton *Lancs* 15 Q19
Riverchapel *Wexford* 40 S11
Riverstick *Cork* 39 U7
Riverstown *Cork* 39 U7
Riverstown *Sligo* 35 P7
Roade *Northants* 11 T22
Roadhead *Cumb* 20 M18
Roberton *Borders* 20 M18
Robertsbridge
  E Sussex 7 W24
Robertstown *Kildare* 37 R10
Robin Hood's Bay
  N Yorks 17 P22
Rocester *Staffs* 11 S20
Rochdale *Gtr Man* 15 Q19
Roche *Cornw'l* 2 X14
Rochester *Kent* 7 V25
Rochester *Northum* 21 M19
Rochford *Essex* 7 U25
Rochfortbridge
  Westmeath 36 R9
Rockchapel *Cork* 38 T5
Rockcliffe *Cumb* 20 N18
Rockcliffe *Dumf/Gal* 19 N16
Rockhill *Limerick* 39 T6
Rockingham
  Northants 12 S22
Rockmills *Cork* 39 T7
Rogart *H'land* 28 F15
Rogate *W Sussex* 6 V22
Roghadal *W Isles* 26 G10
Rolvenden *Kent* 7 W25
Romford *Gtr Lon* 6 U24
Romsey *Hants* 5 W21
Roosky *Leitrim* 36 Q8
Ropsley *Lincs* 12 S22
Roscommon
  Roscommon 35 Q7
Roscrea *Tipperary* 36 S8
Rosedale Abbey
  N Yorks 17 P22
Rosegreen *Tipperary* 39 T8
Rosehall *H'land* 28 G14
Rosehearty *Aberds* 29 G19
Rosemarket *Pembs* 9 U14
Rosemarkie *H'land* 28 G15

Rosenallis *Laois* 36 R9
Roskhill *H'land* 26 H10
Roslin *Midloth* 20 L17
Rosmult *Tipperary* 39 S8
Rosneath *Arg/Bute* 23 K14
Ross *Northum* 21 L20
Ross Carbery *Cork* 38 U5
Ross-on-Wye
  Heref/Worcs 10 U18
Rossaveel *Galway* 34 R4
Rosscahill *Galway* 35 R5
Rosses Point *Sligo* 32 P6
Rossett *Wrex* 10 R18
Rossinver *Leitrim* 32 P7
Rosslare *Wexford* 40 T11
Rosslare Harbour
  Wexford 40 T11
Rosslea *Fermanagh* 32 P9
Rossnowlagh
  Donegal 32 N7
Rostellan *Cork* 39 U7
Rostrevor *Down* 37 P11
Rosturk *Mayo* 34 Q4
Rosyth *Fife* 24 K17
Rothbury *Northum* 21 M20
Rotherham *S Yorks* 16 R21
Rothes *Moray* 29 G17
Rothesay *Arg/Bute* 18 L13
Rothienorman *Aberds* 29 H19
Rothiesholm *Orkney* 30 D18
Rothwell *Northants* 11 T22
Rothwell *W Yorks* 16 Q21
Rottal *Angus* 25 J17
Rottingdean
  Brighton/Hove 6 W23
Roundstone *Galway* 34 R4
Roundwood *Wicklow* 40 R11
Rousky *Tyrone* 32 N9
Rowanburn *Dumf/Gal* 20 M18
Rowlands Gill
  Tyne/Wear 21 N20
Roxburgh *Borders* 21 L19
Roxby *N Lincs* 17 Q22
Royal Leamington
  Spa *Warwick* 11 T20
Royal Tunbridge
  Wells *Kent* 7 V24
Roybridge *H'land* 23 J14
Royston *Herts* 12 T23
Royston *S Yorks* 16 Q21
Royton *Gtr Man* 15 Q19
Rozel *Chan Is* 2 Z19
Ruabon *Wrex* 10 S17
Ruan *Clare* 35 S6
Ruan Minor *Cornw'l* 2 Y13
Ruardean *Glos* 6 U18
Rubery *Heref/Worcs* 10 T19
Rudston
  E Riding Yorks 17 P23
Rufford *Lancs* 15 Q18
Rugby *Warwick* 11 T21
Rugeley *Staffs* 11 S20
Ruislip *Gtr Lon* 6 U23
Rumburgh *Suffolk* 13 T26
Rumney *Card* 4 U17
Runcorn *Ches* 15 R18
Rush *Dublin* 37 Q11
Rushden *Northants* 12 T22
Rushwick
  Heref/Worcs 10 T19
Ruskington *Lincs* 12 R23
Rutherglen *S Lanarks* 19 L15
Ruthin *Denbs* 8 R17
Ruthven *H'land* 24 H15
Ruthwell *Dumf/Gal* 20 N17
Ryal *Northum* 21 M20
Rydal *Cumb* 15 P18
Ryde *I of Wight* 5 W21
Rye *E Sussex* 7 W25
Ryhall *Rutl'd* 12 S23
Ryhope *Tyne/Wear* 21 N21
Ryton *Warwick* 11 T21

S

Sacriston *Durham* 21 N20
Saddell *Arg/Bute* 18 L12
Saffron Walden *Essex* 12 T24
Sageston *Pembs* 9 U14
Saggart *Dublin* 37 R11
St. Abb's *Borders* 25 L19
St. Agnes *Cornw'l* 2 X13
St. Albans *Herts* 6 U23
St. Andrews *Fife* 25 K18

St. Ann's *Dumf/Gal* 20 M17
St. Arvans
  Monmouths 4 U18
St. Asaph *Denbs* 8 R17
St. Athan *V of Glam* 4 V17
St. Aubin *Chan Is* 2 Z19
St. Austell *Cornw'l* 2 X14
St. Bees *Cumb* 14 N16
St. Blazey *Cornw'l* 2 X14
St. Brelade *Chan Is* 2 Z19
St. Breward *Cornw'l* 2 W14
St. Briavels *Glos* 4 U18
St. Bride's Major
  V of Glam 4 V16
St. Buryan *Cornw'l* 2 X12
St. Clears *Carms* 9 U14
St. Columb Major
  Cornw'l 2 X14
St. Columb Minor
  Cornw'l 2 X13
St. Combs *Aberds* 29 G20
St. Cyrus *Aberds* 25 J19
St. David's *Pembs* 9 U13
St. Day *Cornw'l* 2 X13
St. Dennis *Cornw'l* 2 X14
St. Dogmaels
  Ceredig'n 9 T14
St. Dominick *Cornw'l* 3 X15
St. Enoder *Cornw'l* 2 X14
St. Erth *Cornw'l* 2 X13
St. Fergus *Aberds* 29 G20
St. Fillans *Perth/Kinr* 24 K15
St. Germans *Cornw'l* 3 X15
St. Harmon *Powys* 9 T17
St. Helens *Mersey* 15 R18
St. Helier *Chan Is* 2 Z19
St. Issey *Cornw'l* 2 W14
St. Ives *Cambs* 12 T23
St. Ives *Cornw'l* 2 X13
St. John's *I of Man* 14 P14
St. Johns Chapel
  Durham 21 N19
St. Johnstown
  Donegal 32 N9
St. Just *Cornw'l* 2 X12
St. Keverne *Cornw'l* 2 X13
St. Leonards
  E Sussex 7 W25
St. Levan *Cornw'l* 2 X12
St. Mabyn *Cornw'l* 2 W14
St. Margaret's-at-
  Cliffe *Kent* 7 V26
St. Margaret's Hope
  Orkney 30 E18
St. Martin *Chan Is* 2 Z18
St. Martin *Chan Is* 2 Z19
St. Mary Bourne
  Hants 5 V21
St. Mary's *Orkney* 30 E18
St. Mary's Bay *Kent* 7 V25
St. Mawes *Cornw'l* 2 X13
St. Mellons *Card* 4 U17
St. Merryn *Cornw'l* 2 W13
St. Minver *Cornw'l* 2 W14
St. Monance *Fife* 25 K18
St. Neots *Cambs* 12 T23
St. Olaves *Norfolk* 13 S27
St. Osyth *Essex* 7 U26
St. Peter *Chan Is* 2 Z19
St. Peter Port *Chan Is* 2 Z18
St. Sampson *Chan Is* 2 Z18
St. Stephen *Cornw'l* 2 X14
St. Teath *Cornw'l* 2 W14
St. Tudy *Cornw'l* 2 W14
Saintfield *Down* 33 P12
Salcombe *Devon* 3 X16
Sale *Gtr Man* 15 R19
Salen *Arg/Bute* 23 J12
Salen *H'land* 23 J12
Salford *Gtr Man* 15 R19
Salford Priors
  Warwick 11 T20
Saline *Fife* 24 K16
Salisbury *Wilts* 5 V20
Sallachy *H'land* 28 F15
Sallahig *Kerry* 38 U3
Sallins *Kildare* 37 R10
Sally Gap *Wicklow* 37 R11
Sallybrook *Cork* 39 U7
Saltash *Cornw'l* 3 X15
Saltburn by the Sea
  Redcar/Clevel'd 17 N22
Saltcoats *N Ayrs* 18 L14
Salterstown *Louth* 37 Q11
Saltfleet *Lincs* 17 R24
Saltfleetby *Lincs* 17 R24
Salthill *Galway* 35 R5

Saltpans *Donegal* 32 M8
Saltwood *Kent* 7 V26
Sampford Courtenay
  Devon 3 W16
Sanaigmore *Arg/Bute* 18 L11
Sandbach *Ches* 10 R19
Sandbank *Arg/Bute* 23 L14
Sandgate *Kent* 7 V26
Sandhead *Dumf/Gal* 18 N14
Sandhurst *Berks* 6 V22
Sandleigh *Oxon* 5 U21
Sandness *Shet'ld* 31 B20
Sandown *I of Wight* 5 W21
Sandringham *Norfolk* 13 S25
Sandwich *Kent* 7 V26
Sandy *Beds* 12 T23
Sanquhar *Dumf/Gal* 19 M16
Sarnau *Ceredig'n* 9 T15
Sarnesfield
  Heref/Worcs 10 T18
Sarre *Kent* 7 V26
Satterthwaite *Cumb* 15 P17
Saundersfoot *Pembs* 9 U14
Sawbridgeworth
  Herts 6 U24
Sawston *Cambs* 12 T24
Sawtry *Cambs* 12 T23
Saxilby *Lincs* 17 R22
Saxlingham
  Nethergate *Norfolk* 13 S26
Saxmundham *Suffolk* 13 T27
Saxthorpe *Norfolk* 13 S26
Scalasaig *Arg/Bute* 22 K11
Scalby *N Yorks* 17 P23
Scalloway *Shet'ld* 31 B21
Scamblesby *Lincs* 17 R23
Scarborough *N Yorks* 17 P23
Scardoy *H'land* 27 G14
Scarinish *Arg/Bute* 22 J10
Scarning *Norfolk* 13 S25
Scarriff *Clare* 39 S6
Scartaglin *Kerry* 38 T5
Scarva *Down* 33 P11
Scogh *Kilkenny* 40 T9
Scole *Norfolk* 13 T26
Sconser *H'land* 27 H11
Scopwick *Lincs* 12 R23
Scorton *N Yorks* 16 P20
Scotch Corner
  Monaghan 33 P10
Scotch Corner
  N Yorks 16 P20
Scotstown *Monaghan* 33 P9
Scotter *Lincs* 17 Q22
Scourie *H'land* 27 F13
Scousburgh *Shet'ld* 31 C21
Scrabster *H'land* 28 E16
Scraghy *Tyrone* 32 N8
Scramoge
  Roscommon 36 Q7
Screeb *Galway* 34 R4
Screggan *Offaly* 36 R8
Scremerston *Northum* 21 L20
Scribbagh *Fermanagh* 32 P7
Scunthorpe *N Lincs* 17 Q22
Sea Palling *Norfolk* 13 S27
Seaford *E Sussex* 6 W24
Seaham *Durham* 21 N21
Seahouses *Northum* 21 L20
Seamer *N Yorks* 17 P23
Seascale *Cumb* 14 P17
Seaton *Cumb* 20 N16
Seaton *Devon* 4 W17
Seaton Delaval
  Northum 21 M20
Seend *Wilts* 5 V19
Selborne *Hants* 6 V22
Selby *N Yorks* 16 Q21
Selkirk *Borders* 20 L18
Sellafield *Cumb* 14 P17
Selsey *W Sussex* 6 W22
Sennen *Cornw'l* 2 X12
Sennybridge *Powys* 9 U16
Seskinore *Tyrone* 32 N9
Settle *N Yorks* 15 P19
Seven Sisters
  Neath P Talb 9 U16
Sevenoaks *Kent* 6 V24
Severn Beach
  S Gloucs 4 U18
Severn Stoke
  Heref/Worcs 10 T19
Sgarasta Mhor
  W Isles 26 G9

Shaftesbury *Dorset* 5 V19
Shalcombe *I of Wight* 5 W21
Shaldon *Devon* 4 W16
Shalford *Surrey* 6 V22
Shanagolden *Limerick* 38 S5
Shankill *Roscommon* 35 Q7
Shanklin *I of Wight* 5 W21
Shanlaragh *Cork* 38 U5
Shannonbridge *Offaly* 36 R7
Shannow *Cavan* 36 Q9
Shanovogh *Clare* 38 S5
Shantonagh
  Monaghan 37 P10
Shap *Cumb* 15 N18
Sharavogue *Offaly* 36 R8
Sharnbrook *Beds* 12 T22
Sharpness *Glos* 5 U19
Shawbury *Shrops* 10 S18
Shawford *Hants* 5 V21
Shebbear *Devon* 3 W15
Sheerness *Kent* 7 V25
Sheffield *S Yorks* 16 R21
Shefford *Beds* 12 T23
Sheigra *H'land* 27 F13
Shenfield *Essex* 7 U24
Shepherdswell *Kent* 7 V26
Shepley *W Yorks* 16 Q20
Shepshed *Leics* 11 S21
Shepton Mallet
  Som'set 4 V18
Sherborne *Dorset* 4 W18
Sherborne St. John
  Hants 5 V21
Sherburn *N Yorks* 17 P22
Sherburn in Elmet
  N Yorks 16 Q21
Shercock *Cavan* 37 Q10
Shere *Surrey* 6 V23
Sherfield English
  Hants 5 V20
Sherfield on Lodden
  Hants 6 V21
Sheriff Hutton
  N Yorks 16 P21
Sheringham *Norfolk* 13 S26
Sherston *Wilts* 5 U19
Shiel Bridge *H'land* 23 H13
Shieldaig *H'land* 27 G12
Shifnal *Shrops* 10 S19
Shilbottle *Northum* 21 M20
Shildon *Durham* 21 N20
Shillelagh *Wicklow* 40 S10
Shillingstone *Dorset* 5 W19
Shillington *Beds* 12 T23
Shinfield *Berks* 6 V22
Shinrone *Offaly* 36 S8
Shipdham *Norfolk* 13 S25
Shipley *W Yorks* 15 Q20
Shipston-on-Stour
  Warwick 11 T20
Shipton under
  Wychwood *Oxon* 5 U20
Shirebrook *Notts* 11 R21
Shoeburyness *Essex* 7 U25
Shoreham by Sea
  W Sussex 6 W23
Shorwell *I of Wight* 5 W21
Shotley Gate *Suffolk* 13 U26
Shottermill *Surrey* 6 V22
Shottisham *Suffolk* 13 T26
Shotts *N Lanarks* 19 L16
Shrewsbury *Shrops* 10 S18
Shrewton *Wilts* 5 V20
Shrigley *Down* 33 P12
Shrivenham *Oxon* 5 U20
Shrule *Mayo* 35 Q5
Siabost *W Isles* 26 F10
Sible Hedingham
  Essex 13 U25
Sibsey *Lincs* 12 R24
Sidbury *Devon* 4 W17
Sidford *Devon* 4 W17
Sidlesham *W Sussex* 6 W22
Sidmouth *Devon* 4 W17
Silloth *Cumb* 20 N17
Silsden *W Yorks* 15 Q20
Silver End *Essex* 7 U25
Silverdale *Lancs* 15 P18
Silvermines *Tipperary* 39 S7
Silverstone *Northants* 11 T21
Silverstream
  Monaghan 33 P10
Silverton *Devon* 4 W17
Simonsbath *Som'set* 4 V16
Single Street *Donegal* 32 P7
Singleton *W Sussex* 6 W22
Sion Mills *Tyrone* 32 N9

Sittingbourne *Kent* 7 V25
Six Crosses *Kerry* 38 T4
Sixmilebridge *Clare* 39 S6
Sixmilecross *Tyrone* 32 N9
Sixpenny Handley
  Dorset 5 W20
Sizewell *Suffolk* 13 T27
Skeagh *Westmeath* 36 Q8
Skegness *Lincs* 12 R24
Skellingthorpe *Lincs* 17 R22
Skelmersdale *Lancs* 15 Q18
Skelmorlie *N Ayrs* 18 L14
Skelton *Cumb* 20 N18
Skelton
  Redcar/Clevel'd 17 N22
Skerries *Dublin* 37 Q11
Skibbereen *Cork* 38 U5
Skinburness *Cumb* 20 N17
Skipness *Arg/Bute* 18 L13
Skipsea
  E Riding Yorks 17 Q23
Skipton *N Yorks* 15 Q19
Skull *Cork* 38 U4
Slaidburn *Lancs* 15 Q19
Slaithwaite *W Yorks* 15 Q20
Slaley *Northum* 21 N19
Slamannan *Falk* 19 L16
Slane *Meath* 37 Q10
Sleaford *Lincs* 12 S23
Sledmere
  E Riding Yorks 17 P22
Sleights *N Yorks* 17 P22
Sligachan *H'land* 27 H11
Sligo *Sligo* 32 P7
Slisgarrow
  Fermanagh 32 P8
Slough *Berks* 6 U22
Smailholm *Borders* 21 L18
Smarden *Kent* 7 V25
Smethwick
  W Midlands 11 S20
Smithborough
  Monaghan 32 P9
Smithfield *Cumb* 20 N18
Snainton *N Yorks* 17 P22
Snaith *E Riding Yorks* 16 Q21
Snape *Suffolk* 13 T27
Sneaton *N Yorks* 17 P22
Sneem *Kerry* 38 U4
Snettisham *Norfolk* 13 S25
Snodland *Kent* 7 V24
Soham *Cambs* 12 T24
Solas *W Isles* 26 G9
Solihull *W Midlands* 11 T20
Solva *Pembs* 9 U13
Somerby *Leics* 11 S22
Somercotes *Derby* 11 R21
Somersham *Cambs* 12 T23
Somerton *Som'set* 4 V18
Sonning *Berks* 6 V22
Sonning Common
  Oxon 6 U22
Sopley *Hants* 5 W20
Sorbie *Dumf/Gal* 19 N15
Sordale *H'land* 28 E17
Sorisdale *Arg/Bute* 22 J11
Sorn *E Ayrs* 19 L15
Sortat *H'land* 29 E17
Soulby *Cumb* 15 P19
South Anston *S Yorks* 16 R21
South Benfleet *Essex* 7 U25
South Brent *Devon* 3 X16
South Cave
  E Riding Yorks 17 Q22
South Cerney *Glos* 5 U20
South Elkington *Lincs* 17 R23
South Harting
  W Sussex 6 W22
South Hayling *Hants* 6 W22
South Kelsey *Lincs* 17 R23
South Kirkby *W Yorks* 16 Q21
South Molton *Devon* 3 V16
South Ockendon
  Essex 7 U24
South Otterington
  N Yorks 16 P21
South Petherton
  Som'set 4 W18
South Petherwin
  Cornw'l 3 W15
South Queensferry
  C of Edinb 24 L17
South Shields
  Tyne/Wear 21 N21
South Skirlaugh
  E Riding Yorks 17 Q23

South Tawton *Devon* 3 W16
South Tidworth *Hants* 5 V20
South Walsham
  Norfolk 13 S26
South Warnborough
  Hants 6 V22
South Woodham
  Ferrers *Essex* 7 U25
South Wootton
  Norfolk 12 S24
South Zeal *Devon* 3 W16
Southam *Warwick* 11 T21
Southampton
  S'thampton 5 W21
Southborough *Kent* 7 V24
Southend *Arg/Bute* 18 M12
Southend-on-Sea
  Essex 7 U25
Southminster *Essex* 7 U25
Southport *Mersey* 15 Q17
Southwark *Gtr Lon* 6 V23
Southwell *Notts* 11 R22
Southwick *W Sussex* 6 W23
Southwold *Suffolk* 13 T27
Sowerby *N Yorks* 16 P21
Sowerby Bridge
  W Yorks 15 Q20
Spa *Kerry* 38 T4
Spalding *Lincs* 12 S23
Spaldwick *Cambs* 12 T23
Spancelhill *Clare* 39 S6
Sparkford *Som'set* 4 V18
Spean Bridge *H'land* 23 J14
Speenoge *Donegal* 32 M9
Speke *Mersey* 15 R18
Spennymoor *Durham* 21 N20
Sperrin *Tyrone* 33 N9
Spiddle *Galway* 34 R5
Spilsby *Lincs* 12 R24
Spittal *Pembs* 9 U14
Spittal of Glenmuick
  Aberds 25 J17
Spittle of Glenshee
  Perth/Kinr 24 J17
Spixworth *Norfolk* 13 S26
Spofforth *N Yorks* 16 Q21
Spott *E Loth* 25 L18
Spreyton *Devon* 4 W16
Springfield
  Fermanagh 32 P8
Sproatley
  E Riding Yorks 17 Q23
Square *Down* 33 P11
Srahmore *Mayo* 34 P4
Srahnalong *Mayo* 34 Q5
Stadhampton *Oxon* 5 U21
Staffin *H'land* 27 G11
Stafford *Staffs* 10 S19
Staindrop *Durham* 21 N20
Staines *Surrey* 6 V23
Stainforth *N Yorks* 15 P19
Stainforth *S Yorks* 16 Q21
Stainton *Lincs* 17 R23
Stainton Middlesbro' 16 N21
Staintondale *N Yorks* 17 P23
Staithes *N Yorks* 17 N22
Stalbridge *Dorset* 5 W19
Stalham *Norfolk* 13 S27
Stallingborough
  NE Lincs 17 Q23
Stalybridge *Gtr Man* 15 R19
Stamford *Lincs* 12 S23
Stamford Bridge
  E Riding Yorks 17 Q22
Stamfordham
  Northum 21 M20
Standish *Gtr Man* 15 Q18
Standlake *Oxon* 5 U21
Stanford le Hope
  Essex 7 U24
Stanford on Teme
  Heref/Worcs 10 T19
Stanhope *Durham* 21 N19
Stanley *Durham* 21 N20
Stanley *Perth/Kinr* 24 K17
Stannington *Northum* 21 M20
Stansted Mountfitchet
  Essex 12 U24
Stanton *Suffolk* 13 T25
Stanton Harcourt
  Oxon 5 U21
Stanton St. John
  Oxon 5 U21
Stanway *Glos* 11 U20
Stanwix *Cumb* 20 N18

Stapleford *Notts* 11 S21
Staplehurst *Kent* 7 V25
Starcross *Devon* 4 W17
Staunton *Glos* 10 U19
Staunton on Wye
  Heref/Worcs 10 T18
Staveley *Cumb* 15 P18
Staveley *Derby* 16 R21
Staxigoe *H'land* 29 F17
Staxton *N Yorks* 17 P23
Steeple Bumpstead
  Essex 12 T24
Steeple Claydon
  Bucks 11 U22
Stein *H'land* 26 G10
Stenhousemuir *Falk* 24 K16
Stevenage *Herts* 12 U23
Stevenston *N Ayrs* 19 L14
Stewarton *E Ayrs* 19 L14
Stewartstown *Tyrone* 33 N10
Steyning *W Sussex* 6 W23
Stibb Cross *Devon* 3 W15
Stichill *Borders* 21 L19
Stickford *Lincs* 12 R24
Stickney *Lincs* 12 R24
Stillington *N Yorks* 16 P21
Stillorgan *Dublin* 37 R11
Stilton *Cambs* 12 T23
Stirling *Stirl* 24 K16
Stobbs *Borders* 20 M18
Stobo *Borders* 20 L17
Stock *Essex* 7 U24
Stockbridge *Hants* 5 V21
Stockport *Gtr Man* 15 R19
Stocksbridge *S Yorks* 16 R20
Stockton *Warwick* 11 T21
Stockton-on-Tees
  Stockton 21 N21
Stoer *H'land* 27 F13
Stoke *Kent* 7 V25
Stoke Albany
  Northants 11 T22
Stoke Ferry *Norfolk* 13 S25
Stoke Fleming *Devon* 3 X16
Stoke Gabriel *Devon* 3 X16
Stoke Mandeville
  Bucks 6 U22
Stoke-on-Trent *Stoke* 10 R19
Stoke Poges *Bucks* 6 U22
Stoke Prior
  Heref/Worcs 10 T19
Stokenchurch *Bucks* 6 U22
Stokesley *N Yorks* 16 P21
Stone *Bucks* 6 U22
Stone *Glos* 5 U19
Stone *Staffs* 10 S19
Stonehaven *Aberds* 25 J19
Stonehouse *Glos* 5 U19
Stonehouse
  S Lanarks 19 L16
Stoneykirk *Dumf/Gal* 18 N14
Stonham Aspal
  Suffolk 13 T26
Stony Stratford
  M/Keynes 11 T22
Stonyford *Kilkenny* 40 T9
Store *Orkney* 30 D18
Stornoway *W Isles* 26 F11
Storrington *W Sussex* 6 W23
Stotfold *Beds* 12 T23
Stourbridge
  W Midlands 10 T19
Stourpaine *Dorset* 5 W19
Stourport-on-Severn
  Heref/Worcs 10 T19
Stow *Borders* 20 L18
Stow Bardolph
  Norfolk 12 S24
Stow-on-the-Wold
  Glos 11 U20
Stowmarket *Suffolk* 13 T26
Strabane *Tyrone* 32 N9
Strachan *Aberds* 25 H18
Strachur *Arg/Bute* 23 K13
Stradbally *Kerry* 38 T3
Stradbally *Laois* 40 S9
Stradbally *Waterford* 40 T9
Stradbroke *Suffolk* 13 T26
Strade Friary *Mayo* 35 Q5
Stradone *Cavan* 36 Q9
Straffan *Kildare* 37 R10
Straiton *S Ayrs* 19 M14
Strandhill *Sligo* 32 P6
Strangford Down 33 P12
Stranorlar *Donegal* 32 N8
Stranraer *Dumf/Gal* 18 N13

Stratford St. Mary
  Suffolk 13 U25
Stratford-upon-Avon
  Warwick 11 T20
Strathan H'land 28 E15
Strathaven S Lanarks 19 L15
Strathblane Stirl 24 L15
Strathdon Aberds 25 H17
Strathkanaird H'land 27 G13
Strathpeffer H'land 28 G14
Strathy H'land 28 E16
Strathyre Stirl 24 K15
Stratmiglo Fife 24 K17
Stratton Cornw'l 2 W14
Stratton Glos 5 U20
Stratton St. Margaret
  Thamesd'n 5 U20
Streamstown Galway 34 Q3
Streatley Berks 5 U21
Street Som'set 4 V18
Strensall C of York 16 P21
Stretford Gtr Man 15 R19
Stretham Cambs 12 T24
Stretton Ches 15 R18
Stretton Rutl'd 12 S22
Stretton Staffs 11 S20
Strichen Aberds 29 G19
Strokestown
  Roscommon 36 Q7
Stromeferry H'land 27 H12
Stromemore H'land 27 H12
Stromness Orkney 30 E17
Stronachlachar Stirl 24 K14
Strone Arg/Bute 23 L14
Strontian H'land 23 J12
Stroove Donegal 33 M10
Stroud Glos 5 U19
Struy H'land 28 H14
Stubbington Hants 5 W21
Studland Dorset 5 W20
Studley Warwick 11 T20
Sturminster Marshall
  Dorset 5 W19
Sturminster Newton
  Dorset 5 W19
Sturry Kent 7 V26
Sturton Lincs 17 R22
Sudbury Derby 11 S20
Sudbury Suffolk 13 T25
Sulby I of Man 14 P15
Sullom Shetl'd 31 B21
Sully V of Glam 4 V17
Summerhill Meath 37 R10
Sunderland
  Tyne/Wear 21 N21
Sunk Island
  E Riding Yorks 17 Q23
Sunninghill Berks 6 V22
Sutterton Lincs 12 S23
Sutton Cambs 12 T24
Sutton Gtr Lon 6 V23
Sutton Bridge Lincs 12 S24
Sutton Coldfield
  W Midlands 11 S20
Sutton Courtenay
  Oxon 5 U21
Sutton-in-Ashfield
  Notts 11 R21
Sutton Lane Ends
  Ches 15 R19
Sutton-on-Sea Lincs 17 R24
Sutton-on-Trent Notts 11 R22
Sutton Scotney Hants 5 V21
Sutton-under-
  Whitestonecliffe
  N Yorks 16 P21
Sutton Valence Kent 7 V25
Swadlincote Derby 11 S20
Swaffham Norfolk 13 S25
Swalcliffe Oxon 11 T21
Swalecliffe Kent 7 V26
Swan Laois 40 S9
Swanage Dorset 5 W20
Swanley Kent 6 V24
Swanlinbar Cavan 32 P8
Swansea Swan 9 U16
Swatragh
  Londonderry 33 N10
Sway Hants 5 W20
Swindon Thamesd'n 5 U20
Swinefleet
  E Riding Yorks 17 Q22
Swineshead Lincs 12 S23
Swinford Mayo 35 Q6
Swinton Gtr Man 15 Q19
Swinton S Yorks 16 R21
Swinton Borders 21 L19

Swords Dublin 37 R11
Symbister Shetl'd 31 B21
Symington S Lanarks 20 L16
Symonds Yat
  Heref/Worcs 4 U18
Syresham Northants 11 T21
Syston Leics 11 S21

T

Tadcaster N Yorks 16 Q21
Tadley Hants 5 V21
Taghmon Wexford 40 T10
Tain H'land 28 G15
Tal-y-llyn Gwyn 8 S16
Talgarth Powys 10 U17
Talladale H'land 27 G12
Tallaght Dublin 37 R11
Tallanstown Louth 37 Q10
Talley Carms 9 U15
Tallow Waterford 39 T7
Tallowbridge
  Waterford 39 T7
Talsarnau Gwyn 8 S15
Talybont Ceredig'n 8 T16
Talysarn Gwyn 8 R15
Tamerton Foliot
  Devon 3 X15
Tamworth Staffs 11 S20
Tandragee Armagh 33 P11
Tang Westmeath 36 Q8
Tangmere W Sussex 6 W22
Tannadice Angus 25 J18
Tanworth Warwick 11 T20
Taobh Tuath W Isles 26 G9
Tara Meath 37 Q10
Tarbert Kerry 38 S5
Tarbert Arg/Bute 18 L13
Tarbert = Aird Asaig
  Tairbeart W Isles 26 G10
Tarbet Arg/Bute 24 K14
Tarbet H'land 23 J12
Tarbolton S Ayrs 19 L15
Tarland Aberds 25 H18
Tarleton Lancs 15 Q18
Tarporley Ches 10 R18
Tarrant Hinton Dorset 5 W19
Tarskavaig H'land 23 H12
Tarves Aberds 29 H19
Tarvin Ches 10 R18
Tattenhall Ches 10 R18
Tattersett Norfolk 13 S25
Taunton Som'set 4 V17
Taur Cork 38 T5
Tavistock Devon 3 W15
Tawnyinah Mayo 35 Q6
Tayinloan Arg/Bute 18 L12
Taynuilt Arg/Bute 23 K13
Tayport Fife 25 K18
Teangue H'land 23 H12
Tebay Cumb 15 P18
Tedavnet Monaghan 33 P9
Tedburn St Mary
  Devon 4 W16
Teeshan Antrim 33 N11
Teignmouth Devon 4 W16
Telford Shrops 10 S19
Temple Combe
  Som'set 5 W19
Temple Ewell Kent 7 V26
Temple Sowerby
  Cumb 21 N18
Templeboy Sligo 35 P6
Templederry
  Tipperary 39 S7
Templemore
  Tipperary 39 S7
Templenoe Kerry 38 U4
Templepatrick Antrim 33 N11
Templeton Pembs 9 U14
Templetouhy
  Tipperary 39 S8
Tempo Fermanagh 32 P9
Tenbury Wells
  Heref/Worcs 10 T18
Tenby Pembs 9 U14
Tenterden Kent 7 V25
Termon Cavan 32 P8
Termon Donegal 32 M8
Termonfeckin Louth 37 Q11
Terrington N Yorks 17 P22
Terrington St.
  Clement Norfolk 12 S24
Terryglass Tipperary 36 R7

Tetbury Glos 5 U19
Tetney Lincs 17 R23
Tetsworth Oxon 6 U22
Teviothead Borders 20 M18
Tewkesbury Glos 10 U19
Teynham Kent 7 V25
Thame Oxon 6 U22
Thatcham Berks 5 V21
Thaxted Essex 12 U24
The Barony Orkney 30 D17
The Downs
  Westmeath 36 Q9
The Loup
  Londonderry 33 N10
The Mumbles Swan 9 U16
The Sheddings Antrim 33 N11
The Temple Down 33 P12
Theale Berks 6 V21
Thetford Norfolk 13 T25
Thirsk N Yorks 16 P21
Thomas Street
  Roscommon 35 R7
Thomastown Kilkenny 40 S9
Thornaby on Tees
  Stockton 21 N21
Thornbury S Gloucs 4 U18
Thorndon Suffolk 13 T26
Thorne S Yorks 17 Q22
Thorney Cambs 12 S23
Thornham Norfolk 13 S25
Thornhill Dumf/Gal 19 M16
Thornhill Stirl 24 K15
Thornthwaite Cumb 20 N17
Thornton Lancs 15 Q17
Thornton Dale
  N Yorks 17 P22
Thorpe Norfolk 13 S26
Thorpe le Soken
  Essex 7 U26
Thorverton Devon 4 W16
Thrapston Northants 12 T22
Three Legged Cross
  Dorset 5 W20
Threlkeld Cumb 20 N17
Threshfield N Yorks 15 P19
Thrumster H'land 29 F17
Thurcroft S Yorks 16 R21
Thurlby Lincs 12 S23
Thurles Tipperary 39 S8
Thurlestone Devon 3 X16
Thurmaston Leics 11 S21
Thursby Cumb 20 N17
Thurso H'land 28 E16
Ticehurst E Sussex 7 V24
Tickhill S Yorks 16 R21
Tideswell Derby 15 R20
Tighnabruaich
  Arg/Bute 18 L13
Tilbury Essex 7 V24
Tillicoultry Clack 24 K16
Tillingham Essex 7 U25
Tilmanstone Kent 7 V26
Timahoe Kildare 37 R10
Timahoe Laois 40 S9
Timberscombe
  Som'set 4 V16
Timoleague Cork 39 U6
Timolin Kildare 40 S10
Timsbury
  Bath/NE Som'set 5 V19
Tinahely Wicklow 40 S11
Tingewick Bucks 11 U21
Tintagel Cornw'l 2 W14
Tintern Monmouths 4 U18
Tintern Abbey
  Wexford 40 T10
Tipperary Tipperary 39 T7
Tipton W Midlands 10 S19
Tiptree Essex 7 U25
Tisbury Wilts 5 V19
Titchfield Hants 5 W21
Tiverton Devon 4 W17
Tobercurry Sligo 35 P6
Tobermoney Down 33 P12
Tobermore
  Londonderry 33 N10
Tobermory Arg/Bute 22 J11
Toberonochy
  Arg/Bute 23 K12
Toberroe Galway 35 R6
Tobha Mor W Isles 26 H9
Toddington Beds 12 U22
Todmorden W Yorks 15 Q19
Togher Cork 38 U5
Togher Louth 37 Q11
Tolastadh bho Thuath
  W Isles 27 F11

Tollesbury Essex 7 U25
Tolob Shetl'd 31 C21
Tolpuddle Dorset 5 W19
Tomatin H'land 28 H16
Tomdoun H'land 23 H13
Tomintoul Moray 24 H17
Tomnavoulin Moray 28 H17
Tonbridge Kent 7 V24
Tondu Bridg 4 U16
Tong Shrops 10 S19
Tongue H'land 28 F15
Tonyrefail
  Rh Cyn Taff 9 U17
Toomeakady Mayo 34 Q5
Toombeola Galway 34 R4
Toome Antrim 33 N11
Toomyvara Tipperary 39 S7
Toormore Cork 38 U4
Topcliffe N Yorks 16 P21
Topsham Devon 4 W17
Torcross Devon 3 X16
Torness H'land 28 H15
Torphins Aberds 25 H18
Torpoint Cornw'l 3 X15
Torquay Devon 3 X16
Torridon H'land 27 G12
Torroble H'land 28 F15
Torteval Chan Is 2 Z18
Torthorwald Dumf/Gal 20 M16
Torver Cumb 15 P17
Toscaig H'land 27 H12
Totland I of Wight 5 W20
Totley S Yorks 16 R20
Totnes Devon 3 X16
Totton Hants 5 W20
Tow Law Durham 21 N20
Towcester Northants 11 T22
Tower Hamlets
  Gtr Lon 6 U23
Town Yetholm
  Borders 21 L19
Trafford Park Gtr Man 15 R19
Tralee Kerry 38 T4
Tramore Waterford 40 T9
Tranent E Loth 25 L18
Trawsfynydd Gwyn 8 S16
Trecastle Powys 9 U16
Tredegar Bl Gwent 4 U17
Trefeglwys Powys 8 S16
Trefnant Denbs 8 R17
Trefriw Conwy 8 R16
Tregaron Ceredig'n 9 T16
Tregony Cornw'l 2 X14
Tregynon Powys 8 S17
Treharris Merth Tyd 9 U17
Trelech Carms 9 U15
Tremadog Gwyn 8 S15
Trenance Cornw'l 2 X13
Trentham Stoke 10 S19
Treorchy Rh Cyn Taff 9 U16
Tresilian Cornw'l 2 X13
Tretower Powys 10 U17
Treuddyn Flints 10 R17
Trillick Tyrone 32 P9
Trim Meath 37 Q10
Trimdon Durham 21 N21
Trimley Suffolk 13 U26
Tring Herts 6 U22
Trinity Chan Is 2 Z19
Troon S Ayrs 19 L14
Troutbeck Cumb 15 P18
Trowbridge Wilts 5 V19
Trull Som'set 4 W17
Trumpington Cambs 12 T24
Trunch Norfolk 13 S26
Truro Cornw'l 2 X13
Tuam Galway 35 Q6
Tuamgraney Clare 39 S6
Tubber Galway 35 R6
Tuddenham Suffolk 13 T25
Tudweiliog Gwyn 8 S14
Tulla Clare 39 S6
Tullaghan Leitrim 32 P7
Tullaghoge Tyrone 33 N10
Tullaghought Kilkenny 40 T9
Tullagower Clare 38 S5
Tullamore Offaly 36 R9
Tullaroan Kilkenny 40 S9
Tullow Carlow 40 S10
Tully Roscommon 36 Q7
Tully Cross Galway 34 Q4
Tullybeg Galway 35 Q6
Tullycrossmearan
  Fermanagh 32 P8
Tullymacreeve
  Armagh 37 P11
Tullynessle Aberds 29 H18

Tullyverry
  Londonderry 32 M9
Tullyvin Cavan 36 P9
Tulsk Roscommon 35 Q7
Tummel Bridge
  Perth/Kinr 24 J15
Tummery Tyrone 32 P8
Tunstall Suffolk 13 T26
Turloughmore Galway 35 R6
Turnberry S Ayrs 18 M14
Turreen Longford 36 Q8
Turriff Aberds 29 G19
Turvey Beds 12 T22
Tutbury Staffs 11 S20
Tuxford Notts 17 R22
Twatt Orkney 30 D17
Tweedmouth
  Northum 21 L19
Tweedshaws Borders 20 M16
Tweedsmuir Borders 20 L17
Twenty Lincs 12 S23
Twomileborris
  Tipperary 39 S8
Twyford Berks 6 V22
Twyford Hants 5 V21
Twyford Leics 11 S22
Tydd St. Giles Cambs 12 S24
Tydd St. Mary Lincs 12 S24
Tylorstown
  Rh Cyn Taff 9 U17
Ty'n-y-groes Conwy 8 R16
Tynagh Galway 35 R7
Tynan Armagh 33 P10
Tyndrum Stirl 24 K14
Tynemouth
  Tyne/Wear 21 M21
Tyrrellspass
  Westmeath 36 R9
Tywardreath Cornw'l 2 X14
Tywyn Gwyn 8 S15

U

Uckfield E Sussex 6 W24
Uddingston S Lanarks 19 L15
Uffculme Devon 4 W17
Uffington Oxon 5 U20
Ufford Suffolk 13 T26
Ugborough Devon 3 X16
Uig H'land 26 G11
Ulbster H'land 29 F17
Ulceby N Lincs 17 Q23
Ulceby Cross Lincs 17 R24
Uley Glos 5 U19
Ullapool H'land 27 G13
Ulsta Shetl'd 31 A21
Ulverston Cumb 15 P17
Unapool H'land 27 F13
Upavon Wilts 5 V20
Uphill N Som'set 4 V18
Upper Chapel Powys 9 T17
Upper Heyford Oxon 11 U21
Upper Hindhope
  Borders 21 M19
Upper Poppleton
  C of York 16 Q21
Upper Tean Staffs 11 S20
Upperchurch
  Tipperary 39 S7
Uppingham Rutl'd 12 S22
Upton Ches 15 R18
Upton Snodsbury
  Heref/Worcs 10 T19
Upton-upon-Severn
  Heref/Worcs 10 T19
Upwey Dorset 5 W19
Urchfont Wilts 5 V20
Urlingford Kilkenny 39 S8
Urmston Gtr Man 15 R19
Usk Monmouths 4 U18
Usselby Lincs 17 R23
Uttoxeter Staffs 11 S20
Uyeasound Shetl'd 31 A22

V

Valley Angl 8 R14
Veness Orkney 30 D18
Ventnor I of Wight 5 W21
Ventry Kerry 38 T3
Verwood Dorset 5 W20
Veryan Cornw'l 2 X14

Vicarstown *Laois* 40 R9
Vickerstown *Cumb* 14 P17
Vidlin *Shetl'd* 31 B21
Virginia *Cavan* 36 Q9
Virginia Water *Surrey* 6 V22
Voe *Shetl'd* 31 B21
Voy *Orkney* 30 D17

W

Waddesdon *Bucks* 6 U22
Waddingham *Lincs* 17 R22
Waddington *Wexford* 40 T10
Waddington *Lincs* 12 R22
Wadebridge *Cornw'l* 2 W14
Wadhurst *E Sussex* 7 V24
Wainfleet All Saints
  Lincs 12 R24
Wakefield *W Yorks* 16 Q21
Walberswick *Suffolk* 13 T27
Walcott *Lincs* 12 R23
Walderslade *Kent* 7 V25
Waldron *E Sussex* 6 W24
Walford *Heref/Worcs* 5 U18
Walkerburn *Borders* 20 L18
Walkeringham *Notts* 17 R22
Wallasey *Mersey* 15 R17
Wallingford *Oxon* 5 U21
Walls *Shetl'd* 31 B20
Wallsend *Tyne/Wear* 21 N20
Walmer *Kent* 7 V26
Walpole *Norfolk* 12 S24
Walsall *W Midlands* 11 S20
Walsham le Willows
  Suffolk 13 T25
Walsoken *Cambs* 12 S24
Waltham *NE Lincs* 17 Q23
Waltham Abbey
  Essex 6 U24
Waltham Forest
  Gtr Lon 6 U24
Waltham on the
  Wolds *Leics* 11 S22
Walton *Cumb* 21 N18
Walton-on-Thames
  Surrey 6 V23
Walton-on-the-Naze
  Essex 7 U26
Wanborough
  Thamesd'n 5 U20
Wandsworth *Gtr Lon* 6 V23
Wangford *Suffolk* 13 T27
Wansford *Cambs* 12 S23
Wantage *Oxon* 5 U21
Warboys *Cambs* 12 T23
Ward *Dublin* 37 R11
Wardington *Oxon* 11 T21
Wardle *Ches* 10 R18
Ware *Herts* 6 U23
Wareham *Dorset* 5 W19
Wargrave *Berks* 6 V22
Waringstown *Down* 33 P11
Wark *Northum* 21 M19
Warkworth *Northum* 21 M20
Warley *W Midlands* 11 T20
Warminster *Wilts* 5 V19
Warrenpoint *Down* 37 P11
Warrington *Ches* 15 R18
Warsop *Notts* 11 R21
Warton *Lancs* 15 P18
Warwick *Warwick* 11 T20
Wasbister *Orkney* 30 D17
Washaway *Cornw'l* 2 X14
Washford *Som'set* 4 V17
Washingborough
  Lincs 17 R23
Washington
  Tyne/Wear 21 N20
Washington
  W Sussex 6 W23
Watchet *Som'set* 4 V17
Watchfield *Oxon* 5 U20
Waterbeach *Cambs* 12 T24
Waterford *Waterford* 40 T9
Watergrasshill *Cork* 39 T7
Waterhead *Angus* 25 J18
Waterhouses *Staffs* 11 R20
Wateringbury *Kent* 7 V24
Waterlooville *Hants* 6 W21
Waterside
  Londonderry 32 N9
Waterville *Kerry* 38 U3
Watford *Herts* 6 U23

Wath upon Dearne
  S Yorks 16 R21
Watlington *Norfolk* 12 S24
Watlington *Oxon* 6 U22
Watten *H'land* 28 F17
Watton *Norfolk* 13 S25
Waunfawr *Gwyn* 8 R15
Weachyburn *Aberds* 29 G18
Wearhead *Durham* 21 N19
Weasenham *Norfolk* 13 S25
Weaverham *Ches* 15 R18
Weaverthorpe
  N Yorks 17 P22
Wedmore *Som'set* 4 V18
Wednesbury
  W Midlands 10 S19
Wednesfield
  W Midlands 10 S19
Weedon Bec
  Northants 11 T21
Weeley *Essex* 7 U26
Welbourn *Lincs* 12 R22
Weldon *Northants* 12 T22
Weldon *Northum* 21 M20
Welford *Berks* 5 V21
Welford *Northants* 11 T21
Wellesbourne
  Warwick 11 T20
Wellingborough
  Northants 12 T22
Wellington *Shrops* 10 S18
Wellington *Som'set* 4 W17
Wellingtonbridge
  Wexford 40 T10
Wellow
  Bath/NE Som'set 5 V19
Wells *Som'set* 4 V18
Wells-next-the-Sea
  Norfolk 13 S25
Welney *Norfolk* 12 S24
Welshampton *Shrops* 10 S18
Welshpool *Powys* 10 S17
Welton *Lincs* 17 R23
Welwyn Garden City
  Herts 6 U23
Wem *Shrops* 10 S18
Wembury *Devon* 3 X15
Wemyss Bay *Invercl* 18 L14
Wendover *Bucks* 6 U22
Wensley *N Yorks* 15 P20
Wenvoe *V of Glam* 4 V17
Weobley *Heref/Worcs* 10 T18
Werrington *Cornw'l* 3 W15
West Auckland
  Durham 21 N20
West Bergholt *Essex* 13 U25
West Bridgford *Notts* 11 S21
West Bromwich
  W Midlands 11 S20
West Burton *N Yorks* 15 P20
West Calder *W Loth* 20 L16
West Coker *Som'set* 4 W18
West Dean *Wilts* 5 V20
West End *Hants* 5 W21
West Felton *Shrops* 10 S18
West Grinstead
  W Sussex 6 W23
West Haddon
  Northants 11 T21
West Kilbride *N Ayrs* 18 L14
West Kingsdown *Kent* 7 V24
West Kirby *Mersey* 15 R17
West Linton *Borders* 20 L17
West Looe *Cornw'l* 3 X15
West Lulworth *Dorset* 5 W19
West Malling *Kent* 7 V24
West Meon *Hants* 5 V21
West Mersea *Essex* 7 U25
West Moors *Dorset* 5 W20
West Rasen *Lincs* 17 R23
West Thorney
  W Sussex 6 W22
West Wellow *Hants* 5 W20
West Woodburn
  Northum 21 M19
Westbourne
  W Sussex 6 W22
Westbury *Shrops* 10 S18
Westbury *Wilts* 5 V19
Westbury-on-Severn
  Glos 5 U19
Westbury-sub-Mendip
  Som'set 4 V18
Westcott *Surrey* 6 V23
Westerham *Kent* 6 V24
Westfield *E Sussex* 7 W25

Westhill *Aberds* 25 H19
Westhoughton
  Gtr Man 15 Q18
Westleton *Suffolk* 13 T27
Westminster *Gtr Lon* 6 U23
Weston *Staffs* 10 S19
Weston-Super-Mare
  N Som'set 4 V18
Westonzoyland
  Som'set 4 V18
Westport *Mayo* 34 Q4
Westruther *Borders* 21 L18
Westward Ho! *Devon* 3 V15
Wetheral *Cumb* 20 N18
Wetherby *W Yorks* 16 Q21
Wetwang
  E Riding Yorks 17 P22
Wexford *Wexford* 40 T11
Weybourne *Norfolk* 13 S26
Weybridge *Surrey* 6 V23
Weyhill *Hants* 5 V20
Weymouth *Dorset* 5 W19
Whaley Bridge *Derby* 15 R20
Whalley *Lancs* 15 Q19
Whalton *Northum* 21 M20
Whaplode *Lincs* 12 S23
Whatton *Notts* 11 S22
Whauphill *Dumf/Gal* 19 N14
Wheathampstead
  Herts 6 U23
Wheathill *Fermanagh* 32 P8
Wheatley *Notts* 17 R22
Wheatley *Oxon* 5 U21
Wheatley Hill *Durham* 21 N21
Wheaton Aston *Staffs* 10 S19
Wheldrake *C of York* 17 Q22
Whicham *Cumb* 14 P17
Whickham *Tyne/Wear* 21 N20
Whimple *Devon* 4 W17
Whipsnade *Beds* 6 U22
Whissendine *Rutl'd* 11 S22
Whitburn *W Loth* 20 L16
Whitby *N Yorks* 17 P22
Whitchurch
  Bath/NE Som'set 4 V18
Whitchurch *Bucks* 6 U22
Whitchurch *Devon* 3 W15
Whitchurch *Hants* 5 V21
Whitchurch
  Heref/Worcs 4 U18
Whitchurch *Shrops* 10 S18
White Bridge *H'land* 24 H14
White Castle *Donegal* 32 M9
Whitecross *Armagh* 33 P11
Whitegate *Clare* 35 S7
Whitegate *Cork* 39 U7
Whitehall *Orkney* 30 D18
Whitehaven *Cumb* 20 N16
Whitehead *Antrim* 33 N12
Whitehill *Fermanagh* 32 P8
Whitehouse *Arg/Bute* 18 L13
Whitekirk *E Loth* 25 K18
Whiteparish *Wilts* 5 V20
Whitfield *Kent* 7 V26
Whithorn *Dumf/Gal* 19 N15
Whitland *Carms* 9 U14
Whitley Bay
  Tyne/Wear 21 M21
Whitsome *Borders* 21 L19
Whitstable *Kent* 7 V26
Whitstone *Cornw'l* 3 W15
Whittington *Derby* 16 R21
Whittington *Lancs* 15 P18
Whittington *Shrops* 10 S18
Whittington *Staffs* 11 S20
Whittlebury *Northants* 11 T22
Whittlesey *Cambs* 12 S23
Whittlesford *Cambs* 12 T24
Whitwell *Derby* 16 R21
Whitwell *I of Wight* 5 W21
Whitwick *Leics* 11 S21
Whitworth *Lancs* 15 Q19
Whixley *N Yorks* 16 P21
Wick *H'land* 29 F17
Wick *S Gloucs* 5 V19
Wick *V of Glam* 4 V16
Wick *Wilts* 5 W20
Wicken *Cambs* 12 T24
Wickford *Essex* 7 U25
Wickham *Hants* 5 W21
Wickham Market
  Suffolk 13 T26
Wicklow *Wicklow* 40 S11
Wickwar *S Gloucs* 5 U19
Widdrington *Northum* 21 M20
Wide Open
  Tyne/Wear 21 M20

Widecombe *Devon* 3 W16
Widemouth *Cornw'l* 2 W14
Widnes *Ches* 15 R18
Wigan *Gtr Man* 15 Q18
Wigmore *Heref/Worcs* 10 T18
Wigmore *Kent* 7 V25
Wigston *Leics* 11 S21
Wigton *Cumb* 20 N17
Wigtown *Dumf/Gal* 19 N15
Willand *Devon* 4 W17
Willaston *Ches* 15 R17
Willenhall *W Midlands* 10 S19
Willersley
  Heref/Worcs 10 T17
Willesborough *Kent* 7 V25
Williamstown *Galway* 35 Q6
Willingdon *E Sussex* 7 W24
Willington *Beds* 12 T23
Willington *Durham* 21 N20
Williton *Som'set* 4 V17
Willoughby *Lincs* 17 R24
Wilmington *Devon* 4 W17
Wilmslow *Ches* 15 R19
Wilnecote *Staffs* 11 S20
Wilton *Wilts* 5 V20
Wimblington *Cambs* 12 S24
Wimborne Minster
  Dorset 5 W20
Wincanton *Som'set* 5 V19
Winchcombe *Glos* 11 U20
Winchelsea *E Sussex* 7 W25
Winchester *Hants* 5 V21
Windermere *Cumb* 15 P18
Windgap *Kilkenny* 40 T9
Windsor *Berks* 6 V22
Windygates *Fife* 25 K17
Wing *Bucks* 6 U22
Wingate *Durham* 21 N21
Wingham *Kent* 7 V26
Winkleigh *Devon* 3 W16
Winscombe
  N Som'set 4 V18
Winsford *Ches* 10 R18
Winslow *Bucks* 11 U22
Winster *Derby* 11 R20
Winston *Durham* 21 N20
Winterborne Abbas
  Dorset 4 W18
Winterborne Stickland
  Dorset 5 W19
Winterton *N Lincs* 17 Q22
Winterton *Norfolk* 13 S27
Wirksworth *Derby* 11 R20
Wisbech *Cambs* 12 S24
Wisbech St. Mary
  Cambs 12 S24
Wisborough Green
  W Sussex 6 V23
Wishaw *N Lanarks* 19 L16
Witchampton *Dorset* 5 W19
Witchford *Cambs* 12 T24
Witham *Essex* 7 U25
Witheridge *Devon* 4 W16
Withern *Lincs* 17 R24
Withernsea
  E Riding Yorks 17 Q24
Withington *Glos* 5 U20
Witley *Surrey* 6 V22
Witnesham *Suffolk* 13 T26
Witney *Oxon* 5 U20
Wittersham *Kent* 7 V25
Wiveliscombe
  Som'set 4 V17
Wivelsfield *E Sussex* 6 W23
Wivenhoe *Essex* 7 U25
Wix *Essex* 13 U26
Woburn *Beds* 12 U22
Woburn Sands
  M/Keynes 12 T22
Woking *Surrey* 6 V22
Wokingham *Berks* 6 V22
Wolf's Castle *Pembs* 9 U14
Wollaston *Northants* 12 T22
Wolsingham *Durham* 21 N20
Wolverhampton
  W Midlands 10 S19
Wolverton *M/Keynes* 11 T22
Wolviston *Stockton* 21 N21
Wombwell *S Yorks* 16 Q21
Wonersh *Surrey* 6 V22
Wonston *Hants* 5 V21
Woodbridge *Suffolk* 13 T26
Woodbury *Devon* 4 W17
Woodchester *Glos* 5 U19
Woodchurch *Kent* 7 V25
Woodcote *Oxon* 6 U21

Woodenbridge
  Wicklow 40 S11
Woodford *Galway* 35 R7
Woodgreen *Hants* 5 W20
Woodhall Spa *Lincs* 12 R23
Woodhouse *S Yorks* 16 R21
Woodhouse Eaves
  Leics 11 S21
Woodlawn *Galway* 35 R7
Woodley *Berks* 6 V22
Woodstock *Oxon* 5 U21
Woodtown *Meath* 37 Q10
Woofferton *Shrops* 10 T18
Wookey *Som'set* 4 V18
Wookey Hole *Som'set* 4 V18
Wool *Dorset* 5 W19
Woolacombe *Devon* 3 V15
Woolavington
  Som'set 4 V18
Wooler *Northum* 21 L19
Woolwich *Gtr Lon* 6 V24
Wooperton *Northum* 21 M20
Woore *Shrops* 10 S19
Wootton Bassett
  Wilts 5 U20
Wootton Bridge
  I of Wight 5 W21
Wootton Wawen
  Warwick 11 T20
Worcester
  Heref/Worcs 10 T19
Worfield *Shrops* 10 S19
Workington *Cumb* 20 N16
Worksop *Notts* 16 R21
Wormit *Fife* 25 K18
Worsbrough *S Yorks* 16 Q21
Wortham *Suffolk* 13 T26
Worthing *W Sussex* 6 W23
Wotton under Edge
  Glos 5 U19
Wragby *Lincs* 17 R23
Wrangle *Lincs* 12 R24
Wrea Green *Lancs* 15 Q18
Wrentham *Suffolk* 13 T27
Wretham *Norfolk* 13 T25
Wrexham *Wrex* 10 R17
Writtle *Essex* 7 U24
Wroughton
  Thamesd'n 5 U20
Wroxham *Norfolk* 13 S26
Wroxton *Oxon* 11 T21
Wyberton *Lincs* 12 S23
Wye *Kent* 7 V25
Wylye *Wilts* 5 V20
Wymondham *Leics* 12 S22
Wymondham *Norfolk* 13 S26

Y

Yalding *Kent* 7 V24
Yarcombe *Devon* 4 W17
Yardley Hastings
  Northants 12 T22
Yarm *Stockton* 16 N21
Yarmouth *I of Wight* 5 W21
Yarnton *Oxon* 5 U21
Yarrow *Borders* 20 L17
Yate *S Gloucs* 5 U19
Yatton *N Som'set* 4 V18
Yaxley *Cambs* 12 S23
Yeadon *W Yorks* 16 Q20
Yealmpton *Devon* 3 X16
Yelverton *Devon* 3 X15
Yeovil *Som'set* 4 W18
Yetminster *Dorset* 4 W18
York *C of York* 16 Q21
Youghal *Cork* 39 U8
Youlgreave *Derby* 11 R20
Yoxall *Staffs* 11 S20
Yoxford *Suffolk* 13 T27
Ysbyty Ifan *Conwy* 8 R16
Ysbyty Ystwyth
  Ceredig'n 9 T16
Ystalyfera
  Neath P Talb 9 U16
Ystradgynlais *Powys* 9 U16

Z

Zennor *Cornw'l* 2 X12